Contesting Revisionism

Dear Cameron :

Thank you for all
your support !

Kai & Len
Dec. 2021

Contesting Revisionism

China, the United States, and
the Transformation of International Order

STEVE CHAN, HUIYUN FENG, KAI HE,
AND WEIXING HU

OXFORD
UNIVERSITY PRESS

OXFORD
UNIVERSITY PRESS

Oxford University Press is a department of the University of Oxford. It furthers
the University's objective of excellence in research, scholarship, and education
by publishing worldwide. Oxford is a registered trade mark of Oxford University
Press in the UK and certain other countries.

Published in the United States of America by Oxford University Press
198 Madison Avenue, New York, NY 10016, United States of America.

Library of Congress Cataloging-in-Publication Data
Names: Chan, Steve, author. | Feng, Huiyun, 1971– author. |
He, Kai, author. | Hu, Weixing, author.
Title: Contesting revisionism : China, the United States, and the
transformation of international order / Steve Chan,
Huiyun Feng, Kai He, and Weixing Hu.
Other titles: China, the United States, and the transformation of international order
Description: New York : Oxford University Press, 2021. |
Includes bibliographical references and index.
Identifiers: LCCN 2021000924 (print) | LCCN 2021000925 (ebook) |
ISBN 9780197580301 (paperback) | ISBN 9780197580295 (hardback) |
ISBN 9780197580318 | ISBN 9780197580325 (epub) | ISBN 9780197580332
Subjects: LCSH: International relations. | United States—Foreign relations—China. |
China—Foreign relations—United States. | Unipolarity (International relations)
Classification: LCC JZ1242.C444 2020 (print) | LCC JZ1242 (ebook) |
DDC 327.51073—dc23
LC record available at https://lccn.loc.gov/2021000924
LC ebook record available at https://lccn.loc.gov/2021000925

DOI: 10.1093/oso/9780197580295.001.0001

1 3 5 7 9 8 6 4 2

Paperback printed by Marquis, Canada
Hardback printed by Bridgeport National Bindery, Inc., United States of America

Contents

Preface

This book studies states' motivations, specifically, whether a great power has "revisionist" intentions and, if so, what strategies it may employ to fulfill its revisionist agenda. The concept of "revisionism" (or its opposite, a state's commitment to the "status quo") has been a crucial part of international relations scholarship. For example, power-transition theory claims that systemic war is likely to happen when a "revisionist" latecomer rises to challenge a "status-quo" hegemon. Despite the importance of this concept, it has been largely neglected by scholars until relatively recently. It is an especially germane and timely topic for systematic inquiry in view of China's rise in recent years.

In this book, we clarify analytically the different meanings of revisionism, and we discuss the historical origin and evolution of different types of revisionist states and their strategies. We distinguish between "hard" and "soft" strategies to alter the international order, and we introduce different ways of seeking institutional change with illustrations from Chinese and US conduct. Unlike most other prior studies on China, we do not analyze this country as an isolated case, but rather seek to understand it comparatively in the context of other great powers' histories. Moreover, we develop a variety of empirical indicators to track how Beijing and Washington's foreign policy conduct has evolved over time, thus suggesting changes in their respective foreign policy motivation (or intention or orientation). This examination is pertinent to theoretical debates such as whether a rising latecomer will become more revisionist as it gains more power (as offensive realism is inclined to claim), and whether a reigning though declining hegemon would be steadfast in its commitment to and defense of the international order (as power-transition theory tends to argue).

We argue that "hard" revisionist strategies seeking military conquest and domination have become increasingly less likely among contemporary great powers characterized by mutual nuclear deterrence and economic interdependence. Therefore, China's challenges to the existing international order are less likely to take this form than "soft" attempts at institutional reform and resistance. After developing and elaborating on the idea of revisionism conceptually, theoretically, and empirically, we conclude the book with a series of policy recommendations that should contribute to enhancing international stability and diminishing tension in Sino-American relations. The intensifying strategic competition and even enmity between China and the United States during the Covid-19 pandemic augurs a new cold war. It is our hope that this book will deepen our understandings on revisionism in international relations theory, shed some light on the dynamics of international order transition, and offer some insights on how to manage the US-China rivalry peacefully in the twenty-first century.

We are grateful to the two anonymous referees for their constructive comments and suggestions, which helped to clarify and sharpen our arguments in the book. Kai He and Huiyun Feng would like to thank the Australian Research Council (ARC) [Grant IDs: FT 160100355 and DP210102843] and the Korea Foundation (policy-oriented research grant) for financial support, and Weixing Hu would like to acknowledge UMDF research grants from the University of Macau, SRG2019-00183-FSS and CPG2020-00027-FSS. Finally, we thank David McBride, the editor-in-chief in social sciences at Oxford University Press, for his patience and help in bringing this work to its successful fruition.

Steve Chan is College Professor of Distinction, University of Colorado at Boulder; Huiyun Feng is Senior Lecturer of international relations at the School of Government and International Relations, Griffith University, Australia; Kai He is Professor of international relations and Director, Centre for Governance and Public Policy, Griffith University, Australia; and Weixing Hu is UMDF Distinguished Professor and Dean, Faculty of Social Sciences, University of Macau.

1
Basic Rationale and Arguments

The concept of power looms large in discourse on international relations, such as suggested by theories on balance of power, power transition, and power cycles. However, not nearly enough attention has been paid to analyzing states' motivations for seeking power and for using the power in their possession. In other words, there has been more emphasis on the interstate system's structural properties, as defined by the distribution of power among states, than on their leaders' agency in shaping outcomes such as war and peace. This book is motivated by the latter concern about the origin and evolution of leaders' foreign policy intentions or, if you will, their foreign policy motivations and agendas. It is also concerned about how a great power may seek to implement its revisionist agenda under contemporary conditions.

We emphasize the basic distinction between a state's capability (or power) to pursue certain policy, on the one hand, and its intention or motivation to undertake it, on the other hand. If states' relative power were the most important determinant of their behavior, most of them should or would have sided with the Soviet Union rather than the United States, as the Soviet Union was the weaker of the two superpowers in the Cold War. Rather than balancing against a country simply because it has preponderant power (namely, the United States) according to the logic of balance-of-power theory (Waltz 1979), most major and minor states had joined the United States to oppose the Soviet Union. This theory assumes that all states have the same motivation or intention to engage in aggrandizement, and it therefore advises that they should—and moreover expects that they would—balance against the strongest among them because it is the one that poses the greatest threat to them. However, contrary to this advice and expectation, most states' conduct during the Cold War reflected their greater concern with Moscow's likely intention to use its power to harm them, rather than just the fact that the United States was the more powerful country (Walt 1987). Having the capability to do something (such as the means to purchase a house) does not necessarily mean that a person will do so. Similarly, having a capability to cause harm to another state does not imply that a state has the intention (or motivation) to do so. As Vasquez (2009: 99–100) states succinctly, "The inference that, just because there is a capability for war, there will be motivation for war is much too facile." To frame the point differently, it takes both "opportunity" (or capability) and "willingness" (or motivation) to account for a state's behavior (Most and Starr 1989). Both conditions are necessary for explaining its behavior.

International relations scholars' preoccupation with power shifts among states is rooted fundamentally in the idea of "opportunity" or, alternatively, constraints on the range of feasible policy options that leaders can choose from. How leaders will choose from these options, however, depends on their "willingness" or motivation. Naturally, leaders, or the states they represent, can have a variety of motivations. Ned Lebow (2010), for example, mentions fear, interest, status, and revenge as possible motivations that can cause states to fight. These motivations can reflect both deliberate calculations and unconscious psychological impulses, and they need not be mutually exclusive. Our larger point, however, is that we need to connect structural properties at the systemic level of analysis with the motivations or incentives operating at the societal, group, or individual level of analysis. In and of themselves, the interstate distribution of power (a structural variable) cannot tell us the reasons why states behave in the variety of ways that they do. To answer this question, we will have to understand their motivations and the factors that shape these motivations (Gries and Ying 2019). What transmission mechanisms connect power shifts at the systemic level of international relations to officials' formulation and selection of policies at the individual or group level of analysis? This has been the critical missing link in discourse on the so-called Thucydides's Trap thus far (Allison 2017). Although Thucydides is often quoted to have said that the Spartans' fear of Athens's rise was the "inevitable" cause of the Peloponnesian War, proponents of this view have not undertaken systematic studies to investigate how changes in states' power relationships have affected the relevant leaders' emotions (e.g., envy, anxiety, arrogance, overconfidence, in addition to fear), perceptions, and judgments.

Traditional approaches to address the issue of states' motivations have not been satisfactory. "Defensive realists" assume that all states are motivated by their paramount concern for their security and survival in an anarchical world (Waltz 1979), whereas "offensive realists" claim that all states are inherently aggressive and are motivated by the desire to dominate others (Mearsheimer 2001). Power-transition theorists assign different motivations to states depending on their relative power. They argue that the powerful established states are committed to the international status quo, but the rising latecomers tend to be dissatisfied with the existing international order and are interested in overturning it (Organski and Kugler 1980). As these examples suggest, scholars of international relations have generally addressed states' motivations or intentions by rhetorical assertion (or assumption) rather than deep analysis.

Thucydides points to the Spartans' fear of Athens's rise as the reason for the Peloponnesian War, thus suggesting the dominant power's sense of anxiety, insecurity, and even paranoia as the driving motivation for causing war. In contrast to Thucydides, proponents of power-transition theory assign the responsibility for starting war to the rising power's greed and ambition because it is supposed to be motivated by a desire to displace the incumbent hegemon and to upend the existing international order. They thus give a very different explanation of the origin of war than Thucydides.

Fear is also the dominant motivation central to defensive realism's expectation of how states interested in their self-preservation will behave under conditions of structural anarchy (e.g., Waltz 1979). Conversely, greed and ambition are the states' dominant motivation according to accounts presented by offensive realism, which expects them to expand and commit aggression when they gain more power or when they are already in a dominant position (Mearsheimer 2001). This last remark in turn raises the question of why a rising power (e.g., China) should be expected to become more aggressive than an established dominant power commanding a preponderant position (e.g., the United States) if a strong (or stronger) country can always be expected to aggrandize at others' expense (assuming, of course, that all states are motivated to seek more power and therefore whether they will behave aggressively depends on their capability, rather than desire, to do so).

Finally, both defensive realism and offensive realism expect states to balance against the strongest among them, and a situation of balanced power to promise greater international stability (if not also peace). If so, their adherents should welcome the prospect of China reaching power parity with the United States because this development should augur more stable international relations. Yet, power-transition theory (and Thucydides's Trap) presents the opposite proposition, suggesting that the danger of war increases when a rising power catches up to a ruling power. Current discourse in international relations tends to disregard the significant issues just raised. It rarely confronts the tensions, even contradictions, in and between different theoretical positions, and we can sometimes even find these incompatible views being adopted simultaneously in the same study (for a helpful review of the literature in the balance-of-power tradition, see Nexon 2009).

We focus in this book on the concept of revisionism referring to a state's intention to alter or upend the international order. The current literature is generally vague about what it considers to be "*the* international order," and what evidence is to be used to assess a state's revisionist or status-quo intentions. Moreover, it describes states' intentions (or motivations or characters) in a binary manner. Classical scholars have adopted dichotomous categories, such as status-quo versus imperialistic states (Morgenthau 1948), sated versus unsated states (Schuman 1948), satisfied versus dissatisfied states (Carr 1946), status-quo versus revolutionary states (Kissinger 1957), and status-quo versus revisionist states (Wolfers 1962). This practice of assigning states to dichotomous categories (as opposed to evaluating them on a scale or continuum) has continued to this day. Moreover, these dichotomous labels are often used as value-laden code words to indicate an analyst's evident preference for the "status quo" and objection to efforts to alter (or revise) it. There is therefore a palpable status-quo bias in the prevailing discourse, even though "international order" does not necessarily promote the cause of equality, justice, human dignity, or even peace, and even though proponents of power-transition theory (e.g., Gilpin 1981; Organski 1958; Organski and Kugler 1980) have acknowledged forthrightly that the "rules of the game" in the hierarchical world of international relations are rigged to serve the interests of the established powers.

As Turner and Nymalm (2019) point out, one often finds terms such as "status quo," "revisionism," and "international order" embedded in politically constructed narratives separating the West from the non-West, associating the former with morality and progress and the latter with the lack thereof. This tendency is pronounced even though, as these authors suggest and as we will document in our analysis, in many respects the European Union and the United States have behaved more like revisionist states than China. This same tendency has also caused words to be used contrary to their customary meaning so that one encounters the odd phenomenon whereby China is typically labeled as a "revisionist" state even though it professes its commitment to the traditional Westphalian principles of state sovereignty and non-interference in others' domestic affairs, and conversely, the United States is often described as a "status-quo" power even when it engages in frequent foreign military interventions and openly promotes regime changes abroad.

As we stress in the following, international order is always in flux (Buzan 2018; Goh 2019). It is being constantly contested, and it is therefore not a settled matter that commands universal understanding and agreement, as is often implied in the existing literature (whereby analysts can dichotomize states into "revisionist" and "status-quo" categories), especially because there are multiple and even inconsistent ordering norms and principles coexisting in different issue areas (Foot and Walter 2011; Johnston 2019). Instead, in our view the meaning of international order shared by states evolves over time in an ongoing process of negotiation and renegotiation among them, and this transformation often encounters vocal dissenters. It is also important to recognize that states can act to defend some existing norms, rules, and institutions of international order, while also trying to reform, subvert, and replace others at the same time. Therefore, it is not unusual for states to find themselves sometimes disagreeing with the views of other states about what constitutes international order. These views suggest that most states operate in a gray zone between completely embracing the norms, rules, and institutions of international order and rejecting them entirely. They can support some elements of the prevailing international order while objecting to or resisting others. They are norm entrepreneurs that can play both defense and offense at the same time. This view suggests that it is unhelpful to assign states into binary categories of being "revisionist" and "non-revisionist." States can also be "selective revisionists" (Medeiros 2019) in the sense that they are not always consistent in applying their avowed principles, such that China can profess non-interference in other countries' internal affairs, except in the cases of apartheid South Africa and racist Rhodesia, and the United States can promote humanitarian intervention, except in the case of Rwanda's genocide, and opposition to armed occupation (such as Iraq's annexation of Kuwait), except in the case of Israel's takeover of Arab land.

We also argue that revisionism should not be deployed as a pejorative term to indicate one's objection to a state or its policy. An analyst can sometimes find herself agreeing with or supporting a policy even though it is profoundly revisionist in undermining and challenging the existing "rules of the game" in international relations. The introduction and propagation of ideas such as "crimes against humanity and peace," "responsibility to protect," and "preemptive (preventive) war" come to mind as examples of US and Western countries' attempts to reshape the norms, rules, and institutions of the existing international order. Other examples come to mind, such as the Global South's campaigns to promote a "new international economic order" and to challenge apartheid and other forms of racial discrimination (which were of course once condoned and legitimated by the "international order").

Finally, we disagree with a common tendency in the current literature to treat "international order" as the same thing as the existing distribution of power among states, or to "assume that order and the interests of the hegemon or dominant state are mutually constitutive" (Johnston 2019: 12). This tendency considers any attempt by a state—any state except the hegemon—to improve its international position as a disturbance to the international order, and it has the effect of casting any quarrel that a state may have with the hegemon as a challenge to the entire international community. By conflating the international order and the hegemon's interests, this tendency also rules out, by definition, any consideration that the dominant state can act in a manner inconsistent with the international order (or orders) as commonly understood by the rest of international community.

Why Study Revisionism? And Why We Disagree with the Existing Literature

The topic of revisionism has received increasing recent attention from scholars of international relations (e.g., Behravesh 2018; Breuer and Johnston 2019; Chan et al. 2019; Cooley et al. 2019; Davidson 2006; Goddard 2018a, 2018b; Hurd 2007; Johnson 2003; Murray 2019; Ren 2015; Thies 2015; Thies and Nieman 2017; Turner and Nymalm 2019; Wilson 2019; Xiang 2001). This general recognition among scholars shares the basic view that it is meaningless and even misleading to be only concerned with states' changing power relations without also attending to their respective intentions or their respective foreign policy motivations and agendas. What motivates a state in its use of its power? This question is important because, for example, officials should respond differently, depending on whether a counterpart is motivated by fear or greed (Davis 2000; Schweller 1994). In one case, the appropriate response should be reassurance, and in the other, deterrence. This question is pertinent and timely in the context of China's dramatic rise in the recent past. What will a more powerful China want (Legro 2007, 2015), and hence, what will it do? Depending on the answer to this question, other states may adopt different policies toward China, such as accommodation versus confrontation, engagement versus containment, and reassurance versus deterrence.

Determining another state's motivation or intention is of course difficult (Chan 2017). There is the ever-present danger that one's counterpart would engage in strategic deception to deliberately mislead and misinform. Moreover, as realists are fond of reminding us, a state's intention can change in the future. Even if we trust another state's current leaders, can we count on their future successors to remain faithful to their promises? They therefore see attempts to discern states' intentions to be a hopeless endeavor. In Mearsheimer's (2001: 31) words, "states can never be certain about other states' intentions. Specifically, no state can be sure that another state will not use its offensive military capability to attack [others]." Rosato (2014/2015) agrees that we cannot infer states' intentions from their statements, conduct, or institutions. This view implies that states should always assume the worst about others and behave according to the maxim that "it is better to be safe than sorry."

This advice can produce a self-fulfilling prophecy. By acting as if the other side is hostile, one's own action can cause it to respond in a hostile manner. As MacDonald and Parent (2018: 10) conclude, "the biggest danger may not be the impending Sino-American transition itself, but the widespread belief it makes war more likely." If both sides behave as if the other side cannot be trusted, their action brings about a suboptimal outcome, causing them to forfeit the benefits that they could have otherwise gained if they had cooperated (Axelrod 1984; Jervis 1978). That a state's intentions are subject to change also means the possibility of positive evolution, such as when it changes from challenging to supporting international norms and institutions. This possibility in turn suggests that states sometimes have an incentive to cooperate with others in the hope that they can influence the latter's future intentions (Edelstein 2002). This has been, for example, a common argument advanced by those US officials and scholars advocating engagement with China.

We also believe that many realists' view on the impossibility of gauging states' intentions is too pessimistic. Although there is always uncertainty in discerning states' future intentions, this does not mean that states are completely helpless in trying to communicate their intentions to others or to reduce uncertainties in their judgments about others' intentions (e.g., Jervis 1976; Kydd 2000, 2005; Edelstein 2002; Yoder 2019; Yoder and Haynes 2015). For example, contemporary Germany's embeddedness in the institutions of the European Union and the North Atlantic Treaty Organization (NATO) suggests that it would be very difficult and costly for it to revert to militarism. Alarm bells would go off long before Berlin could reverse its commitments, and such a reversal of course would surely encounter vigorous domestic opposition. China's embeddedness in cross-border production chains, multilateral financial arrangements, and more broadly, its policies to engage in globalization and market reform would also meet strong resistance from vested domestic stakeholders who would be hurt if there were to be a policy U-turn. Therefore, it is not quite true that there is nothing to stop officials from a change of heart.

To the extent that many empirical indicators point to the same conclusion about a state's intentions and to the extent that these indicators suggest costly investments in its reputation and institutional commitments, they provide more credible signals than just "cheap talk" (Fearon 1995, 1997). Recent research suggests that even "cheap talk" can be highly informative in disclosing states' intentions and strategies (e.g., Goddard 2018b; Pu 2019; Yoder et al. 2019). Indeed, if officials had really believed that it was impossible to discern others' intentions and that all states were equally hostile and untrustworthy, they would have sided with the Soviet Union rather than the United States during the Cold War in accordance with the traditional logic of balance of power. We also would not have seen the emergence of "security communities" consisting, for example, of countries in the North Atlantic region, where the idea of going to war against each other has become unthinkable (Deutsch et al. 1957).

How do we infer a state's intentions or motivations? We do so by observing its behavior—its words and deeds. In this book's analysis, we resort to a variety of behavioral indicators to infer intentions and motivations. As just acknowledged, this attempt is necessarily challenging and fraud with the possibility of errors. Moreover, reasonable people can come to different conclusions when considering the same evidence. Therefore, it is important to be clear and transparent about one's evidence and the logic used to interpret this evidence. Because each individual item of evidence may be questionable, we shall resort to an ensemble of indicators from a variety of sources. This collection of evidence should be more credible than isolated anecdotes. We should also be on firmer ground when we assess the available data to contrast a state's own past and current conduct and when we compare it to the conduct of its peers. We engage in these efforts in Chapter 3. Even though making inferences about states' intentions is difficult, and even though differences of opinion may persist among analysts, it is important to make such attributions based on systematic data rather than rhetorical assertion.

As suggested already, we cannot bypass the difficulties of grappling with discerning states' intentions because this determination is basic to any attempt to explain and predict their conduct. It is at the heart of international relations discourses and debates (e.g., Brooks 1997; Edelstein 2002; Goddard 2018b; Jervis 1978; Kydd 2000; Rosato 2014/2015). For example, in our later discussion of prospect theory, we argue that officials' intentions are influenced by whether they find themselves in a domain of gain or loss; this theory suggests that people are motivated to take greater risks when seeking to avert or reverse losses, but are inclined to act more cautiously when trying to preserve gains. An understanding of a counterpart's intentions is obviously also indispensable to formulating sound policies toward it. So, to extend this example, we propose in our later discussion of policy implications that reassurances will be a more sensible approach than threats when dealing with a counterpart that is fearful of suffering a setback (in contrast to one that is trying to advance its gains).

Mistaken judgments or inferences about another state's intentions can be consequential. In the parlance of statistical analysis, we should recognize the risks of committing both Type 1 and Type 2 errors—that is, the danger of mistaking a "revisionist" state as a "status-quo" state, and also the danger of failing to recognize a "status-quo" state for what it actually is—or confusing a distributive revisionist with a radical revisionist (Ward 2017 introduces this distinction, in addition to a third category which he calls normative revisionism; we will discuss the former two types later). Hans Morgenthau was quoted to have said, "A nation that mistakes a policy of imperialism for a policy of the status quo will be unprepared to meet the threat to its own existence which the other nation's policy entails. [However, a] nation that mistakes a policy of the status quo for a policy of imperialism will evoke through its disproportionate reaction the very danger of war which it is trying to avoid" (Davis 2000: 40–41). Neville Chamberlain is remembered by history as someone who had failed to recognize Hitler's aggressive ambitions (but see Ripsman and Levy 2008). Conversely, John Foster Dulles might have made the opposite mistake of dismissing Moscow's détente signals in the 1950s (Holsti 1962), thereby missing an opportunity to end the Cold War three decades earlier.

We seek to understand in this book the emergence of revisionist states and their strategies—especially great powers that can challenge the prevailing international order and thus potentially become a source of international instability and even devastating conflicts like the two world wars. We argue that revisionism is not a fixed attribute of a rising power. Rising powers are not hard-wired to become revisionist challengers to the international system (Davidson 2006; Schweller 2015; Thies and Nieman 2017; Ward 2017). This view differentiates us from the predominant view that rising states are destined to be revisionists—except, of course, for reasons that are not usually explicated, the prevailing scholarship typically considers the United States to be a "status-quo" power during its years of ascent.

Other states' behavior can make a difference in turning a rising power into a revisionist challenger or integrating it peacefully into the global community. For instance, Japan in the 1920s and 1930s resented its treatment by the established powers, and its frustration due to perceived discrimination against it in turn altered its domestic balance of power to the advantage of this country's ultra-nationalists, leading eventually to Tokyo's fateful decision to attack Pearl Harbor. The punitive Versailles Treaty and the trials and tribulations of the Weimar Republic also had reverberations in Germany's domestic political economy, paving the path for the rise of the Nazis and their revisionist agenda. In contrast, Britain made concessions that facilitated the establishment of US hegemony in the Western Hemisphere, and it also accommodated other rising powers such as Russia and Japan. Its diplomacy enabled it to create a more powerful coalition that helped it defeat Germany in World War I. More recently, China has become a more constructive stakeholder in international relations. Although Beijing was extremely isolated economically and politically in the 1960s, it has since become deeply enmeshed in the global political economy and it is now very active in international institutions and multilateral diplomacy (such as United Nations peacekeeping missions and efforts to curb nuclear proliferation) that it had once opposed strenuously.

The analysis of states' revisionist or status-quo motivations is especially germane and timely in view of power-transition theory's recent popularity (Organski and Kugler 1980; Tammen et al. 2000; for reviews of this literature, see DiCicco 2017; DiCicco and Levy 1999, 2003; Tammen et al. 2017). This theory warns that the danger of a systemic war (a large conflict between the world's two leading powers to dominate the interstate system, one that can produce a fundamental change in international order) increases when a revisionist rising power overtakes or reaches parity with an incumbent hegemon. It claims that such war is caused by this upstart's revisionist agenda to challenge the hegemon's global dominance and to overturn the international order that this hegemon allegedly supports and defends. The relevant historical evidence, however, does not support this proposition, as dominant states and rising states rarely fight each other; both are more likely to pick "soft targets" presented by weaker opponents and declining powers (Lebow 2010: 116–117). Power transition was not associated with any of the wars among great powers since 1648 (Lebow 2010: 18). Some of the wars included in the analysis of power-transition theory, such as the Franco-Prussian War and the Russo-Japanese War, were clearly not about a struggle to determine which of these belligerents should determine the international order. Moreover, wars fought among the great powers are more likely to stem from the aggressiveness of the more dominant states than the ambitions of cocky, impatient upstarts. As Lebow (2010: 124) remarks,

> Dominant states are generally not content with their status and authority. They seek more power through additional conquests, and by doing so hope to be able to impose their preferences on others. Habsburg Spain, France under Louis XIV and Napoleon, Wilhelminian and Nazi Germany and the United States in the post-Cold War era are cases in point. They went to war because they thought they were powerful enough to become more powerful still.

MacDonald and Parent (2018: 178) remark, "even in familiar and favorable cases, the evidence in favor of power transition theory is thin" (see also Chan 2008, 2020a). Based on their research of sixteen historical cases, they question propositions advanced by formulations such as Thucydides's Trap and power-transition theory, and suggest that "both rising and declining powers display pervasive caution, and transition periods are in effect less dangerous than non-transition periods" (MacDonald and Parent 2018: 66). Declining states do not usually undertake provocative policies that can trigger war, nor do rising states always seek confrontation. Especially in a multipolar world, a rising state can very well support a declining state if it perceives that this policy can help it to counter threats from other states and if it feels that it has little to fear militarily from the declining state (Shifrinson 2018).

Besides its questionable empirical support, the interpretive logic behind power-transition theory is problematic. It presents several important puzzles. If a rising state has improved its position in the interstate system, why should it remain dissatisfied and continue to harbor a revisionist agenda to undermine the very international order that has permitted and even facilitated its rise? Why should it not wait for the ongoing trend to further improve its international position so that it may gain dominance peacefully? Why would it want to precipitate a premature war? Indeed, if the revisionist upstart has already gained the upper hand, why did it lose the war it has started? Indeed, modern history shows that "every dominant and great power that initiated a systemic war [or a hegemonic bid] was defeated" (Lebow 2010: 119). Given this historical record, why would China want to repeat the same mistake again? Does anyone seriously think that starting such a war would enhance its security and improve its chances of survival sufficiently to warrant the prospective costs and risks (Kirshner 2012)? If not, what could incline a rising but still weaker country to accept and even to initiate a conflict with a stronger opponent, such as when Japan attacked Pearl Harbor even though its leaders knew that the United States was eight or nine times more powerful (Russett 1969)? Of course, China had also fought the United States in Korea long before anyone was talking about a possible power transition between these two countries. Moreover, if we consider power transitions involving countries other than the world's most powerful country (such as when power-transition proponents included the Anglo-German dyad, the Franco-Prussian dyad, and the Russo-Japanese dyad in their analyses), there have been quite a few peaceful transitions, such as when Germany overtook Russia, France, and Britain, and when China overtook Japan, Russia, and Germany in recent decades. Thus, it appears that a power transition is neither a necessary nor a sufficient condition for war to occur. Moreover, judging from the recent episodes of transition, whether the overtaking country or the country being overtaken is a democracy or is ostensibly revisionist is irrelevant to whether war or peace will ensue (all these episodes had a peaceful outcome; on how domestic political structure can affect the incentive to launch a war, see Schweller 1992).

Moreover, if the "rules of the game" are rigged in favor of a few established states, wouldn't most other states be inclined to join a revisionist coalition, an expectation that seems to be contradicted by evidence from the two world wars? Conversely, if a declining hegemon has become less preponderant under the existing international order, why should it remain committed to this order? Indeed, why would this hegemon be disinclined to change the "rules of the game" even when it is gaining more power relative to the rest of the world? After all, offensive realism would expect this country to persist expanding its power until it has become the world's undisputed master (Mearsheimer 2001). According to this view, more power should always be better because it makes a country more secure. If relative power gain by a rising latecomer gives it more capabilities to upend the international order, thus causing it to pose a greater threat to this order, why should this reasoning not also apply to the reigning hegemon when it becomes more dominant, such as when it becomes a unipolar power after the demise of its chief competitor (such as the Soviet Union)? That is, why shouldn't the hegemon try to alter the international order to align it even more closely to its interests and values, and to further consolidate and extend its dominance? Existing studies of power-transition theory have not generally taken up these questions. Moreover, they have been almost exclusively concerned with only one of this theory's two independent variables—namely, the shifting power balance between the two supposed competing states—to explain and predict the occurrence of a systemic war, and they have generally overlooked the need for systematic analysis of this theory's other independent variable, the ostensible revisionist intention of a rising upstart.

Current prevailing discourse suggests that a rising state's revisionism escalates in tandem with its increased power, but for some reason a hegemon's commitment to defend the international order remains unchanged, despite its relative decline. This discourse shuttles its logic by emphasizing a rising latecomer's relative power gains that would augment its capability to challenge the existing international order, while overlooking the possibility that these gains would also have given this country a larger stake in this order and hence a stronger incentive to preserve it (Chan et al. 2019). Conversely, this literature claims that a hegemon is committed to the international order because it has the largest stake in its preservation, while neglecting the fact that with its relative decline this stake would have become smaller and the hegemon should therefore have less incentive to defend or uphold this order. At the same time, as this hegemon still possesses more power than other countries, it continues to have the greatest capability to revise this order to arrest and reverse its decline. As implied by these remarks, we do not see revisionism to be an exclusive or innate characteristic of rising states. Established states, including the reigning hegemon, can also be revisionist. What observations and inferences can we make about changing Chinese and American motivations as their foreign policy conduct has evolved over time? Has China become a more status-quo country and the United States a more revisionist country, as recent power shifts have produced relative gain for one and relative loss for the other? Ultimately, questions such as these will have to be settled by empirical evidence rather than dogmatic assertion.

Support or rejection of international order is never a matter of all or nothing. Therefore, the current literature grossly oversimplifies matters when it dichotomizes countries into revisionist and status-quo categories. As already mentioned, international order is always in flux and is always being contested. There is continuing tension between complicity and resistance, that is, states are always concurrently accepting or acquiescing to and even actively supporting or promoting some international rules, norms, and principles while questioning, objecting to, and even seeking to dismantle and replace other rules, norms, and principles (Goh 2013, 2019). A state can be a norm entrepreneur, advocating a new vision of some elements of international order while rejecting some other elements. It can even challenge a principle such as sovereignty in some circumstances, such as when it argues in favor of the "responsibility to protect" against humanitarian tragedies abroad, while asserting this same principle to protect its own borders against illegal immigration or to deny international investigators the authority to pursue possible war crimes committed by its own citizens.

Stated simply, while China does not wholly subscribe to the current international order, it is also not demanding that it be overhauled immediately and in its entirety. As we will elaborate in subsequent chapters, it is important to recognize that international order consists of multiple dimensions and that "China will play multiple roles at the same time as supporter, reformer, and challenger—in shaping the current international order" (He and Feng 2020: 24). It can operate in the gray zone just like other countries, including the United States. Most analysts have been concerned with the danger that a rising revisionist state will use military violence to overthrow the existing order, a possibility that in our view has become less likely in the contemporary world because of mutual nuclear deterrence and economic interdependence. In contrast to such "hard revisionism," a revisionist state is more likely nowadays to adopt various "soft" strategies to seek institutional change (a topic for Chapter 4).

International order is always a social pact between the powerful and the less powerful, and as such it involves reciprocal and conditional exchanges of promises (Goh 2019: 620). This bargain is subject to constant renegotiation and is therefore an evolving rather than settled deal—a distinctly different position than the one taken by power-transition theory's proponents. Our view also argues that international order cannot be simply imposed by a powerful state unilaterally but rather requires the consent of "follower" states. Cox (1987: 7) sees this order to be "based ideologically on a broad measure of consent." Others agree and emphasize that legitimacy is an important part of the explanation for why an international order endures (Clark 2005; Finnemore 2009; Lake 2009). It seems natural for a country to try to extend its domestic values and institutions to its sphere of influence and beyond (Kupchan 2014). But for a revisionist challenger to undermine and challenge an existing order, it must be able to introduce new norms, rules, and identities that are appealing and acceptable to other countries. This is surely not an easy undertaking at which a rising state can be assumed to succeed (Drezner 2019), and for reasons given by Allan et al. (2018), China's values and identities will have a difficult time finding resonance in other countries where democracy and neoliberalism have taken deep roots in elite and public attitudes. It seems to us that the view that if US power declines, or if the United States disengages from its international commitments, China will be able to step in and rewrite the rules of international order, is based much more on facile assumption than rigorous analysis.

Because it is a two-way bargain, international order requires not just the less powerful states, but also the most powerful state to restrain its own use of power in observance of the rules, norms, and principles that have the consensual support of the international community. This observance gives the most powerful state legitimacy and accords it the status of a hegemon—as distinct from the idea of primacy, which refers only to its preponderance in the interstate power distribution without any implication that other states perceive its dominance to be rightful or legitimate. We draw the readers' attention to this important distinction between the interstate balance of power, on the one hand, and the international order (or society), on the other. Indeed, we are inclined to argue that given its enormous power, international order should be especially relevant for checking a dominant country's possible wanton exercise of power. Whether a small, weak state has revisionist inclinations is less consequential because it lacks the capability to act on them. It is, however, a different matter for a large, strong state which has the capability to carry out its revisionist agenda. When a state is preponderant without any peers, its foreign policies are more likely to reflect its own natural instincts, domestic politics, and its leaders' personalities. Its intentions are therefore highly consequential. These remarks again suggest that contrary to the predominant tendency of the existing literature, we do not view revisionism to be an exclusive trait belonging only to rising states. An established, ruling state can also be revisionist.

This line of argument introduces another important implication: changes in states' material capabilities are in themselves insufficient to cause transitions in international order because such transitions will also require a concomitant transformation of norms and institutions (He and Feng 2020). Put alternatively, an existing international order may persist even in the face of a shifting balance of power (or material capabilities) between, say, the United States and China, while important norms and institutions of this order remain essentially intact. Thus, an international order can survive a change in the identity of world's dominant power. Power transition does not necessarily mean order transition—and the US-dominated order may continue after the passing of US hegemony (Ikenberry 2001, 2008, 2012; Keohane 1984). After all, the one undisputed power transition that the post-1815 era has witnessed—the peaceful transition of world leadership from Britain to the United States—did not produce, in the eyes of most analysts, a basic change in the then-existing international order. As He and Feng (2020: 8) have noted, although there seems to be an agreement among analysts that a power transition is a necessary condition for order transition, there is disagreement about whether it is a sufficient condition. It is also germane to note that although most analysts are preoccupied with the danger that an existing international order may be overthrown and replaced by a rising revisionist state's resort to military violence, we should not overlook the prospect that this order may also be transformed as a result of peaceful reform (a topic we will take up in Chapter 4).

If we treat revisionism as a variable, rather than as a state's fixed trait, we are naturally led to ask: what can change a state's commitment to international order? As alluded to in the preceding discussion, the United States under George W. Bush and especially Donald Trump has taken decisive steps to disengage from and even to challenge various international norms, institutions, and agreements. What can account for this phenomenon? As another example, Japan had fought ostensibly on the side of the established powers in World War I, but has been usually considered a revisionist power both before this conflict (e.g., in the Russo-Japanese and Sino-Japanese Wars) and subsequently (i.e., in World War II). What happened to cause such "switches," which the existing literature has hardly tried to answer? Are different meanings of revisionism being used, thus causing confusion? Are the labels "revisionist" and "status-quo" powers simply post hoc designations and political constructions referring to whether a country has fought on "our" side or "theirs"—or to communicate a writer's personal approval or disapproval of the foreign policy agenda of the country in question?

To what extent can we consider both Wilhelmine Germany and Nazi Germany to be revisionist? Or Brezhnev's Soviet Union and Putin's Russia to be revisionist? How about Maoist China compared to today's China under Xi Jinping? To the extent that the term "revisionism" or "revisionist" has been applied to all these regimes, are we not mixing apples, oranges, and pineapples? The danger of concept stretching (Sartori 1970) is evident. While suggesting a writer's evident objection to these states' foreign policy agendas when the label "revisionist" is applied, this concept has been used in an extremely casual and inconsistent way that misleads and obscures rather than illuminates. The analyst using this term pejoratively almost always sidesteps the question of what exactly the pertinent states are trying to "revise"—or for that matter, how the supposed revisionist states have behaved differently from the supposed status-quo states.

Clearly, the supposed revisionist states cannot be *just* trying to revise the existing interstate distribution of power, seeking to improve their relative positions in the interstate hierarchy. Which state after all does not have this aspiration? If used in this sense, then all states would be considered revisionists because they would all presumably prefer more power and higher status to less power and lower status (including the United States during the late 1800s when it sought to oust British influence from the Western Hemisphere and to establish its own hegemony in this region). This remark would be especially apposite for the so-called established, status-quo states. How else did they acquire their dominant status? Didn't they resort to war and territorial expansion to gain their dominance in the first place? Mearsheimer (2001: 238) quotes Henry Cabot Lodge saying that during the years of its ascendance, the United States had compiled "a record of conquest, colonization, and territorial expansion unequaled by any people in the nineteenth century." We may also ask what process had produced the phenomenon that "the sun never sets on the Union Jack." The prevailing discourse claims that some countries, such as imperial Germany and interwar Japan, were expansionist and were therefore ipso facto revisionist countries. But were they not just following the precedents established by the British, French, and Americans? We thus disagree with the use of the word "revisionism" to refer to a state's attempts to alter the "status quo," defined as the existing interstate distribution of power, to its relative advantage (e.g., Lim 2015). After all, a state's power can grow simply because other countries have fallen behind or collapsed, as in the case of the former Soviet Union (of course, US policies had also contributed to the Soviet Union's demise). Its growing power does not necessarily translate to an increase in its revisionist motivation which, according to the existing literature, typically means a disposition to resort to violent military means to challenge the ruling hegemon and overthrow the existing international order (even though, as we have remarked, states can seek to gain more power and alter the international order by non-military means).

We want to emphasize and elaborate further on a point made in the preceding paragraph. By "revisionism" we cannot and should not mean attempts to alter the existing balance of power among states. Kissinger (2014: 9) clarifies this distinction between the international order as reflected by the shared norms and expectations of international society and the interstate system as defined by the distribution of power among states, when he describes world politics to consist of "a set of commonly accepted rules that define the limits of permissible action and a balance of power that enforces restraints where rules break down, preventing one political unit from subjugating all others." Buzan (2018) has similarly called attention to the distinction between the social structure of the international society and the material structure of the interstate system. When arguing that the liberal international order is bound to fail, Mearsheimer (2019) also recognizes that the international order and the interstate distribution of power are two distinct though causally connected realms. When people treat a state's improvement in its relative power as prima facie evidence of its assault on international order, they are conflating (deliberately or otherwise) these two different analytical concepts and empirical domains. When they do this, they equate international order with the ruling state's power dominance and, by this sleight of hand, turn any bilateral conflict that a country has with the ruling state into a challenge to the entire international community or international order. By sanctifying the ruling state's dominance and questioning the legitimacy of any attempt to challenge its dominance, this tendency manifests a status-quo bias.

Naturally, our statement does not deny that international order and interstate distribution of power are related so that, for example, a hegemon's power derives not just from its material capability but also from the legitimacy conferred by other states' widespread acceptance of the prevailing order, consisting of the norms and institutions that it has sponsored and supported (Clark 2005; Lake 2009). In Reus-Smit's (2004: 43) words, power is constituted "by social institutions, broadly construed as complexes of norms, rules, principles, and decision-making procedures and strong actors are constituted by these intersubjective resources. They therefore have an internal and inherent incentive to comply with the existing structure of international norms." Thus, when a dominant state disregards the rules, norms, and institutions of international order, it suffers a legitimacy deficit and it "rules without right" (Reus-Smit 2007). East Asia between 1300 and 1900 had featured a hierarchical and Sino-centric system based more on legitimacy than coercion (Kang 2003, 2007, 2010). This phenomenon again underscores the importance of consent on the part of subordinate actors in supporting and sustaining an international (or regional) order.

The causal arrow can also point in the other direction. For example, Mearsheimer argues that a unipolar power is necessary to sustain a liberal international order. He states succinctly that "an order is an organized group of international institutions that help govern the interactions among the member states," and "international institutions, which are the building blocks of orders, are effectively rules that the great powers devise and agree to follow, because they believe that obeying these rules is in their interest" (Mearsheimer 2019: 9). In his and many others' view (e.g., Bull 1977; Gilpin 1981; Organski and Kugler 1980), these institutions serve primarily the interests of those states that had created them, and they are not necessarily designed to promote the causes of justice, equality, liberty, or other desiderata such as human dignity. This observation in turn relates to our concerns expressed earlier about the tendency for the existing literature to reify international order as the existing interstate hierarchy and to uphold it as sacrosanct.

As just suggested, we want to keep conceptually distinct and separate a state's satisfaction with its position in the interstate balance of power and its disposition toward the international order. Thus, we differ from Cooley et al. (2019), who have developed a typology of revisionism based on whether a state seeks to change the interstate balance of power and whether it wants to revise the international order. In our view, all states would like to improve their international position (that is, to alter the distribution of power to their advantage), but not all states want to mount a fundamental challenge to the international order, defined as the prevailing rules, norms, and institutions regulating their conduct. Revisionism to us refers *only* to the latter consideration—whether a state wants to alter the fundamental nature of the existing international order (as we will explain later, revisionist states may pursue different policies—such as peaceful reform or violent revolution—to realize their agenda). Our view may sound radical, but it is not actually very unorthodox. As already remarked, the existing literature has argued that the United States was not revisionist when it was a rising power, even though most analysts would agree that it was an expansionist state, seeking to evict British and Spanish influence from the Western Hemisphere.

Our view reflects the original theoretical motivation for introducing the concept of revisionism to international relations research. A "positional revisionist," in the terminology of Cooley et al. (2019)—one that seeks to change the interstate balance of power to its advantage but one that does not seek to change the prevailing international order—is not in our view a revisionist state at all. Similarly, when a state seeks to replace and overhaul this order (as distinct from seeking relatively minor alterations), we consider it to be revisionist regardless of whether it accepts the current interstate balance of power (a developing country may acknowledge and accept its relatively weak international position while joining other similar states in demanding fundamental reform of the international order, such as exemplified by the campaign to promote a "new international economic order;" this example also suggests that a state may entertain a revisionist desire but lacks the capability to achieve this desire). Thus, when Cooley et al. (2019) suggest that the United States is satisfied with the current interstate balance of power but wishes to alter the international order, this suggestion would mean to us that it is at least potentially a revisionist state—depending on how seriously and extensively it rejects the basic tenets and institutions of the existing international order. We believe that our analytic stance in this regard follows more closely existing scholarship, as suggested by Kissinger's remark quoted in the preceding paragraph and by the original intention motivating the formulation of power-transition theory.

This theory invokes two variables—the relative power of the world's two most powerful states and the motivation or character of the rising state—to be determinative of the danger of a systemic war. Given this formulation, the rising state's revisionism is obviously not the same thing as a power shift to its relative advantage, or else the two variables of power-transition theory will be duplicative and redundant. To anticipate later discussion, Ward (2017) has distinguished "distributive revisionism" (a state's interest in having a larger share of interstate resources reallocated to it) from "radical revisionism" (a state's interest in overhauling the international order). In the following discussion, we use the term "revisionism" to refer to a state's desire and intention to alter the ordering principles of international society or the most basic "rules of the game" for international conduct. This being the case, our perspective differs from many others who see, for example, Beijing's policies to improve its power as prima facie evidence that it has a radical revisionist agenda. Our position also means that we disagree with the argument that in a unipolar world, a country's challenge of US preponderance (that is, its attempt to contain, hinder, or diminish US power or, for that matter, to oppose Washington's efforts to rewrite the rules of international order) to be necessarily an expression of this country's revisionism or its intention to challenge the international order (e.g., Schweller and Pu 2011). Moreover, resistance to US hegemony does not necessarily entail an armed challenge. As we will discuss in Chapter 4, recent scholarship has shown that various tactics of "soft balancing" are available to states to frustrate a hegemon (e.g., Paul 2018).

Finally, and as just remarked, revisionism is in our view a matter of degree and can be pursued by different strategies. A revisionist state does not necessarily seek to overhaul or upend the entire international order (it may be unhappy with only certain aspects of the existing order), and military violence is not the only strategy to be expected from a revisionist state. In other words, revisionism can involve more limited demands for institutional reform, and these demands may be pursued by non-military means. In these latter respects, our view of revisionism differs from Ward's (2017) discussion of radical revisionists, and it is closer to Goddard's (2018a) analysis with its explicit recognition that revisionist states may take different paths and adopt different policy approaches.

Our position suggests that other states can engage in power competition with a dominant state or even seek a larger share from the interstate allocation of benefits (tangible and intangible) without necessarily challenging the basic norms and foundational principles of international order. As already mentioned, a change in the identity of the ruling hegemon does not necessarily presage a change in international order. Thus, we do not accept as a foregone conclusion that if China were to overtake the United States in power, this development would automatically mean that a new international order reflecting Chinese views and preferences would be introduced and successfully established. We also do not rule out the possibility that international order can change without an incumbent hegemon being displaced—indeed, this change in international order can be brought about by this hegemon's own actions, such as when it decides to withdraw its support for the rules, norms, and institutions underpinning this order, or even to actively sabotage these rules, norms, and institutions.

As also already mentioned, we contend that no country, not even a hegemon, can unilaterally and single-handedly install an international order. Although this dominant state plays a critical leadership role in creating and sustaining this order, the consent and cooperation of "follower" states are also necessary. Although stated less strongly than our assertion, Ikenberry and Nexon (2019: 418) observe that "hegemons rarely enjoy sufficient power to completely overhaul order entirely." The viability and persistence of international order thus depend also on other states' common expectations and shared sense that the rules, norms, and institutions supporting this order are just, proper, and legitimate.

As already mentioned but needs to be emphasized again, the other implication of this discussion is that unless China can present values and identities that resonate with other countries, especially other great powers, the current international order will persist even if US power declines. Other great powers may continue to feel that the current order is more congenial to their values, identities, and interests, and they can work together to sustain this order when/if the United States loses its unprecedented dominance in modern history. Again, power transition does not necessarily presage an order transition (Ikenberry 2008, 2011; Keohane 1984; Ruggie 1982), a proposition that should be evident to those who claim that the passing of international leadership from Britain to the United States was not followed or accompanied by a change of international order. As Allan et al. (2018: 840) argue, "when the reigning hegemonic ideology is supported by the distribution of identity, then the hegemonic order is likely to remain stable even if the leading state is declining."

This discussion suggests that international order does not necessarily require the existence of a single, preponderant power, as is sometimes suggested by proponents of hegemonic stability theory (Kindleberger 1973). Britain never achieved the same degree of preponderance as the United States, and it was only primus inter pares among the other great powers. After the Napoleonic Wars, Europe's order was provided not by a single dominant state, but rather by a concert of great powers along the lines of the k-group discussed by Snidal (1985). Instructively, the demise of this concert system came about not because of rejection or abandonment by its conservative or autocratic members, but rather because of deliberate subversion and dismantlement by its liberal members, Britain and France (Kupchan 2010).

To reiterate, we believe that "revisionism" and "status-quo commitment" are a variable rather than a constant to be used in describing the foreign policy motivations or intentions of *all* states, not just those states that are gaining relative power. Established states, including the ruling hegemon and those that are suffering (or poised to suffer) relative decline, can also have a revisionist agenda. The reality of international relations is such that all states play both offense and defense at the same time (Crawford 2003), and their behavior and motivations may very well differ according to the issue areas in question (Chin and Thakur 2010; Foot and Walter 2011; Ikenberry and Lim 2017; Johnston 2019; Kastner et al. 2016). A state may be committed to existing rules and norms in some cases, but also seek to replace them with new ones in other cases. For example, the United States and other Western states have challenged the traditional concept of sovereignty, and they have supported "responsibility to protect" and have even promoted "regime change" in situations of grave violations of human rights. They had also introduced, after World War II, conventions to punish officials guilty of crimes against peace and humanity. In these examples, the United States and other Western countries have acted as "norm entrepreneurs" to introduce new expectations and principles to replace old ones. They were/are, in other words, revisionists in these instances. This view is of course a significant departure from the customary tendency in the existing literature to use "revisionist" and "status-quo" motivations as code words for an analyst to designate "hostile" and "friendly" states, respectively.

As suggested by the preceding examples, the norms, rules, and institutions of international order can evolve without a systemic war. Peaceful reform and changing elite and public attitudes can alter widely shared views and understandings about the "rules of the game." Thus, while colonialism and racial discrimination (e.g., South Africa's apartheid, US laws banning Chinese immigrants) were accepted practices at one time, they are no longer tolerated in today's world. Recent reform to the International Monetary Fund's voting quotas to reflect more accurately the world's changing distribution of economic power offers another example of peaceful change. Surely, norms against the use of nuclear weapons have gained strength over time (Tannenwald 1999, 2005). Moreover, until the US invasion of Iraq in 2003, there was an emerging international consensus that military intervention abroad should require some effort to obtain United Nations authorization (Thompson 2006: 2). And as already noted briefly, the idea that foreigners have a responsibility to protect innocent people, even if this means violating the traditional principle of state sovereignty, has gained international support, though it remains controversial (Bellamy 2009).

Our view also sees states usually operating in a gray zone between complete acceptance or rejection of the international order, thus concurring with Goh's (2019: 641) advice that "we need to stop thinking solely in terms of opposition and revolt, and instead look for a shifting balance between complicity and resistance . . . a rising hegemonic challenger like China can choose to operate in that grey area between complicity and resistance, while not revolting outright against the existing hegemonic order." Our agreement with this perspective should make it clear that we do not see China as somehow absolutely or irrevocably a revisionist state. This view of course also dissents with the idea that the United States is absolutely or irrevocably committed to the defense of the international order. Such dichotomy, as we have already stressed, is descriptively inaccurate and analytically unhelpful. Both countries, like others, can be "selective" revisionists (Medeiros 2019), being revisionist on some occasions and on some matters, which in turn means that their revisionist tendencies can vary according to issue areas and over time (Foot and Walter 2011).

The preceding remarks also call attention to the fact that a state's words and deeds need not correspond. For example, Washington has (along with China) declined to join the International Criminal Court, and it has in fact barred international personnel investigating possible rights abuses committed by Americans in Afghanistan from entering the United States. Washington also did not have any compunction in imposing a naval "quarantine" against Cuba in 1962, although today it routinely invokes freedom of navigation in response to China's sovereignty claims in the South China Sea, despite its own refusal to join the United Nations Convention for the Law of the Sea (UNCLOS), which China has signed. Although it has criticized Beijing for rejecting the Permanent Court of Arbitration's jurisdiction in China's sovereignty dispute with the Philippines in the South China Sea, the United States has also refused to acknowledge the International Court of Justice's ruling that it had violated international law when it mined Nicaragua's ports. These examples point to the role that hypocrisy plays in international relations (Finnemore 2009). This role mediates the tension caused by the conundrum of enforcing international laws and promoting lofting ideals, on the one hand, and accepting the reality of power politics, on the other hand. Recognition of this conundrum suggests that we rarely see states evincing absolute support for or outright rejection of international order—in other words, most states' commitment or opposition to international order is not a matter of all or nothing. As we have tried to emphasize, we object to the existing literature's tendency to classify states in binary categories of being either revisionist or committed to the international order (usually treating the United States as a "status quo" country and China as a "revisionist" one, without much discussion or evidence). We view interstate interactions to be a constant process of negotiation and adjustment. As Johnston (2019: 58) has put it, "[the status quo versus revisionist] binary make[s] no conceptual sense in a world of multiple and often inconsistent orders." Not only is this approach empirically unsound, it is also, in our view, normatively biased.

Historical Illustrations, Analogies, and Lessons

Revisionism stems from some serious discontent with the prevailing rules, norms, and institutions of the existing international order. This discontent, however, does not necessarily suggest a desire to overthrow the existing order entirely or an intention to resort to military means in this effort ("hard revisionism"). Revisionist states may pursue non-military means to alter the existing order or some parts of this order ("soft revisionism"). Moreover, and as we have emphasized earlier, an expansionist state may engage in aggression and conquest (in order to alter the balance of power in its favor) without, however, seeking to upend the basic tenets and foundational principles of international order. Finally, a state may espouse a revisionist (revolutionary) ideology without, however, having the capability or the intention to implement this ideology. Thus its "bite" may not match its "bark."

In our view, Napoleonic France and Bolshevik Russia (the Soviet Union) were revisionist states because they had propagated and sought to implement a new ideology (republicanism and the dictatorship of international proletariat, respectively) to overturn the foundational principles (monarchical rule and territorial states, respectively) of international relations prevailing at their time. Mao's doctrine of people's war can also be considered a challenge to the existing international order because it advocates armed insurgency to overthrow ruling bourgeois governments (Beijing, however, did not have the necessary capabilities to carry out its revisionist agenda much beyond its immediate neighborhood during the Maoist years). This reasoning also suggests that the Monroe Doctrine presented a radical challenge to the then-prevailing rules of international relations because it asserted an exclusive regional sphere of influence for the United States and, in the so-called Roosevelt Corollary, an absolute right for the United States to intervene in the domestic affairs of *any* state located in the Western Hemisphere for *whatever* reason Washington sees fit. The idea of "American exceptionalism" of course also implies that Washington claims that it is not bound by the usual rules that apply to other states. Finally, the emergence of the European Union with its supranational institutions and its vision of a "single (borderless) Europe" naturally introduces a revolutionary, new ordering principle, and presents a radical break from the existing order based on sovereign, territorial states. As these examples suggest, the current literature's denotation of the term "revisionist" has been rather vague and inconsistent, even though its connotation in referring to "troublemakers" is relatively clear. We seek to reverse the tendency often found in the current practice to deploy it to convey a normative judgment rather than as an empirical observation.

Power-transition theorists (Organski and Kugler 1980) see revisionist states as challengers to the existing "international order." But what is "the international order"? Despite its analytic and conceptual prominence in the international relations literature, there is a relative dearth of systematic work on international order (e.g., Kegley and Raymond 1994; Lebow 2018). We draw on the seminal work of Hedley Bull (1977) in discussing international order. As one of the founders of the so-called English school, he has pioneered the idea of an international society with widely recognized rules, norms, and institutions shared by most states most of the time. Since the advent of modern states, the prevailing international order has encompassed the institution of sovereignty and the idea of the juridical equality of all states, the principle of non-interference in other states' domestic affairs, the inviolability of states' territorial integrity, the sanctity of treaty commitments, mutual respect for the great powers' traditional spheres of influence, and conventions regarding warfare, combat (for example, with respect to the treatment of civilians and prisoners of war), and diplomatic immunity. These are widely recognized "rules of the game" that provide stability and facilitate peace in international relations. They contribute to these desiderata by propagating and consolidating common expectations about what constitutes proper and legitimate conduct in international relations. Presumably, a revisionist state is one that disagrees with these precepts and violates them flagrantly and repeatedly. We will address more extensively these tenets and principles of international order in subsequent discussions. We will present a variety of empirical indicators to discern the extent of Chinese and US revisionism in Chapter 3. We will also introduce Buzan's (2010, 2018) ideas on the primary and secondary institutions of international order when discussing revisionist strategies in Chapter 4.

For now, we want to just mention briefly that it is not clear to us why the label "revisionist" is appropriate for some states that have been described as such. Wilhelmine Germany and imperial Japan come to mind as such cases. These were surely expansionist and aggressive states that had pursued military conquest to increase their power. It is not clear, however, in what ways they had sought to change the existing international order in terms of the various tenets and principles mentioned in the preceding paragraph. In many ways, their conduct—such as in engaging in territorial expansion, seeking spheres of influence, undertaking gunboat diplomacy, demanding commercial privileges and access to foreign markets, and violating rules on the use of force—did not differ from the so-called established, status-quo powers that were victorious in their military conflicts. In fact, the policies undertaken by Wilhelmine Germany and imperial Japan were following the precedents of imperial expansion and military and economic aggrandizement established by Britain, France, and the United States. In other words, they were not so much challenging the "rules of the game" as much as they were imitating and following the established powers' practices to play the same game. Moreover, it is not clear how Wilhelmine Germany and imperial Japan's understanding or vision of international order differed radically from the then-prevailing one, based on a hierarchical system of sovereign, territorial states dominated by a few powerful countries ruling over a vast number of subjugated peoples denied of citizenship or statehood.

As the reader may have already realized, our analytic position questions whether a country's rising power will necessarily cause it to develop a more offensive or aggressive posture, causing it to become involved in more militarized interstate disputes and to mount a more serious challenge to the prevailing international order. The conventional wisdom of US scholars argues that when the United States was rising, it was a status-quo power. This argument, however, is usually asserted, rather than thoroughly explained or documented, and the United States is typically treated as an exception to the rule that rising powers tend to be revisionist powers. However, the evidence from Thies and Nieman's (2017) analysis of BRICS (Brazil, Russia, India, China, and South Africa) is quite decisive in *rejecting* the facile assumption made by structural theorists of international relations, claiming changing power relations among states to be the primary source of rising states' revisionist impulses and hence a main cause of major wars. Shirk (2007) appears to be making this claim when she states, "History teaches us that rising powers are likely to provoke war" (quoted in Lebow and Valentino 2009: 389), although it is not clear whether she also had the United States in mind among history's rising powers (or for that matter, Britain, the Netherlands, and Portugal during their respective years of ascendance).

Even a casual observer of China can see that during this country's years of rapid rise (since the late 1970s when Deng Xiaoping launched his program of economic reform), the incidence and severity of Beijing's resort to military force have declined conspicuously when compared to the years before its rise. In other words, the pertinent trends contradict rather than confirm offensive realism's claim and power-transition theory's insinuation that increasing power will make a country like China more aggressive, expansionist, and revisionist. It would also be instructive to inquire how many wars a rising China has fought, say, since 1979 (when it had a border conflict with Vietnam), compared to the incidence of wars fought by the United States as an established ruling power and this country's overt use of military force abroad (e.g., Afghanistan, Grenada, Iraq, Libya, Panama, Serbia, Syria). Because territorial contests are the most common source for wars and militarized interstate disputes (Vasquez 1993, 2009; Vasquez and Henehan 2011) and because China shares a border with more countries than any other in the world (in comparison, the United States has land borders with only two countries), the difference in these countries' respective incidence of being involved in wars and militarized interstate disputes is even more stark than the raw figures, without adjusting for the number of their neighbors, would suggest. This phenomenon explains in part our bewilderment in the existing literature's attribution of relative aggressiveness, bellicosity, or assertiveness to these countries. Moreover, contrary to the expectation of offensive realism, China has not appeared to have become more aggressive, bellicose, or assertive in its foreign policy, even though its power has grown in recent years. This is at least a debatable question to be settled by systematic evidence (Jerden 2014; Johnston 2013). Contesting the prevailing US view, Zhang (2019: 156) notes, "China has not become more militarily aggressive over time" as it becomes more powerful relative to the other South China Sea contestants.

Structural theorists who emphasize power shifts as a cause of war tend to overlook agency (that is, leaders' capacity to shape events), the domestic sources of foreign policy, including a society's self-conception (Shih and Yin 2013), and people's capacity to learn from history. The mechanical way in which many structural theorists apply historical interpretations as ostensible analogies or precedents for contemporary China is especially problematic (e.g., Allison 2017). For example, the so-called Thucydides's Trap invites people to imagine ancient Athens (a rising power) as an analogy for contemporary China and ancient Sparta (presumably, the ruling power on the eve of the Peloponnesian War) as an analogy for contemporary United States. But how valid are such analogies when we consider that Sparta was an oligarchy relying on an agrarian economy and deriving its strength from its powerful infantry (the hoplites), whereas Athens was a democracy according to the standards of its time and drew its strength primarily from its maritime and commercial prowess? We would have to dismiss these important differences in regime characteristics, economic base, and military orientation, and to also overlook important developments in the intervening 2,500 years, such as the advent of modern states, nationalism, and nuclear weapons, in mediating the effects of bilateral power shifts on the probability of a war breaking out (Chan 2020a). Other observers have explicitly introduced Wilhelmine Germany, "a country that felt it had been denied its 'place in the sun,' that believed it had been mistreated by the other powers, and that was determined to achieve its rightful place by nationalistic assertiveness" (Wolfowitz 1997: 8), as a parallel for today's China. It is not clear, however, why a motivation to improve a country's international position and even its grievances against the established powers should be construed ipso facto as evidence of its revisionist agenda. Although historical analogies can be helpful in formulating sound policies, they can also be misused (Khong 1992; May 1973). Kang (2003, 2007, 2010, 2020) has been most forceful in arguing that analysts cannot uncritically transfer theories based on Western experiences to study China, and that East Asia's past suggests that contemporary Western discourse on Thucydides's Trap and power-transition war is seriously misinformed. Thus, he contends that we should not simply project Western countries' past conduct to understand Chinese behavior, but must instead take seriously this country and East Asia's own traditions. Chan (2020a, 2020b) argues that even when assessed on their own terms, these formulations are highly problematic.

Naturally, historical analogies such as that offered by Thucydides's Trap argue that since leaders are boxed in by the circumstances that they find themselves in, they have only limited influence in overcoming the structural pressures and constraints. These structural conditions incline the leaders to repeat the same mistakes. But why should we assume that leaders are incapable of learning from history? Presumably, Chinese leaders can draw lessons from the successes and failures of other countries' experiences, such as those of Japan, Germany, the Soviet Union, and the United States (Buzan and Cox 2013; Feng 2006; Kirshner 2012; Medeiros 2009; Wolf 2014). Why should we expect that Chinese leaders would be motivated by the same impulses and would pursue the same agenda that structural forces had supposedly caused earlier rising and, for that matter, declining powers to risk war? A "naïve" rationalist view would instead suggest that the more often prior aggressive states seeking imperial expansion have been defeated in their bid for regional or global hegemony (e.g., Napoleon, Hitler, Mussolini, Tojo, Brezhnev), the less likely others will follow their example. The idea that rising powers will again and again resort to military means to challenge a dominant hegemon and the prevailing international order suggests that their leaders are somehow trapped by the same structural conditions and are condemned to repeat the same mistakes. Realists, including proponents of power-transition theory, assume that states are rational actors who compare benefits and costs. If so, why would leaders of a late rising power like China fail to update their beliefs in view of their predecessors' experiences (including lessons provided by the successful example set by the United States in reaching its hegemonic status in a peaceful transition)? As we will argue more extensively later, we see various institutional strategies to shape and influence international order to be more likely pursued by revisionist states nowadays than military conquest and subversion. And as we have implied thus far and as we will argue later, there is a strong element of social and political construction—if you will, revisionist history—in the presentation of great-power encounters in the past and the prognosis of Sino-American relations in the future.

In addition to failing to consider people's capacity to learn from the past, there is a bias in the current literature dominated by structural theorists who tend to overemphasize the dynamics of competition in interstate relations and who fail to give enough consideration to the effects of socialization and stakeholding in shaping the motivations and incentives of rising states. China's changing perspective on and role in multilateral diplomacy offer a dramatic example (Johnston 2008). The dominant Western narratives are preoccupied with a rising country's power to overthrow the prevailing international order without considering that with its improved international position, this country will have a larger stake in preserving the order that has enabled its upward mobility. These same narratives tend to manifest a lack of comparative historical perspective, such as when they criticize contemporary China for free-riding on the provision of international public goods while overlooking US isolationism and protectionism (e.g., its absence from the League of Nations, its Smoot-Hawley legislation that exacerbated the Great Depression) long after it had become the world's dominant power (circa 1870 but certainly by the 1890s). Furthermore, much of the US discourse on China's rise tends to be autobiographical (Pan 2012), describing or predicting Chinese conduct that reflects conscious or unconscious reasoning based on its own past conduct. Thus, Washington claims that Beijing is a revisionist country because it wants to push the United States out of the Asia Pacific region—without, however, realizing the irony that it is accusing Beijing for trying to do what it had itself practiced. The Monroe Doctrine had sought an exclusive US sphere of influence in the Western Hemisphere and successfully so because the United States has thus far been the only country that has secured a regional hegemony.

Organization of the Book

Having stated our rationale for studying revisionism and our critique of existing treatments of this topic, we organize the remainder of the book in four chapters. In Chapter 2, we discuss the origin and evolution of a revisionist state. We include in our analysis cases from the present and the past, such as Wilhelmine and

Nazi Germany, the Soviet Union during the Cold War and contemporary Russia, imperial Japan between the 1880s and 1940s, the United States during its years of ascendance and today, and China in the 1950s and 1960s compared to now. This chapter also discusses how domestic and foreign conditions interact to influence revisionist impulses, and how these impulses and frustrations with perceived resistance to a revisionist state's aspirations can lead to war.

In Chapter 3, we offer our views on the key elements of international order. We introduce specifically two different conceptions of this order, one that is based on widely accepted norms and the other based on rules and institutions. We then introduce a battery of indicators to track the evolution of Chinese and US foreign policy behavior and use these indicators to infer the changing motivations or intentions of their leaders. We conclude from our analysis that while Beijing's behavior points increasingly to a more status-quo agenda, Washington's conduct has moved in the opposite direction of becoming more revisionist. This conclusion, based on multiple convergent indicators, challenges the prevailing view presented by the current literature that a rising power tends to be revisionist, whereas an established ruling power is necessarily committed to the preservation of international order.

In Chapter 4, we turn to a discussion of various strategies available to revisionist states. We argue that although a systemic war will surely be a catastrophic event for both the belligerents and bystanders, this danger preoccupying most analysts working in the tradition of power-transition theory or Thucydides's Trap is not very likely among today's great powers because of their mutual nuclear deterrence and economic interdependence. "Hard revisionism" in the form of overt, massive use of military force to gain territory, confront a ruling hegemon, and mount a direct challenge to the existing international order appears to us much less probable than non-military strategies or "soft revisionism" to influence existing institutions or to create alternative institutions (Drezner 2019). Which strategy a revisionist state will select would depend on its perceived benefits (relative to costs) from an existing institution and its comparative advantage to shape this existing institution or to foster a competing alternative.

Finally, in Chapter 5 we summarize the highlights of our analysis and present some ideas that we hope would reduce tension in Sino-American relations and facilitate the peaceful transformation of international order. This transformation presents a daunting challenge because, on the one hand, its rules, principles, and institutions should be sufficiently binding and authoritative to command widespread respect and compliance, and, on the other hand, they should be sufficiently flexible to adapt to changing circumstances and accommodate compromises in view of the harsh reality of power politics and potential objection from great powers. Naturally, power shifts can engender a variety of psychological or emotional reactions, such as fear, anxiety, arrogance, overconfidence, distrust, and uncertainty. When a large amount of power shift occurs within a short period of time, these reactions and the danger of misjudgment tend to be exacerbated.

Prospect theory suggests that people in the domain of loss are likely to become more risk-acceptant (Boettcher 2005; He 2016a; Kahneman and Tversky 1979; McDermott 1998). A rising state may fear that a declining but still more powerful ruling state is motivated to block its ascent and even to consider launching a preventive war before it catches up (Copeland 2000; Levy 1987, 1996). Conversely, a declining albeit still dominant state may be concerned that it cannot trust the ascending state's promises because the latter can renege on its commitments after gaining more power in the future (Fearon 1995). This mutual trust deficit (Chan 2017; Lieberthal and Wang 2012) can be further compounded by domestic partisan competition, shrinking the "win set" of each country's leaders and therefore their bargaining space (Putnam 1988). Domestic politics engendering incentives for nationalist demagoguery, resort to scapegoating foreigners, and attempts to outbid one's opponents in "getting tough" on real or imagined foreign adversaries can further exacerbate international tension (Colaresi 2005). In view of these difficulties, prudent statecraft requires reassurance, reciprocity, and empathy. Empathy points to the need for care and sensitivity, so that one's actions do not place the other side's leaders in a domain of loss (including these leaders' domestic standing) whereby they would be more inclined to accept confrontation and even conflict.

The study of states' revisionist or status-quo motivations is an important but long-neglected topic for scholars of international relations. Although there has been a recent uptick of interest in this topic given popular, scholarly, and of course official fascination with and concern about China's rapid rise, there is still a dearth of work reflecting both thoughtful conceptual refinement and thorough empirical analysis. In the remainder of this book, we will pursue multiple objectives that are often missing in the current literature: we will engage in both theoretical development and policy relevance; we will undertake historical analysis and compare China with other major states (thus avoiding treating this country in isolation or as sui generis); and we will examine multiple data sources to track over time the changes in Beijing and Washington's foreign policy orientation or motivation. We will not take a country's revisionist or status-quo motivation for granted or as a fixed attribute, and we will try to explain its origin and evolution as a result of the pressures and opportunities presented by its external environment and the nature of its changing domestic politics. Finally, we will make the case that revisionist states will not always pursue "hard" strategies relying on military means to displace the incumbent hegemon or to overthrow the existing international order. We urge instead greater attention to various "soft" strategies available to a revisionist state to leverage its resources and achieve its agenda. In other words, we will try to say something about how different revisionist states will pursue different strategies given their different resources and situations, and what factors incline them to become revisionist in the first place.

2

The Origin and Evolution of Revisionism

Revisionism refers to a specific kind of motivation or orientation that a state can have in its foreign policy. It refers to a desire or intention to revise or make changes to a doctrine, norm, principle, or institution. The changes being sought by a revisionist can be "limited" or "unlimited" (Schweller 1994, 2015). This distinction corresponds roughly with the difference between "distributive revisionism" and "radical revisionism" (Ward 2017) mentioned in the previous chapter. The former type refers to a state seeking to redistribute resources (tangible or intangible) in its favor, whereas the latter type refers to a state's deeper sense of dissatisfaction with the basic rules and principles that determine the allocation of these resources and its desire or intention to alter and replace these basic rules and principles. Another variation is offered by Behravesh (2018), who refers to a state's offensive campaign to redistribute resources in its favor as "thick revisionism" and expressions of defiance against or dissatisfaction with the "status quo" as "thin revisionism." He views Nazi Germany's territorial conquests and Russia's recent annexation of Crimea as examples of the former, whereas Iran and North Korea's nuclear programs exemplify the latter. As we will explain later, we prefer the terms "hard" and "soft revisionism," whose definition differs from other analysts' concepts.

Naturally, classification categories suggest ideal types because all states can be to a greater or lesser extent dissatisfied with their share of resources or benefits (whether they be export revenues, colonial possessions, geostrategic position, or diplomatic prestige). They can also be to a greater or lesser extent dissatisfied with some aspects of the existing "rules of the game" for conducting international relations. Therefore, when analysts make categorical assertions about whether a specific state is revisionist or committed to the "status quo," they are arguably engaging in simplification. All states would obviously like to improve their share of resources or benefits, and they can all lend support to the prevailing rules and principles in some issue areas but would prefer to see them changed or replaced in other issue areas (Foot and Walter 2011; Johnston 2019). When the term "revisionism" is used by international relations analysts, they customarily mean "radical revisionism" as defined by Ward (2017). Moreover, they usually have in mind attempts by the pertinent state to subvert, challenge, and overthrow the existing rules and principles of international order by coercive and non-consensual means, and hence the "thick revisionism" suggested by Behravesh (2018).

This last distinction is important because while a country can be dissatisfied with its current share of resources or benefits and while it can even be upset with the existing rules, norms, and institutions of international order, it can still try to promote change by peaceful reform and consensual adjustment. Several recent studies on China's conduct in dealing with international financial institutions, such as the International Monetary Fund and the Asian Infrastructure Investment Bank, conclude that Beijing has behaved in this manner (e.g., Ren 2015; Wilson 2019). As Ren (2015: 2025) has emphasized, "peaceful rise does not exclude rule change, so long as this is made not through force or coercion, but rather through mutual accommodation." We concur with his view that "history may show that all rising powers seek rule change one way or another. The real question is the way in which a rising power seeks rule change" (Ren 2015: 2026). Indeed, we do not see why his observation should be limited to only rising powers because in our view established powers can also have revisionist motivations and agenda.

We consider a state that is motivated to change the basic norms, rules, and institutions of international order to be revisionist. To us, its method or strategy for pursuing this agenda is important. It can adopt what we call "hard revisionism" by relying mainly on military means (note, however, that such conduct might be condoned by the then-prevailing "rules of the game" and thus not considered as revisionist by us). Or it can pursue "soft revisionism," emphasizing primarily non-military means to alter and shape international institutions in a direction more congenial to its values and interests. States characterized by the latter tendency are interested in introducing and promoting gradual adjustments of international order, in contrast to the former tendency's aim of upending and replacing it by military conquest and coercion. Naturally, as ideal types, this dichotomy does not capture all possible variations in states' conduct, but seeks rather to point to a difference of relative emphasis in their respective strategies. The option of pursuing "hard revisionism" is not as readily available to smaller states given their more limited resources. In contrast, "soft revisionism" as a strategy should be available to all states, and its adoption is therefore not limited to just the great powers.

This discussion leads us to four topics for inquiry. First, we would want to ask about the sources of revisionist motivation, which in this book refers to a desire to change the basic norms, rules, and institutions of the prevailing international order. What combination of domestic and foreign factors can give rise to this motivation? How do perceptions of opportunities and pressures contribute to such motivation? Second, what conditions are pertinent in enabling or disabling states with such revisionist motivation in carrying out their policy program? Naturally, one such condition is the belief that this country has the requisite capability to execute its revisionist program. Shifting power relations among states can thus influence this belief. Another condition can be the pertinent leaders' judgments about their counterparts' relative resolve. Which country is more determined to defend the existing international order or to challenge it? Third, what conditions tend to influence the established powers' response to the rising latecomers' demand for recognition? In other words, what considerations are likely to affect the established powers' willingness to accommodate the rising powers? Naturally, this accommodation—or the lack thereof—can be one of the determinants of whether a state develops a revisionist motivation. Since revisionism can also motivate an incumbent hegemon or dominant power, one would also want to know how the conditions and conduct of other countries can affect its policies. Finally, what considerations tend to shape a revisionist state's choice of strategy? Significantly, even when a country has a revisionist agenda and even when it has substantial capability, it may not necessarily resort to waging a systemic war. It may adopt an isolationist or reclusive policy. This state can also pursue a strategy of soft revisionism, as explained earlier.

We will postpone until Chapter 4 to discuss the fourth topic of inquiry just mentioned, specifically concerning the different strategies that revisionist states can adopt. We will review the pertinent literature, which includes social identity theory and this theory's expectations of the conditions under which a state may adopt emulation, competition, or creativity as its strategy for upward mobility (e.g., Larson and Shevchenko 2010, 2019). Additionally, Goddard's (2018a) recent work shows that a revisionist state's strategy (including peaceful integration) depends on its position in international networks and its access to international institutions. Finally, there is Hirschman's (1970) classic work on how firms, organizations, and states respond to decline by choosing among "voice, exit, and loyalty." As suggested by the last remark, we see revisionism to be a motivation that can apply to declining as well as rising states. Even a ruling hegemon can have this motivation if it feels that it is not adequately recognized or compensated by the current international order as befitting its dominant position.

In the remainder of this chapter, we will take up the other three topics mentioned previously. What are the historical conditions that can produce grievance and even anger on the part of rising powers, causing their leaders and people to feel that their just aspirations have been thwarted by the established powers? What opportunities and pressures both at home and abroad can abet or dampen their revisionist impulses? As just mentioned, revisionism can also characterize established powers, both when they are gaining even greater preponderance and when they are suffering relative decline. How can their emotions, such as anxiety or arrogance, and a "windows logic" encourage a revisionist agenda? Moreover, under what conditions are established powers more likely to accept and accommodate rising powers? We will give much less attention in our discussion to the topic of power shifts because it has been the dominant and even exclusive focus of the existing literature, including those reflecting concerns of analysts working in the tradition of balance-of-power theory, power-transition theory, and power-cycle theory (e.g., Doran 1991; Mearsheimer 2001; Modelski 1987; Organski and Kugler 1980; Waltz 1979). Allison's (2017) discussion of Thucydides's Trap is but the most recent, prominent formulation in this tradition that gives the analytic pride of place to the role of changing power balance among major states in producing large wars.

We will emphasize here, however, that although much ink has been spilled over the idea that China is catching up to the United States, there remains an enormous gap between these two countries. Whether in terms of their relative economic, technological, or military power, the preponderant position enjoyed by the United States will be invulnerable to any Chinese attempt to match it, not to mention to overtake it, for at least several decades (if then)—and this remark does not even take into account important US allies who can further contribute to its huge advantages (Norrlof and Wohlforth 2019). As Nye (2019: 74) states succinctly, "no other country—including China—is about to replace the American position in the world in terms of its overall power." The idea of an imminent or impending power transition between China and the United States is quite fanciful and even ludicrous (e.g., Beckley 2011/2012; Brooks and Wohlforth 2016a, 2016b; Buzan 2004a; Chan 2020c; Danzman et al. 2017; Gilli and Gilli 2019; Lieber and Press 2006; Posen 2003; Russett 1985; Starrs 2013), and the United States continues to maintain a large edge in structural power (Barnett and Duvall 2005; Chan 2020c; Strange 1987; Farrell and Newman 2019). In a 2014 speech, President Barack Obama declared, "America has rarely been stronger relative to the rest of the world. Those who argue otherwise— who suggest that America is in decline, or has seen its global leadership slip away—are either misreading history or engaged in partisan politics" (quoted in MacDonald and Parent 2018: 190).

Such a transition is much more unlikely in today's world of unipolarity than in the bygone era of European balance of power because the technological distance separating the United States from the rest of the pack is much greater (in contrast, this gap was much narrower among the great powers in earlier eras, such as between Sparta and Athens, Rome and Carthage, France and the Habsburgs, Napoleon and his adversaries, and even prior to World War II when Nazi Germany was able to remilitarize in a few short years to pose a threat to Britain and France). It is unimaginable, for example, that China can in a few short years leapfrog the United States to become more powerful militarily, as Nazi Germany managed to do relative to Britain in the 1930s. That the United States enjoys and will almost certainly continue to enjoy its preponderant position for at least several decades to come in turn raises the question of why the fascination and, indeed, obsession with a prospective power transition between the two countries, reflecting perhaps sensationalist and even alarmist construction with a political agenda.

This statement should not be interpreted to deny that China can pose a problem for the United States even without having caught up (Christensen 2001) or that it has made significant strides in improving its relative position in the interstate distribution of power, but it is quite a different matter to frame the relevant discourse in terms of an ongoing or impending power transition. Moreover, it confuses what may be a contest for regional dominance as a global struggle over the fate of *the* international order. In our view, power-transition theorists misconstrue and misrepresent the two world wars as a German challenge to Britain's worldwide preeminence (and even less persuasively, to claim that Japan's bid for a regional sphere of influence constitutes such an attempt). As Levy (2020: n.p.) has asked with insight about China and the United States: "Is [their] competition between a rising regional power and a global power for regional dominance, or a competition for dominance in the global system?" The dynamics involved in these different kinds of rivalries are quite different (Levy and Thompson 2005: 2010). And as Levy (2020: n.p.) notes, "the [latter], but presumably, not the former, might involve a remaking of the rules and norms of the global system that Organski posited was at the heart of power transitions."

That states need to have the requisite capability to act on their motivation naturally leads analysts to focus on power shifts among major states as the starting point of their inquiry. Sharp, abrupt changes in relative power can empower revisionist states to act on their vision or ambition. There is another reason for focusing on power shifts as the starting point of inquiry: improvements in a country's relative power position can introduce an incongruity in its perceived accomplishments and its status as ascribed by other states. This discrepancy can in turn cause a sense of frustration and relative deprivation, motivating an upwardly mobile state to demand appropriate recognition. When its demand for this recognition or accommodation is met with repeated resistance, its distributive demands can turn into a desire to revise the international order itself.

Parenthetically and conversely, a refusal to downsize its self-appointed role or to adjust its outdated sense of entitlement can also cause status incongruity for a declining state. Thus, the founders of power-transition theory (Organski 1958; Organski and Kugler 1980) considered a declining hegemon's adjustment of its role and expectations, and the speed of a power transition that can affect its ability to make this adjustment, among those factors that can influence whether this transition will have a peaceful or violent outcome. Various psychological and bureaucratic reasons can stand in the way of this country making the necessary adjustments—which in turn means that a rising power's greed, ambition, or impatience are not the only reason for a war to occur. It would be more reasonable and valid to see this occurrence as a bargaining failure caused by both

Changes in power balance (relative increase or decrease). →
Status discrepancy and dissatisfaction with the existing distribution of benefits. →
Demands to revise the existing distribution of benefits. →
If accepted, a new status quo is established; if rejected, turning to demands to revise the norms, rules, and institutions of the existing international order. →
These demands are further affected by foreign pressures and opportunities. →
These encounters can be amplified or dampened by domestic conditions. →
Which can in turn create a feedback loop to interact with foreign conditions. →
Depending on a state's calculation of its costs and benefits, and its comparative advantages in different issue areas, it may pursue hard or soft revisionism.

Figure 2.1 Genesis and evolution of revisionism.

sides' inability to reach a settlement to avoid conflict (DiCicco and Levy 2003; Levy 2020).

We present in Figure 2.1 a flowchart showing the genesis and evolution of revisionism on the part of a rising state.

Relative Deprivation and International Order

Dominance has its advantages. For example, consumers pay more, sometimes substantially more, for gasoline in other countries than in the United States. The dominance of the US dollar as the premier international currency gives American tourists convenience while traveling abroad, and it enables the United States to run chronic budget deficits and export the inflationary impact of its fiscal extravagance to other countries. Naturally, economic dominance (including the power of the dollar as the preferred instrument of commercial settlement and as the world's reserve currency) also gives Washington the leverage to compel other countries to join its sanctions against Iran and Russia, lest they be denied access to US financial institutions and the US market. Indeed, as Farrel and Newman (2019) have shown, the United States has "weaponized" interdependence, taking advantage of its central position in international financial and information networks, to advance its interests and to coerce or punish opponents. As another example of the advantage enjoyed by a hegemon (Britain in the past and the United States today), English as the world's lingua franca confers upon Americans not only convenience but also a competitive edge in areas such as mass media and everyday communication.

These advantages do not just come "out of the blue," but rather have a historical and institutional legacy. We will discuss in more detail the nature of international order in the next chapter, but it is pertinent to note here that its rules and institutions do not just emerge mysteriously because of some neutral, impersonal force. As Organski (1958) has observed, they were created by the established powers to serve their interests and to the detriment of other countries. He writes, "the powerful and dissatisfied nations are usually those that have grown to full power after the existing international order was fully established and the benefits already allocated. These parvenus had no share in the creation of the international order, and the dominant nation and its supporters are not usually willing to grant the newcomers more than a small part of the advantages they receive" (quoted in Organski and Kugler 1980: 19). Given this view that international order is a source of privilege for the powerful, it is only natural that Organski (1958: 328, 332) warns his readers not to confuse the defense of this order with "a peace with justice." Gilpin (1981: 29), another well-known scholar who has written on the subject of power transition, has made similar observations, remarking that "in international society the distribution of power among coalitions [of states] determines who governs the international system and whose interests are principally promoted by the functioning of the system," and that the "dominant states have sought to exert control over the system in order to advance their self-interests."

It is natural to conclude from these observations that there are in this world "surplus" and "deficit" countries, according their relative power positions in the international system and the resources or benefits they receive from this system. These are, respectively, countries that are "over-compensated" and "under-compensated" in the amount of resources and benefits (including intangible ones like status) that they receive compared to their actual capabilities, performance, or relative power position. Examples include the discrepancies in the weighted vote that different countries receive in the International Monetary Fund (compared to the relative size of their economy and their financial contribution to this organization), and the designation of a country as a permanent member of the United Nations Security Council and the veto power that comes with this designation (compared to the size of its economy, population, and contributions of money and personnel to this organization). More intangible forms of recognition or the lack thereof can come from membership in select clubs such as the G8 and G20 or, conversely, exclusion from even organizations with universal membership, such as when Beijing was denied its right to represent China in the United Nations before October 1971.

It is not difficult to surmise from power-transition theory as originally formulated that revisionist motivation arises from a serious discrepancy between a rising latecomer's relative power and its share of tangible and intangible benefits received from the international system. This happens when its improved power position is not readily and sufficiently compensated by the amount of additional benefits that it expects to receive from the international system. Thus, rising states tend to be "deficit" countries in the sense that they are not given as much recognition or resources as they think they deserve because of their relative power gains. This discrepancy can become a source of disappointment and grievance, even resentment and anger. It can also happen to an established power, including a hegemon that is becoming even more powerful, when its power gains are not sufficiently recognized and accorded with even greater deference and accommodation by other countries. Many statements from former US president Donald Trump suggested an annoyance, even resentment, that the United States had not been adequately compensated in its alliance and trade relations, and that it had been unfairly taken advantage of by its allies and trade partners.

Powell (1999: 199) has argued that "if the distribution of benefits mirrors the distribution of power, no state can credibly threaten to use force to change the status quo and the risk of war is smallest. If, however, there is a sufficiently large disparity between the distribution of power and benefits, the status quo may be threatened regardless of what the underlying distribution of power is." A contest of arms will only make sense for a dissatisfied revisionist if it believes that its capabilities will enable it to demonstrate on the battlefield that it deserves to be allocated more resources and benefits than its counterparts would be willing to concede in the absence of this demonstration of its capabilities. This observation also explains why "status-quo" states—that is, those "surplus" states that receive more than their "fair" share of resources and benefits (including intangible ones like status)—are disinclined to enter into conflicts because they can expect to lose those privileges and entitlements that are largely a legacy of their past dominance. These states cannot hope to improve even more their already over-compensated share.

Relative deprivation (Gurr 1970) due to inadequate compensation for a state's rising stature, then, is the main reason for its disenchantment and dissatisfaction. The greater its perception of the gap between its relative power and its share of resources and benefits, the greater is its sense of grievance. When its demands for recognition and accommodation are rebuffed repeatedly, this grievance intensifies and changes from demands to redistribute resources and benefits to demands to revise the norms, rules, and institutions of the international order. Significantly, a country's relative power and its share of resources and benefits are a matter of subjective perception and feeling. People (including officials) can disagree about both.

As just explained, wars happen because of a difference of opinion on the part of officials representing the opposing sides about their countries' relative strength and entitlements. They resort to a contest of arms to disclose to the other side that their demands for resources and benefits are justified by their strength, which the other side has declined to recognize in the absence of this demonstration on the battlefield (Fearon 1997). If everyone had agreed on their relative power and their just share of resources and benefits, war would not have been necessary to make the adjustments. Under such circumstances, the relevant states should be able to reach a settlement peacefully. War would then be irrational because the combatants would have to bear the costs of waging it without any chance to improve their share of resources and benefits (we set aside here the other chief impediment to settlement mentioned by Fearon, the so-called commitment problem). As Mark Twain has been quoted saying, a difference of opinion makes a horse race.

There is a reasonably large body of literature investigating status inconsistency (that is, the discrepancy between a country's achieved status and its ascribed status) as a cause of international violence and instability (e.g., East 1972; Gochman 1980; Maoz 2010; Midlarsky 1975; Ray 1974; Renshon 2016, 2017; Volgy and Mayhall 1995; Wallace 1973; Ward 2019). The general conclusion of this literature is that there is a positive relationship between these two variables so that status inconsistency is a precursor to war or militarized interstate disputes. Results from Renshon's (2017) recent research suggest that this relationship is quite resilient under different conditions, and conflict initiation serves an instrumental purpose for those states suffering a status deficit to gain the recognition that they aspire to. That is, starting militarized disputes or waging wars "pays" in the sense of gaining improved status recognition for the state suffering from relative deprivation that initiates these conflicts, especially when it prevails in these conflicts. Note that this observation suggests that even when this state loses a military confrontation, it may still gain increased international recognition and stature, such as for Anwar Sadat's Egypt after it launched but lost the Yom Kippur War against Israel.

Renshon (2017) makes an important point in observing that people (and therefore the states that they represent) do not typically update their perceptions of the interstate hierarchy (or, more specifically, states' relative ranking in this hierarchy) constantly or quickly. We also know from prospect theory (Boettcher 2005; Kahneman and Tversky 1979; McDermott 1998) that those who have made gains are likely to update quickly their reference point (often characterized as the endowment effect), whereas those who have suffered losses are more reluctant to accept these losses and to revise their reference point as quickly to acknowledge their setback. This discrepancy in timing can therefore be a natural source of the frustration and disappointment felt by rising upstarts that accommodation to their newly improved international position is tardy and/or inadequate. In addition to the psychological reason just noted, there can also be political and institutional reasons for established states in decline to resist reforms that can undermine their existing roles, entitlements, self-image, and/or vested bureaucratic interests.

By bringing in relative deprivation, status inconsistency, and prospect theory to our analysis, we are better able to connect developments at the macro or systemic level of analysis, such as power shifts among the major states with psychological variables at the individual, group, or organizational levels of analysis. These theories help us bridge the gap we often find in discourses on power-transition theory and Thucydides's Trap, specifically, the question about what transmission mechanisms operate to make the effects of structural changes at the systemic or interstate levels of analysis felt at the individual, group, or societal level of political discourse and decision-making. For example, we can point to the tendency for disappointment, frustration, annoyance, resentment, envy, and even outright anger to affect political and decision-making processes when leaders of a rising latecomer feel that their efforts to seek appropriate recognition and compensation for their improved international position have been repeatedly blocked and thwarted by the established states. As in domestic politics and interpersonal relations, a feeling that one has been "disrespected" can be the source of strong emotional reactions. In international relations, this perceived denial or disrespect can engender a powerful sense of "status immobility," which can turn distributive demands into challenges to alter and even overthrow the existing international order (Ward 2017). As Ward (2019) rightly points out, much work still remains to be done in extending and refining how social psychological explanations about status anxiety based on research about individuals can be fruitfully applied to studying the behavior of states, as existing approaches tend to anthropomorphize states and to overlook the alternative paths that domestic politics may take to influence how leaders can respond to such anxiety in different ways.

Assessing Revisionism

We argue that revisionism is not a static attribute, but is rather a changing variable. We also agree with Davidson (2006) that whether a state has a revisionist or status-quo agenda is not based on its structural position in the international system; it is rather a contingent matter and reflects situational variations. There is no reason to expect that just because a state is a rising latecomer, it must have revisionist intentions or motivations. Indeed, this point should be quite evident to those scholars who argue that the Anglo-American power transition was peaceful because the United States was a status-quo power. Whether or not this characterization is valid, this argument indicates that revisionism is not an inherent trait of all rising powers.

Indeed, a moment's reflection should also tell us that, far from seeking to challenge the international order, Japan during its years of ascendance had tried to imitate Western customs and institutions in the hope of being accepted as a member of the "civilized" community of nations. Thus, as Khong (2001: 40) observes, Japan had "proved [to be] an example par excellence in conforming its government institutions, legal system, and general international practices to the interests, rules, and values of 'civilized' international society, as prescribed by Western nations." Of course, Japanese leaders and people became increasingly resentful and angry as they encountered repeated denial and obstruction due to what they perceived to be deliberately humiliating and hypocritical rejections from the established, Western powers. For instance, these countries (the United States, Britain, and Australia) turned down Japan's demand at the Versailles Peace Conference that they recognize the principle of racial and sovereign equality of all nations. Moreover, domestic legislation in the United States discriminated against people of Japanese ancestry (and other Asians), limiting their legal immigration and barring them from owning land (Buzas 2013; Ward 2017). These actions had a blowback effect in Japan, causing domestic discourse there to turn increasingly in a radical direction. In other words, the actions of the established powers hurt moderate voices and empowered the more militant and nationalist elements in Japanese society, because these actions created a pervasive impression that Japan was being discriminated against and humiliated on racial grounds. The more general point to be underscored by this discussion of Japan's experience is that whether a rising power becomes revisionist depends critically on the nature of the existing international order. Is this order—especially its rules regarding admission to the club of great powers—open to new entrants? We will return to this question later.

As just noted, the nature of an international order can entail domestic consequences (such as the effects that a racist international hierarchy had on interwar Japan). It has become more evident recently that populist politics in Europe and the United States has been greatly abetted by the domestic consequences of a liberal international order promoting globalization and, in the case of Europe, regionalization as well. These trends arguably have exacerbated domestic social and economic inequities and increased racial tension and anxieties on the part of those who perceive their social status, cultural identity, and income and employment prospects to be imperiled. These feelings have engendered opposition to immigration, free trade, and foreign intervention. They have also increased distrust of and decreased support for international institutions. Politicians such as Donald Trump have exploited these feelings of resentment and alienation. But politicians on the political left have also voiced opposition to US interventionism and international trade regimes. The more general point is, of course, that international order can have a blowback effect on domestic politics or, in Ikenberry and Nexon's (2019: 421) words, it "can reconfigure the interests and domestic orders of participants."

It is of course true that Japan from, say, 1875 to 1945 was an ambitious, expansionist power. It fought wars against China and Russia, colonized Korea and

Taiwan, and aspired to create an exclusive sphere of influence in East Asia. But this behavior was not exceptional, and it reflected customary conduct under the rules of the game prevailing at that time. After all, Britain and France had also fought wars against China and Russia in the second half of the nineteenth century, pursued colonialism all over the world, and sought to carve out spheres of influence in East Asia (and elsewhere) and extraterritorial jurisdictions inside China. Similarly, the United States had also waged war against Mexico and Spain, sought territorial expansion abroad (e.g., Puerto Rico, Guam, Hawaii), and conducted a bloody anti-insurgency campaign in the Philippines to colonize that country. It had also proclaimed and, by the start of the twentieth century, had indeed secured an exclusive sphere of influence in the Western Hemisphere. It is not clear why Japan should be considered any more a revisionist state than the established, Western states. Although it resorted to violence and aggression to pursue its aggrandizement—like Britain, France, Russia, and the United States— it was not seeking to challenge or displace the existing international order. Tokyo resorted to war to implement its program of expansion, but the intention or motivation behind this aggression was not a radical attempt to install a new international order. Although Japan had wanted to create a regional hegemony, it did not seek to introduce a new order in the sense of installing new rules and practices that would have been alien to the established, Western powers. Japan sought distributive gains in Asia, but its attempt to create an exclusive East Asia Co-Prosperity Sphere undermined the regional order because it threatened Washington's "open door" policy toward China. Tokyo's attempt in this regard had been preceded by Washington's declaration of the Monroe Doctrine, which had similarly sought to exclude European influences from the Western Hemisphere.

We also do not consider imperial Germany before World War I to be a revisionist state. Kaiser's Germany surely sought to expand its influence—but which of the other rising powers during those years did not? Compared to imperial Germany, Russia and the United States had made much larger territorial conquests at the expense of their neighbors. Again, this remark does not deny that Berlin had an ambitious program and exhibited considerable bellicosity in its foreign policy. However, Berlin's pursuit of overseas colonies and markets, its naval buildup, and its *Weltpolitik* to acquire influence and prestige in general could not be said to undermine or challenge the then existing rules of the game. If anything, it was following prevailing practices and established precedents created by Britain and France. Although its policies caused tension and elevated distrust, this result does not in itself mean that Berlin was trying to install a new international order with different norms, rules, and principles. As a counterfactual thought experiment, how would the international order be different if Kaiser's Germany had won World War I? Naturally, this development would mean that Britain, France, and Russia's influence would be diminished, and their relative international position would suffer. But this is very different from saying that the norms, rules, and principles for conducting international relations would be altered fundamentally.

Which countries could be considered revisionist? Napoleon's France arguably would qualify because it propagated a new republican form of government to replace the then prevailing monarchical system of hereditary rule by royalty and aristocracy. It challenged the divine right of kings and introduced novel ideas of popular will and citizen army. Bolshevism and the communist ideology of armed revolution, class struggle, workers' dictatorship, and proletarian internationalism promoted by the Soviet Union and China at one time would also suggest an attempt to challenge the existing international order and to replace it with a set of new norms, principles, and doctrines. However, one may question the extent to which the Soviet Union before World War II and China in the first half century of the People's Republic had possessed the necessary capabilities to implement their revisionist agenda. Of course, since China's recent rise, Beijing has disavowed its earlier revolutionary ideology that challenged the legitimacy of ruling bourgeoisies in other countries. Russia has also done so. Only the Soviet Union during the Cold War years appeared to have both the motivation and capability to carry out a program of revisionism. However, even this attribution may be questionable because the Soviet Union was always much weaker than the United States (its allies were also much weaker than the Western coalition). It was only able to match the United States in strategic weapons; in all other areas of competition, Moscow was at a severe disadvantage. The Soviet Union during the Cold War competed with the United States in armament and for foreign allies and influence. At the same time, it adopted an "exit" strategy abstaining from deep involvement in the global political economy dominated by the capitalist countries, preferring instead to mainly associate itself with its ideological partners in Eastern and Central Europe.

We do not see today's China and Russia as revisionists because neither of them challenges the basic (primary) institutions of the existing international order or, for that matter, seeks to displace the United States as the global hegemon (Chan et al. 2019; Krickovic 2018; Larson and Shevchenko 2019). If anything, both are more interested in preserving, defending, or aspiring to a position of regional leadership and in demanding that the United States accord them this recognition in their respective neighborhood. Ironically and contrary to many people's perceptions in the West, both Moscow and Beijing see themselves more on the strategic defense in responding to US pressures and initiatives, and both also chafe under what they perceive to be persistent and overwhelming US power in their near abroad, in contrast to US concerns about a resurgent Russia and a rising China in the process of catching up. Both Moscow and Beijing would be happy to accept a concert system with the United States. Neither harbors, in our view, an ambition to seek global hegemony or to install a new international order in the sense of instituting basic changes to the current prevailing norms, rules, and principles of international relations.

One may argue that Russia's annexation of Crimea challenges this last observation, but this action was at least based on a popular referendum in Crimea. Washington's policies in other situations of secession—such as in the former Yugoslavia—have insisted on a people's right of self-determination. It has also made this argument against China's attempt to force Taiwan to accept reunification—although it abandons this position when addressing Israel's annexation of Arab land. Washington has also claimed that the entire Ukrainian people should have a voice in deciding Crimea's secession and that this secession should follow Ukraine's constitutional process—an argument that ironically reflects Beijing's position on Taiwan.

Nazi Germany comes closer to a state that advocated a radical ideology and that commanded at the same time the economic and military capabilities to implement this ideology. Hitler and his associates proclaimed the imperative for Germany to acquire its *Lebensraum*, and they had not been bashful in resorting to military conquest and coercion to pursue this agenda and to proclaim the doctrine of "might makes right." Perhaps the most distinctive feature of Nazi ideology pointing to a radical motivation was its racist doctrine. This doctrine proclaimed a new international order based on a racial hierarchy with the Aryans at its apex. Thus, Nazi Germany sought distributive gains, but had at the same time also tried to replace the existing international order with a radical new one based on race. This statement of course does not deny that other countries at the time had also practiced racial discrimination and espoused racist views, such as "white Australia." The indigenous peoples in Australia, Canada, South Africa, and of course the United States have all suffered serious deprivations under domination by settlers of European descent. And, as remarked earlier, the prevailing order had even after World War I endorsed a racist hierarchy that had excluded Japan. Although he is often remembered today for his support for people's right to self-determination (although only for Europeans and not those indigenous peoples who were victims of colonialism), President Woodrow Wilson was an avowed racist in US domestic politics. Only the Nazis, however, had advocated and implemented a deliberate and concerted program of exterminating "inferior" races.

What about the United States? American exceptionalism and Manifest Destiny have been the hallmarks of this country's self-perception. It often considers itself to be exempt from the norms and rules that apply to others. For example, there has been widespread and persistent outrage expressed about Russia's meddling in the US presidential election of 2016, with little acknowledgment, however, that the United States has been documented to have interfered repeatedly and flagrantly in many countries' elections, as far back as at least the 1948 Italian election, in which it had sought to prevent the Communist Party from coming to power (Levin 2017, 2018, 2020). Washington was also complicit in violent coups that overthrew democratically elected leaders, such as Iran's Mohammad Mossadegh and Chile's Salvador Allende. Americans have historically professed a disdain for the "Old World" and a fear of foreign entanglements and yet, at the same time, have shown a missionary zeal to transform the rest of the world in their own image. Schweller (2015: n.p.) asks his readers to "imagine another globally dominant power, say China or Russia, [had] acted on its beliefs that: (1) its mission is to rid the world of evil by spreading what it claims are its universal values; (2) its security requires waging preventive wars; and (3) international norms, rules, and law apply to everyone else but not to itself because world order requires that it acts differently from all other states. Would we not consider that to be a revisionist power?"

During the years of its rise, the United States had asserted unilaterally the Monroe Doctrine, which tried to expel European influence from the Western Hemisphere. In responding to US Secretary of State Richard Olney's invocation of this doctrine in the boundary dispute between Venezuela and British Guiana, British Prime Minister Robert Salisbury retorted, "no nation, however powerful, [is] competent to insert into the code of international law a novel principle which was never recognized before, and which has not since been accepted by the government of any country" (quoted in Zakaria 1998: 150). This doctrine had since been followed and expanded by the so-called Roosevelt Corollary, which proclaimed that Washington had the absolute right to intervene in the domestic affairs of any country located in the Western Hemisphere for whatever reason that it saw fit. Although isolationism has been frequently used to describe US foreign policy during this period, Washington had intervened militarily and repeatedly in its near abroad and it had also sought to "open" Japan and China. In Khong's (2001: 49) words, the United States "increasingly [tried] to establish its own rules in competition with others, and to play its own game beyond its regional sphere."

In the years after the Cold War, Washington has promoted vigorously the doctrine of regime change abroad (including military intervention and/or economic coercion to remove objectionable regimes in Iraq, Libya, Afghanistan, and, thus far unsuccessfully, in Iran, Syria, and Venezuela). It also proclaimed its right to wage a preventive war in invading Iraq in 2003. The George W. Bush administration claimed that Saddam Hussein had connections with Al Qaeda and that he had or was about to have weapons of mass destruction—claims that have since been shown to be false. In its fight against terrorists, Washington has resorted to kidnapping (extra-legal "rendition"), secret detentions, detentions without trial, drone attacks, and "enhanced interrogation" methods—all of which appear to contradict its professed values. It has even literally seized another country's leader (Panama's Manuel Noriega) and assassinated its official in a third country (Iran's General Qasem Soleimani in Baghdad). Whether one agrees or disagrees with these actions and pronouncements, they clearly suggest radical changes to the existing norms, rules, and principles of international order.

In contrast to other revisionist states, the United States has been in an incomparably preponderant position. Commenting on the US military supremacy, historian Paul Kennedy has noted, "Nothing has ever existed like this disparity of power, nothing. . . . I have returned to all of the comparative defense spending and military personnel statistics over the past 500 years that I compiled for *The Rise and Fall of the Great Powers*, and no other nation comes close" (quoted in Ikenberry et al. 2009: 10). This preponderance is important because other countries are less able to restrain the United States; instead, they will have to rely more on this preponderant state's self-restraint based on its own values and impulses— that is, on Washington's voluntary observance of and adherence to the norms, rules, and principles of international order, especially when it does not have to fear pushback from other countries.

The United States qualifies more than any other past or current great power that entertains a radical and expansive view of what a new world order should be and one that is also truly peerless in its power to implement this view. Significantly, moreover, it has also not been bashful about adopting a unilateral, assertive approach, including frequent resort to arms, to carry out its vision of international order. The United States has fought more foreign wars and it has been involved in more militarized interstate disputes than any country since 1945—and by a wide margin. The frequency of its military interventions abroad has risen after the Cold War's end, increasing from 46 during 1948–1991 to 188 during 1992–2017 (Toft 2017). The last time China fought a war was against Vietnam in 1979, and it has generally limited its sovereignty contests in the South China Sea with the deployment of coast guard vessels rather than naval assets (after an armed clash with Vietnam in 1988). In contrast to the United States, all its armed conflicts were located near or at its border, whereas most of those fought by the United States have been in its "far abroad" (especially the most protracted and costly ones in Korea, Vietnam, Iraq, and Afghanistan). Physical distance is informative because, everything else being equal, it is indicative of whether a state has an offensive or defensive motivation (the farther away, the more offensive motivation). Thus, the United States meets our definition of revisionism more than other great powers— even though it has been simultaneously the "top dog" in the interstate system, enjoying unprecedented primacy after the Soviet Union's collapse.

Ward (2017) has studied imperial Germany, interwar Japan, and Nazi Germany, all of them considered by him to be radical revisionists. His criteria to define and assess radical revisionism are different from our terminology of hard revisionism. According to him, radical revisionism manifests itself when a state refuses to accept arms control agreements, withdraws from international institutions, and seeks to overthrow the existing interstate hierarchy or balance of power. Imperial Germany's refusal to accept restraints on its naval competition with Britain and its withdrawal from multilateral consultative conferences are taken by him to be signs of its radical revisionism. Similarly, interwar Japan's withdrawal from the League of Nations and the Washington naval agreement and its push to establish its a sphere of influence in East Asia after the Mukden Incident are also interpreted as indications of its radical revisionism. Nazi Germany's rejection of the Versailles Peace Treaty (especially its refusal to accept reparations and its reoccupation of Rhineland) and its withdrawal from the League of Nations produce a similar conclusion that it was a radical revisionist. The common theme running through these three cases points to a refusal to join or remain in international organizations and a refusal to accede to international agreements (especially on arms control) as evidence of radical revisionism. Another sign would be a strong resentment produced by perceived national humiliation and indignity inflicted by the established powers.

In addition to the preceding considerations, Ward (2017) refers to a country's concerted attempt to alter the existing interstate balance of power as a sign of radical revisionism, especially its heavy investment in armament. Other scholars (e.g., Lemke and Werner 1996) have also used extraordinarily high military spending to indicate revisionism. Despite its favorable geographic position (being flanked by two oceans and having just two weak contiguous neighbors), the United States has led the world in this spending. In recent years, it has spent more on its military than the *combined* defense expenditures of the next seven to eleven highest countries. At one time shortly after the Cold War, it spent nearly as much on its military as the rest of the world *combined*. Imperial Germany, interwar Japan, and Nazi Germany never had attained this level of military supremacy measured by defense expenditures. In this regard, rather than being the proverbial 800-pound gorilla in the room, the United States has been the 330,000-pound blue whale!

In the 1950s and 1960s, China had rejected the United Nations and other international organizations. In its public statements, it has emphasized (and continues to recall) its "century of national humiliation" due to aggression and encroachment committed by foreign countries against it. More recently, however, China has joined various international organizations so that its membership in these organizations has reached a level comparable to its peers in the international community. As we will discuss more extensively in the next chapter, Beijing has also signed and ratified most international accords and conventions. Indeed, it has joined some—such as the United Nations Convention on the

Law of the Sea (UNCLOS), the Basel Convention, the Convention to Eliminate Discrimination against Women, and the Convention on the Rights of the Child—that Washington has thus far declined to join (Trump had pulled the United States from the Paris climate agreement but Biden has reversed this decision to rejoin this accord).

In 1999, the US Senate had refused to ratify the Comprehensive Test Ban Treaty despite President Bill Clinton's support for it. Along with China, the United States has remained outside the Treaty to Ban Landmines and the International Criminal Court. George W. Bush and Donald Trump, moreover, withdrew the United States from the Anti-Ballistic Missile Treaty and the Intermediate-Range Nuclear Forces Treaty, in 2002 and 2018, respectively. Trump also pulled the United States from multilateral institutions such as the Trans-Pacific Partnership, the United Nations Human Rights Council, the United Nations Education, Scientific, and Cultural Organization (UNESCO), the United Nations Global Compact on Migration, the multilateral agreement to curb Iran's nuclear program (the Joint Comprehensive Plan of Action, or JCPA), and most recently, the Arms Trade Treaty, the Open Skies Treaty, and the World Health Organization (Biden has announced that the United States will rejoin this organization). He denounced the North American Free Trade Agreement as the "worst trade deal [the U.S. has] ever signed," (https://www.cnbc.com/video/2016/09/26/donald-j-trump-says-nafta-the-worst-trade-deal-ever-signed.html), insisting that it be renegotiated with Mexico and Canada to gain more favorable terms for the United States. One may also recall that in an earlier era, the US Senate had refused to approve US membership in the League of Nations and the International Trade Organization (the Havana Charter). Given this record pertaining to international organizations and arms control agreements, the United States—especially after the Cold War's end—would presumably meet Ward's criteria for radical revisionism if his study had included it (many of the events mentioned in this paragraph happened after his book's publication). His indicators are instructive, but to us, Washington's propagation of novel doctrines that challenge existing international principles, such as its pronouncements on preventive war and regime change, are even more informative of a revisionist agenda.

Washington also appeared to have been motivated by a revisionist agenda during the years of its rise, especially during the administration of Theodore Roosevelt. In Allison's (2017: 90) words, during the late 1800s and early 1900s,

the US [had] declared war on Spain, expelling it from the Western Hemisphere and acquiring Puerto Rico, Guam, and the Philippines; threatened Germany and Britain with war unless they agreed to settle disputes on American terms; supported an insurrection in Colombia to create a new country, Panama, in order to build a canal; and declared itself the policeman of the Western Hemisphere, asserting the right to intervene whenever and wherever it judged necessary—a right it exercised nine times in the seven years of TR's [Theodore Roosevelt's] presidency alone.

In the mid-1800s, the United States had also acquired a massive amount of new territory from Mexico (comprising all or parts of Arizona, California, Colorado, Nevada, New Mexico, Utah, and Wyoming). Mearsheimer (2001: 238) observes, "Indeed, [it] was bent on establishing regional hegemony, and it was an expansionist power of the first order in the Americas." We have emphasized on several previous occasions that although deplorable, territorial conquest does not necessarily in our view constitute evidence of a revisionist agenda referring to an attempt to challenge and overhaul the existing international order. This said, it is difficult to argue that based on this record of expansion, the United States was any more a status-quo power during its years of ascendance compared to, say, imperial Germany and Japan. Naturally, and it should be obvious, that we do not consider acts of systematic racist discrimination, competition for spheres of influence, or commission of armed aggression to be inconsistent with the "rules of the game" in the era of colonialism and imperialism does not mean that we condone or approve such conduct.

Conditions for Revisionism

The preceding discussion should immediately call our attention to several important differences separating Nazi Germany before World War II, the Soviet Union during the Cold War, and the United States during approximately the three decades before World War I and during the three decades since the end of the Cold War. We have argued that all these cases showed a revisionist agenda.

However, the United States is different from Nazi Germany and the Soviet Union during the Cold War because it had already become the world's leading power by the late 1800s. Indeed, while one may conceivably argue that the other two countries were "rising powers," the United States had already risen to its preeminent position in international relations and, moreover, it has extended its preponderance even further after the Soviet Union's demise in 1991.

Second and consequently, relative deprivation—a sense of frustration and annoyance that one's country has not been accorded respect, deference, and recognition in proportion to its power—has not been usually applied to explain the US case as this argument has been customarily applied to other countries. Yet our logic argues that given its preponderant position and especially in the face of its further power gains, a hegemon can also feel that it is entitled to even more resources and benefits (including intangibles such as "respect"), in addition to those that it is already receiving from the international system. Content analysis of Donald Trump's speeches show that "great" and "greatest" are among the most frequently used words, and their reference "almost always applies to America"— "It is the greatest nation in the world and should be recognized by others as such. American leaders should recognize their power and not buckle in to the demands or free-riding of others" (Lebow 2018: 213). Trump called for restoring America's greatness (as in "Making America Great Again") by reasserting its power in the world. He spoke revealingly: "We're like the big bully that keeps getting beat up. You ever see that? The big bully that keeps getting beat up" (quoted in Lebow 2018: 215). As Lebow (2018: 215) opines, "Being a bully seems fine. But there is something inherently unfair about being the biggest and meanest dude around and being stepped on by others."

Third, the United States was/is already an established, dominant power (certainly after the Soviet Union collapsed), and it has enjoyed a peerless position in international relations since 1991. While German (before the two world wars) and Soviet (during the latter part of the Cold War) leaders were concerned that their country was poised to suffer relative and even absolute decline and, indeed, the Soviet Union had already begun to experience this setback for some considerable time before the end of Cold War (e.g., Copeland 2000; Van Evera 1999; Wohlforth 2003), US leaders have faced an opposite situation such that they could look forward to an even more preponderant position for their country. German leaders were facing a disappearing window of opportunity and an approaching window of vulnerability, and Soviet leaders had by the 1980s and perhaps even earlier, in the 1970s, already seen a process of steady decline for their country and were facing the prospect of further deterioration that would exacerbate their country's difficulties. These leaders were therefore in the domain of actual or potential loss, whereas in contrast, US leaders found themselves in the domain of actual and prospective gain. This difference points to an important distinction between policies being motivated by a sense of vulnerability versus a sense of opportunity. Whereas fear, insecurity, and gambling to recover from actual or prospective loss might describe German and Soviet leaders' motivations, confidence (perhaps even overconfidence) and hubris would offer a better description for the policies of George W. Bush and Donald Trump.

Finally, anger and resentment provide a part of the explanation for mass and elite dissatisfaction on the part of interwar Germany and Japan as well as post-1949 China—at least for the earlier years of the People's Republic. This widespread and strong feeling of having been mistreated and disrespected by the international community provided powerful fuel for revisionist impulses (Murray 2019; Ward 2017). It affected the nature of domestic discourse in these countries, tilting this discourse in favor of nationalists who prefer a more confrontational approach to foreign policy. This sense of victimhood and national humiliation has not been typically invoked to describe the United States and yet, as Trump's statement quoted earlier suggests, the feeling that the United States has been exploited by other countries and has not been given proper respect and deference by them is pervasive among his political supporters. This sense of victimhood has become more visible recently as globalization has exacerbated domestic inequities, causing a political backlash against existing trade regimes and rising support for "America First" policies. There has moreover been a surge of anti-immigrant feelings. Even with respect to Washington's traditional allies, there has been a palpable sense of resentment against their inadequate burden-sharing in providing collective security and even public threats that the United States would reconsider its defense commitments to these allies if they fail to respond to its demands adequately (in late July 2020, the Trump administration announced that it would withdraw 12,000 US military personnel from Germany, apparently without prior consultation with German officials). In combination, these forces have caused a rising tide against the post-1945 liberal international order (Ikenberry 2001, 2012) and, as reported earlier, a series of decisions suggesting US disengagement from and even abandonment of multilateral diplomacy and international institutions and conventions.

Relative deprivation and the resentment resulting from this feeling do not, however, tell the entire story. Revisionism on the part of the United States can also stem from another source characteristic of liberal internationalists who are motivated by messianic impulses and a missionary zeal to convert the rest of the world in their own image (liberal internationalists of course hold very different views on foreign policy compared to Trump's political base, which is more conservative and isolationist). With respect to China, proponents of a US policy of "engagement" have openly professed an agenda to convert its people so that they will eventually become more aligned with American values and interests. One recalls similar motivation in an earlier era, when many American missionaries went to China to convert the Chinese to Christianity. This impulse was aptly captured by the memorable words of Nebraska's Senator Kenneth Wherry, "with God's help, we will lift Shanghai up and up, until it is just like Kansas City" (https://www.wanderingeducators.com/hidden-treasures-shanghai-just-kansas-city.html).

Although external pressure typically provides part of the explanation for German, Japanese, and Chinese foreign policy, this explanation applies to a much less extent to the United States, for which external opportunity plays a larger role in shaping its motivation and behavior given its preponderant power in the international system. Moreover, and as already mentioned, the more powerful a country is in the world, the more strongly will its domestic politics and values shape its foreign policy (Jervis 2009), everything else being equal. Other countries will be less able to check a preponderant hegemon, which is therefore more empowered to behave according to its predisposition reflecting its domestic rather foreign conditions and which is also naturally in a more advantageous position to respond to external opportunities rather than being put in a position of having to react to pressures coming from abroad. The "pull" of domestic politics and international opportunities are therefore more influential than the "push" of external pressures and constraints in deciding the foreign policy of a preponderant hegemon.

These remarks suggest that the United States presents the exception rather than the rule with respect to the sources of its revisionism. Its international preponderance distinguishes it from other great powers. Davidson (2006) has studied four key cases (revolutionary France, fascist Italy, Britain in 1911, and interwar France) to determine the origins of their respective revisionism or status-quo commitment. He considers the influence of both domestic and foreign conditions and concludes that foreign conditions are more decisive. Foreign conditions can pertain to either a state's heightened concerns for its security and autonomy, or this state's assessment of the international balance of power and resolve. Davidson contends that the former dimension affecting a state's incentives (or "willingness," in the terminology of Most and Starr 1989) is more important than the latter dimension reflecting its capability (or "opportunity," according to Most and Starr). In the absence of strong incentives, a rising state will not become revisionist even if it has the requisite capability. In Davidson's view, domestic variables are not as important as foreign variables. Domestic variables, however, can compound or mitigate the effects of foreign variables. Domestic politics can therefore be significant in influencing a state's foreign policy orientation if it does not clash with international pressures and opportunities (Davidson 2006: 132). But, as we have argued in the preceding paragraph, as a country gains an overwhelmingly powerful position in international relations (as in the case of the United States), Davidson's conclusion is reversed: for such a country, domestic politics and values tend to override the influence of external conditions as other countries are much less able to constrain it.

Although interwar Japan and Germany were not among the cases he has studied, the general outline of Davidson's explanation fits reasonably well with the phenomenon of these countries becoming increasingly revisionist and strident over those years. Japanese leaders had been acutely concerned about their country's reliance on foreign markets and supplies of raw resources, and they had concluded that this economic and resource dependency was a basic cause responsible for Germany's defeat in World War I. They therefore set out to address this serious vulnerability facing their country, but instead of improving their situation, their expansion to China met increasing resistance from not just the Chinese, but also the Americans and the British, whose economic embargo against Japan put even more pressure on its resource constraints (Barnhart 1987). Concomitantly, domestic politics in Japan had increasingly turned in a more militant and bellicose direction due to a pervasive feeling that this country's aspirations had been repeatedly blocked by the established powers (Buzas 2013; Ward 2017). Ultimately, their dwindling stockpile of resources (especially petroleum) was the decisive factor inclining the Japanese leaders to take a gamble in starting war against the United States—lest their country suffer the fate of slow economic strangulation and defeat without having fired a shot. The domestic conditions were facilitative, but the foreign pressure stemming from Japan's dire resource situation was decisive.

Several scholars have also studied the so-called windows logic in influencing German leaders' decision to launch a preventive war against Russia/the Soviet Union in 1914 and again in 1941 in the belief that with the passage of time, their country would face increasingly long odds against a formidable challenger to their east (Copeland 2000; Lebow 1984; Van Evera 1999; this view that declining states tend to initiate a preventive war has been recently challenged by MacDonald and Parent 2018, who argue that declining states are actually more likely to retrench and those that retrench have been able to recover with some regularity). This sense of international pressure was compounded by a strong sense of relative deprivation due to Germany being denied its rightful place "in the sun" and, in the case of World War II, due to its mistreatment and humiliation by the oppressive Versailles Peace Treaty. Naturally, the domestic coalitions and log-rolling deals among the militarists, industrialists, and others supporting an overseas empire have also been part of the story explaining Germany's (and as explained previously, Japan's) expansion, just as domestic discord had played a role in the incoherent and tardy responses from its democratic adversaries (Snyder 1993; Schweller 1998, 2006). Hitler's invasion of the Soviet Union in 1941 was also motivated by a desire to alleviate the resource constraints facing his country and to acquire *Lebensraum* and a large resource base to help Germany develop a military and industry that could compete effectively with the United States on a continental scale (Mercante 2012). The timing of war, as opposed to the onset of revisionism, represented a window of opportunity for Germany in 1914 and again in 1939, occasioned by the peaking of this country's military might and, concomitantly, tardiness on the part of its opponents (Britain, France, and the Soviet Union) in ratcheting up their military preparedness. In contrast, Japan's decision to attack Pearl Harbor in 1941 reflected a sense of urgency and even desperation to act before this country succumbed to the mounting pressure caused by the relentless US-led embargo of strategic materiel.

As already mentioned, the interaction of foreign and domestic pressures does not fit as well to explain the case of US revisionism. After the settlement of the boundary dispute between Venezuela and British Guiana in 1899, Britain had essentially conceded to US hegemony in the Western Hemisphere (Bourne 1967; Friedberg 1988; Rock 1989, 2000). There was therefore no foreign pressure to speak of for Washington in this region. It rather faced great opportunities to expand its influence. The Spanish-American War was clearly a war of choice rather than a war forced upon Washington. In roughly the period between 1853 and 1913, the United States was actively engaged in the Western Hemisphere and in the Asia Pacific despite its supposed isolationism. There were certainly many outspoken voices in domestic politics in favor of US expansion to pursue its Manifest Destiny. The more important point here is that the general situation facing the United States was one consisting much more of opportunity than pressure. This is also the gist of Zakaria's (1998) thesis when he argues that once the US executive branch had gained the necessary authority in its struggle for power with Congress and had acquired the necessary institutional resources, the country embarked on a path of expansion in the late 1800s. This interpretation highlights opportunistic behavior, one that gives more weight to the "pull" factors in both domestic and foreign conditions than the "push" factors receiving much greater emphasis in Davidson's (2006) account.

The more recent—that is, post–Cold War—picture of US foreign policy also corresponds to the preceding interpretation. After the Soviet Union's demise, the United States reached a unipolar status with no peer competitor in sight. The George W. Bush administration tried to take advantage of the historically un-precedented primacy enjoyed by the United States to fashion a new international order (Jervis 2003, 2005; Daalder and Lindsay 2005). A permissive international environment was reinforced by a window of opportunity created by the political rally around the administration after the 9/11 terrorist attack. Congress and public opinion were both permissive and even supportive of an expansive and aggressive foreign policy agenda in the name of fighting international terrorism. Walt (2005: 23) observes,

> the United States is in a position that is historically unprecedented, and . . . it has used its power to mold a world that would be compatible with U.S. interests and values. The United States has not acted as a "status quo" power: rather, it has used its position of primacy to increase its influence, to enhance its position vis-à-vis potential rivals, and to deal with security threats.

As this comment suggests, Washington has not just a desire for distributive gains. More importantly, it has been motivated to create a new international order. This motivation is the hallmark of revisionism and distinguishes it from China, Russia, and most other countries in the world. With respect to China, Wolfowitz (1997) was quoted earlier referring to Beijing's desire to seek "a place in the sun," just as Kaiser's Germany did before World War I. Without denying that China harbors ambitions as well as grievances, the attribution of an offensive motivation to Beijing in pursuit of regional and even global hegemony is more open to question. Instead of this ostensible motivation, Pollack (2005) has described Beijing's efforts to be mainly concerned with staying out of Washington's "strategic headlights." Goldstein (2005: 12) describes Beijing's grand strategy in a similar vein:

> [It] aims to engineer China's rise to great power status within the constraints of a unipolar international system that the United States dominates. It is designed to sustain the conditions necessary for continuing China's program of economic and military modernization, as well as to minimize the risk that others, most importantly the peerless United States, will view the ongoing increases in China's capabilities as an unacceptably dangerous threat that must be parried or perhaps even forestalled. China's grand strategy, in short, aims to increase the country's international clout without triggering a counterbalancing reaction.

As a third example, Xiang (2001: 16) avers:

> Chinese security policy seeks "a place in the shade"—obscure, comfortable and unharried. This defensive posture rests on the fact that the reform-minded Chinese élite understands the political danger of riding the nationalist tiger. Nationalist agitation will disturb political stability. In an authoritarian state, nationalist fervour can provide the cover for the public airing of radical views that the government finds difficult to control, and which can be easily turned against the regime itself.

Drezner (2017) remarks in a similar vein in challenging the conventional view that China is a revisionist power. He reports that "China's compliance with adverse WTO [World Trade Organization] rulings was better than that of either the United States or the European Union," and concludes, "China, far from acting like a spoiler, acted primarily as a responsible stakeholder to reinforce the preexisting rules of the global economic game" during and after the Great Recession of 2008 (Drezner 2017: 82, 91).

Broz et al. (2020: 432) report that, in contrast, "the United States has made more frequent use of WTO exceptions to protect domestic industries from foreign competition than any other nation. . . . Foreign nations have initiated more complaints at the WTO against the US for violating trade-exception rules than against any other nation or region, including the European Union."

Turning to variations in countries' propensity to use force, Jacques (2019) writes:

> As the world once more enters dangerous waters, in my view our concern should not so much be China but the United States. One of the remarkable things about China is how relatively peaceful it has been during its rise: contrast that with the US in its equivalent period, notably between 1860 and 1914, with the wars of westward expansion against Spain, Mexico, the annexation of Hawaii and the conquest of the Philippines. The same can be said, by the way, of the UK, France and also Japan, all of which fought many wars of expansion during their rise. In contrast, China's rise has been characterised by an extraordinary restraint, a fact that is largely, if not overwhelmingly, ignored.

Finally, Kang (2020: 140) quotes Kishore Mahbubani's (Singapore's former ambassador to the United Nations) observation that "China is the only great power today that has not fired a single bullet across its borders in 30 years [as of 2010]." "By contrast, even under the peaceful American presidency of Barack Obama, the U.S. dropped 26,000 bombs on seven countries in 2016 (Lee 2019)" (Kang 2020: 140).

Chinese foreign policy thus appears quite different from the usual portrayal of Beijing as an assertive and impatient upstart seeking to elbow away other countries in its effort to claim its "place in the sun." Moreover, and especially when juxtaposed against Washington's self-image as a status-quo power and its actual conduct, whether now or when it was a rising state, standard references to China as a revisionist power in current prevailing narratives in mass circulation and even scholarly discourses strongly support the view that "revisionism is not an objective description of a rising power's aggressiveness or orientation toward the status quo, but rather is a social construction" (Murray 2019: 66). This idea or label is often deployed and propagated by the established powers to denounce and denigrate those newcomers who are, in their view, "troublemakers"— without pausing to ask how they themselves managed to reach their current dominant positions.

Is China a revisionist state? It is certainly unhappy with some aspects of the current international order and would like to see changes in them. But it would be a stretch to claim that it wants to undermine and overthrow the entire international order. Although China has clearly made significant gains in its relative position in the interstate hierarchy, it has not promoted or propagated any ideology or vision that can be construed as an attempt to replace the current norms, rules, and principles of international order with new ones. Lind (2017: 82) states succinctly, "Beijing has not tried to export an ideology around the world. Washington has." China of course wants and prefers to improve its international rank, raise its status, and gain more power—or, if you will, to turn the current international distribution of resources and benefits to its advantage. As we have explained, however, this intention or desire represents distributive revisionism, in Ward's (2017) terminology, and it hardly distinguishes China from other countries. As we have asked earlier, which country would have the opposite intention or desire to have a smaller share of resources or benefits from their international relations? Thus, that states are distributive revisionists strikes us as a truism.

The more appropriate question is which countries want to rewrite the basic rules and foundational principles of international order, especially by unilateral application of military force. Which countries have a revisionist motivation or agenda, and which ones have also the necessary capabilities to carry out this motivation or agenda and are moreover likely to do so by resorting to violent, unilateral assertion? Naturally, whether unilateral assertiveness is likely depends on how much a country is out of step with the rest of the world. If its views and preferences are mostly congruent with the international community, then unilateral assertiveness would not be necessary, as most other countries would voluntarily join the "coalition of the willing" in promoting a new international order. Unilateral assertiveness becomes possible and even likely in view of power preponderance only if a country finds itself seriously outside the international consensus regarding the rules, norms, and expectations of proper international conduct. In the next chapter, we will present evidence showing that the United States has become increasingly isolated from international consensus and, conversely, that China's policy positions have become increasingly aligned with this consensus.

This said, it is also important to return to a point brought up earlier, specifically, the importance of legitimacy in sustaining a hegemon's rule and maintaining the international order (Clark 2005; Lake 2011). China's authoritarian political system and its form of state-led capitalism (or in Beijing's words, socialism with Chinese characteristics) are unlikely to resonate with the prevailing views of elites and mass publics of most other countries, at least the more important countries in global politics and economics. In other words, China is isolated from the dominant ideology and identity shared by these other countries, with their widespread support for democracy and somewhat more ambivalent support for neoliberalism. This serious discrepancy between Chinese values, preferences, and identity and those of other countries suggests that China will encounter serious difficulties, indeed resistance, to gain admission to the select club of established powers, and that it "is unlikely to become the hegemon in the near future" (Allan et al. 2018: 839). These authors further remark, "China is unlikely to be able to attract powerful followers into a counterhegemonic coalition" (Allan et al. 2018: 841). Even though there may be some discontent with the current international order, China is not in a position to offer a competitive alternative to it—and the Chinese leaders should be quite aware of this situation. All of this leads us to argue that it is too facile to assume or claim that if the United States suffers a decline in its relative power, China somehow will be able to rewrite the rules of international order. However, it should be noted that international norms and legitimacy are also socially constructed and contested. It is hard to predict how international legitimacy will change or be changed along with China's rise and the international order transition.

In our view, China faces a much more constrained environment than the United States. Its geostrategic situation is such that it has the largest number of neighbors in the world (including other great powers that share a land border with it or that are located within close distance to it), and it has a long, exposed coastline that the US navy and air force have heretofore enjoyed unhindered access to. Moreover, as a trading state with a heavy dependence on foreign markets and resources, the sea lanes for its shipping are vulnerable to interdiction and blockade. In comparison, the United States has an enviable geostrategic position such that it has only two relatively weak countries and fish as its neighbors. Although Beijing is trying to turn to domestic consumption as the main engine for its economic growth, China continues to depend heavily on exports to foreign markets and to a much larger extent than the United States, for which domestic consumption is much more important for its economy. And, of course, the United States commands an enormous military advantage, which includes forward deployment of its military assets along China's borders, in addition to its vast network of alliances. Thus, China's external environment presents more pressures than opportunities compared to the United States. It faces a much less enviable security situation than the United States, even without considering the additional contributions that powerful allies can make to enhance even further Washington's already preponderant position.

Presiding over an authoritarian government, Chinese leaders arguably face fewer domestic constraints than their US counterparts. They should face fewer domestic veto groups and are less tethered to public opinion. Therefore, the situation for the two countries in terms of pressures facing their respective leadership is reversed in the domestic realm. This said, Beijing can also suffer domestic "audience costs" from increasingly vocal nationalists (Weeks 2008, 2012; Weiss 2012, 2014). The current alignment of domestic interest groups in China seems to suggest that those with an internationalist outlook and favoring economic development as the national priority are still dominant. This situation should bode well for checking others who advocate a more confrontational foreign policy. However, this balance between "nationalists" and "internationalists" and between "militants" and "moderates" can change. The recent Sino-American trade dispute has affected the domestic distribution of power and interests in both countries. For example, the biggest Chinese casualties of tariffs imposed by the United States are likely to be the more internationalist and moderate stakeholders located in China's coastal provinces. Media reports suggest that there were recurrent battles between internationalists and nationalists inside the US government and Trump's White House, indicating that the nationalists had gained an upper hand. Washington's reactions to Beijing's infringement of Hong Kong's autonomy and over its lack of transparency in the early phase of the Covid-19 pandemic suggest a further escalation of tension in their bilateral relations. Domestic struggles can have international repercussions to the extent that they affect the nature and direction of political discourse in other countries to the advantage of nationalists or internationalists. Domestic politics in the United States has shown deep partisan divisions that can affect the fundamental tenets of its foreign policy. We have already mentioned many recent US decisions that communicate a disenchantment with and even a disdain for and opposition to multilateral institutions and the liberal economic order that Washington has supported in the past. Changes in US foreign policy can affect how other countries, including China, will respond by influencing these other countries' domestic politics and their political factions' incentives and outlooks. As we have already mentioned, Japanese and German bellicosity during the interwar years reflected their resentment of being mistreated and even humiliated in past encounters with the established powers. This resentment was reflected primarily in these countries' domestic politics, which in turn influenced the foreign policy choices made by their respective elites. This remark of course does not deny these countries' own aggression and ambition, and therefore their responsibility for undertaking disastrous policies at enormous costs to their people and to others.

Conditions for Accommodation or Escalation

Paul (2016b: 4) remarks: "The process of accommodation in international relations is exceptionally complicated, as it involves status adjustment, the sharing of leadership roles through the accordance of institutional membership and privileges, and acceptance of spheres of influence: something established powers rarely offer to newcomers."

Paul's remark underscores an important point made by other scholars, such as Goh (2019) and Buzan (2018), who argue that international order is always in the process of being renegotiated, and Murray (2019), who sees the emergence of a revisionist state as the result of social interactions between a rising state and the established states. In other words, whether a rising state becomes a revisionist state is not just a function of its innate qualities or relative power position in the interstate system, but rather reflects also whether this state and the established ones can make reciprocal adjustments in their expectations and behavior to facilitate accommodation. This view stresses that the relevant process is always a two-way street, and it explains our emphasis on not studying China's conduct in isolation or as sui generis, but rather on the need to compare it with that of other states like the United States and treating it in the context of what these other states are saying and doing.

Whether a country becomes revisionist depends on how others treat it. He (2016b) distinguishes "accommodation for identity" and "accommodation for interest." These are naturally ideal types, and real-world situations do not therefore fully meet their descriptions. "Accommodation for identity" suggests that one accedes to a counterpart's demands because one considers these demands to be legitimate and that this counterpart deserves the recognition being bestowed on it. It is difficult to imagine examples of this type of accommodation stemming from the feeling that it is only right and proper to accommodate another country because of a common identity. The Anglo-American rapprochement (discussed later) offers perhaps the closest example of "accommodation for identity," even though it is still a stretch to apply this description.

"Accommodation for interest" suggests an instrumental purpose for both sides to cooperate, often on a transient basis. The Sino-American rapprochement during the 1970s and 1980s to oppose the Soviet Union offers an example; the Nazi-Soviet Pact of Non-Aggression suggests another example. Naturally, as they reflect temporary marriages of convenience, these partnerships can easily dissolve when circumstances change. In retrospect, the arrangements reached by Mikhail Gorbachev and his Western counterparts reflected more an "accommodation for interest" than a true meeting of minds based on "accommodation for identity." The arrangements reached by the two sides turned out to be built on a fragile base.

The distinction between "accommodation for identity" and "accommodation for interest" is important because, as McLauchlin (2016: 308) argues, "A rising power needs to be sure that it is being granted privileges because it is a great power—that is, because there is some normative recognition that it *deserves* those privileges—rather than just to defuse it as a threat" (emphasis in original). He continues, "when a rising power's demand is imbued with status anxiety, it is not just a matter of concessions, but a demand about *the reasons that the other party makes concessions*" (emphasis in original). Thus, for example, when Beijing was finally able to gain membership in the United Nations and its Security Council in October 1971, Washington's acquiescence to this decision by the General Assembly was *not* an instance of voluntary "accommodation for identity," reflecting its belief that Beijing deserved to represent China. It was rather a decision forced upon it by circumstance. Had it conceded earlier to Beijing's right to represent China and to claim a permanent seat on the Security Council with veto power, this act could have been plausibly interpreted as an "accom-modation for identity." Thus, the timing in making accommodation matters in distinguishing whether it was a result of common identity or a result of shared interest—or neither, as suggested by the previous example of China's admission to the United Nations.

Conventional wisdom in the United States argues that this country was not a revisionist state during the period of its rapid rise. This view emphasizes that shared culture and common democratic institutions were responsible for the peaceful transition when the baton of world leadership was passed from Britain to the United States. Yet neither country was obviously democratic during the period in question because women suffrage was not introduced in both countries until after World War I, and in the case of the United States, voting rights for its black citizens did not begin to be protected and realized until the 1960s. During much of the 1800s, Britain and the United States were rivals in the Western Hemisphere, and they came close to blows on several occasions (Bourne 1967; Layne 1994). Compared to a common culture and shared liberal ethos, Britain's decision to accommodate the rise of the United States, especially its conces-sion to US hegemony in the Western Hemisphere, was much more impactful in averting an armed conflict between the two countries. This observation of course does not deny that British and American self-identification as members of the same Anglo-Saxon family (Murray 2019; Rock 1989) facilitated the former's rec-ognition of the latter as a new great power, in contrast to Japan's quest for recog-nition by a select group of established powers having a different race and culture. Whether or not this Anglo-American affinity contributed to Britain's belated recognition of America's ascendance (it probably played only a minor role), it was at least not a hindrance to this recognition. Countries sharing this affinity (such as Prussia and Austria, and Japan and China) have after all been known to go to war (as did Britain and the United States in 1812).

As Layne (1994) has argued, the harsh reality of an increasingly unfavor-able balance of power forced Britain to make concessions to the United States. These concessions included the recall of British naval forces from the Western Hemisphere, London's acceptance of international arbitration as Washington had demanded in the boundary dispute between Venezuela and British Guiana in 1896, the abrogation of the Clayton-Bulwer Act and its replacement in 1901 by the Hay-Pauncefote Treaty giving Washington the right to build and fortify the Panama Canal, and the settlement of Alaska's boundary with Canada on terms almost entirely favorable to the United States. Zeren and Hall (2016: 113) state straightforwardly about the Anglo-American transition,

> [T]here is little sense in talking about "passing the baton" of liberal hegemony.
> It is very important not to accept such language. For one thing, Great Britain

never exercised hegemonic power, being but one of a small number of great powers; the situation of the United States, both at the end of World War II . . . and still more from 1989, has been entirely different. For another, the manner in which the United States took powers from Great Britain was altogether more brutal.

Newcomers almost always must apply sharp elbows, often much more than that, to gain admission to the select club of great powers. The established powers rarely make concessions to them except when confronted with an unfavorable balance of power or resolve. In its various encounters with Britain, the United States demonstrated growing power and greater resolve, enabling it to increasingly gain the upper hand with the passage of time. Growing US power and greater resolve to use it accounted for the evolving relationship from being contentious to being amicable, albeit one that became increasingly dominated by the United States over time. Common heritage cannot quite account for this evolution because it is obviously difficult to explain change by pointing to a constant feature—after all, these countries had fought in 1812 and during 1775–1783 in the American Revolutionary War. Something else must account for the different outcomes (tense and even hostile relations in the earlier years, and more amicable relations in the later years). "For London, the 'special relationship' was a myth devised 'to enable Britain to withdraw gracefully' from those areas where British interests clashed with Washington's, and its function was to make the 'pill' of appeasing the United States 'more palatable to swallow'" (Layne 1994: 27–28).

Timing appears to be another important determinant in deciding the prospects of accommodation. By the late 1800s, London was facing multiple rising powers challenging its interests in different places. In addition to the United States, Germany, Russia, and Japan were also rising powers. Britain's increasing problem with strained resources forced it to conciliate with and accommodate some of them such as the United States, to settle account with others such as Russia and Britain's perennial rival France, and to even join an alliance with Japan (Chan 2004a; Claar and Ripsman 2016; Vasquez 1996). London practiced what can be described as "smart appeasement" of these countries so that it could focus its efforts on the threat coming from a source closest to its home islands, namely, Germany (Treisman 2004; Kennedy 2010; Rock 1989, 2000; Walker 2013). The timing of the ascendance of multiple great powers was fortuitous, but Britain's response to its strategic predicament was deliberate. By making the concessions and accommodations that it did, London was able to prevail in the subsequent global conflict. That France, Russia, Japan, and the United States fought on its side was decisive in determining the outcome of World War I, and Britain's prior diplomacy could take much of the credit for this outcome.

There are of course also several rising or re-emergent powers today, in addition to China. Russia, Japan, Germany, India, and Brazil also play an important role in their respective region, if not on the global stage as well. Significantly, the US position in today's international system is incomparably stronger than the one Britain had faced in the late 1800s and early 1900s. Except for Russia, Washington can count on practically all the major powers to support its cause if it should have a confrontation with China. Moreover, like Germany, China lives in a congested neighborhood surrounded by several large powers. In contrast and as already mentioned, the United States has two small and friendly neighbors, and is protected by the "stopping power of water" (Mearsheimer 2001) on its two flanks. It can rely on the instinct of China's neighbors to balance against its rising power and to seek support from the United States. In other words, China's neighbors would be more concerned about a potential nearby threat and would align themselves with a more distant power as their ally to balance against this threat. Of course, even without the assistance of allies, the United States commands vastly superior capabilities compared to China (Brooks and Wohlforth 2016a; Buzan 2004a). This consideration alone distinguishes the present situation from the one faced by Britain in the late 1800s and early 1900s.

As hinted in the last paragraph, geography in the sense of sheer physical distance may be another factor in influencing the prospects of accommodation (Domke 1988; Zeren and Hall 2016). The farther two countries are separated by distance, the more easily and likely they should be able to demarcate the geographic boundaries of their competition and to achieve some modus vivendi in recognizing each other's sphere of influence. Moreover, because territorial disputes are the most common cause for wars and military confrontations (Vasquez 1993, 2009; Vasquez and Henehan 2011), physical distance removes this source of interstate contention. This was a consideration in Anglo-American relations, even though British Canada shared a border with the United States. The United States (as well as Russia and Japan) was much farther away from the British homeland, whereas Germany was much closer.

Although the United States and China are separated by an ocean and although they do not have any direct territorial dispute, US allies have been parties to such disputes with China. For example, Japan has a dispute with China over the Diaoyu/Senkaku islands in the East China Sea, and the Philippines has been embroiled in disputes with China over islets in the South China Sea. Moreover, although not a formal US ally, Taiwan has tacit US support, and it has put up a long-standing resistance against Beijing's efforts to reincorporate it as part of China. Thus, the United States can easily become entangled in a confrontation with China stemming from its alliance relations. In the summer of 2020, the Trump administration abandoned its previously announced neutrality to reject Beijing's sovereignty claims in the South China Sea, thus involving the United

States more directly in China's disputes with several Southeast Asian states. This was part of more comprehensive changes of Washington's China policy under Trump, viewing their relationship predominantly as a great-power competition (Hu 2020; Smith 2018). The contagion caused by such entanglement has been described as chain-ganging (Christensen and Snyder 1990; Snyder 1997). It has been the principal mechanism for local conflicts to become large conflagrations in the past, as exemplified by the events following the assassination of Archduke Ferdinand in Sarajevo in 1914 and the German invasion of Poland in 1939. In World War I, Britain became involved because of its indirect ties with various alliances (Serbia was a Russian ally, and Russia was in turn an ally of France). The United States of course has an extensive network of alliances and has positioned its military assets in forward deployment within close distance to China's borders. In this sense, it is practically a "resident" country in East Asia, and in this case, the barrier to conflict created by physical distance does not have its typical inhibitive effect on the occurrence of conflict.

Factors such as those pertaining to geography, alliance, and forward deployment of military assets can combine to present a dangerous brew for conflict escalation, as shown by the Cuban Missile Crisis in 1962, when the world came closest to a direct military conflict between two nuclear powers. Of course, in that crisis "the shoe was on the other foot"; it was the United States that faced a recalcitrant neighbor at its doorstep, providing a military base for an extraregional great power. This episode can be instructive because Taiwan offers a close parallel. What would the United States do if China were to announce a "quarantine" of this island?

Yet another factor facilitating accommodation relates to the economic relationship between the established power and the rising power. Of course, this relationship did not stop war from happening between Britain and Germany in 1914 and again in 1939. Several scholars have observed that to the extent that powerful domestic interest groups have a large vested interest in preserving important commercial ties, the prospects for accommodation—or at least the prospects for containing the escalation of conflict—should be brighter (Claar and Ripsman 2016; Rock 1989). Therefore, strong Anglo-American economic ties were supposed to have facilitated their mutual adjustment. According to this view, this variable should also stabilize Sino-American relations; the economies of these two countries have been described as "superfusion" given their extensive interlocking commercial and financial ties (Karabell 2009). Recent increase of tension between China and the United States, however, suggests that the effects of economic interdependence may be exaggerated. Despite many pundits' expectation that both sides would be hurt by an escalation of tariffs and countertariffs, their trade dispute has become more protracted and intense, suggesting that politics is trumping economics. Thus, the proposition that close commercial and financial relations can ease the frictions of power transition may not be as powerful as previously thought. It is of course true that just as there are some domestic groups that benefit from economic openness and interdependence, there are also other groups that are hurt by them and that would benefit from protectionism favoring import-substituting producers. Some time ago, Waltz (1979: 138) has observed that "close interdependence means closeness of contact and raises the prospect of occasional conflict." Other scholars have studied the question of whether economic interdependence promotes peace, and have reached different conclusions (e.g., Barbieri 2002; Mansfield and Pollins 2003; Russett and Oneal 2001).

Significantly, as Zhang (2020: 168) has reminded us, "The international economy was not as connected in previous power transitions as in the contemporary US-China relations. The connection between the British and US economies was far smaller in the 1900s than that of US-China relations [today]." Therefore, there is a qualitative difference distinguishing today's international interdependence from the past (say, the world before World War I). The consequences of disrupting today's Sino-American economic ties would be much more serious than that between Britain and the United States, or between Britain and Germany in an earlier epoch. These situations are not comparable, and it would moreover be fundamentally misleading to recall the Cold War as an analogy to describe today's Sino-American relations because their economic relations are many, many times greater than those between the Soviet Union and the United States during the Cold War.

Still another factor mentioned by the current literature in facilitating or hindering an established power's accommodation of a rising latecomer relates to the former's self-identity and its domestic politics. Racial discrimination against the Japanese and Japanese Americans provides a historical example. Playing the race card can be deployed by strategic elites to mobilize their political base and gain domestic popularity, even if this effort may be couched in covert terms to appeal to hidden racial prejudices. It is not an accident that Japanese Americans, but not German or Italian Americans, were sent to internment camps during World War II and that Japan was the target of two atomic bombs. We can still hear today in public discourse veiled racial attacks aimed at immigrants and asylum seekers from Central America and Muslim countries. Such attacks can sometimes be heard even from the highest level of a government and against one's own minority citizens and political representatives, as evidenced by Trump's not-so-subtle media tweets telling four congresswomen of color to "go back [to] . . . the totally broken and crime infested places from which they came" (https://www.vox.com/2019/7/14/20693758/donald-trump-tweets-racist-xenophobic-aoc-omar-tlaib-pressley-back-countries). Woodrow Wilson had also held racist views on blacks and Asians. Such nativist and racist attitudes may be further reinforced by similar prejudices held by allies. Ward (2017) mentions that Washington's re-luctance to recognize Japan's demand for racial equality was in part influenced by British and Australian objections to this demand. It would of course not be surprising that decisions on whether to accommodate a rising power would in part depend on an established power's consideration of this policy's effects on its allies—such as how US policies toward China would have ramifications for its relations with Japan and South Korea. A country's identity can of course ex-tend beyond race; we have referred to the study by Allan et al. (2018) on elite and mass support for and conception of democracy and neoliberalism, and Rousseau (2006) and Oren (2003) have written more generally about the role of identity politics in international relations.

Recent research suggests that states, including both rising and declining powers, aspire to a high symbolic status, sometimes even more so than they are interested in making greater material gains (Deng 2008; Krickovic and Zhang 2020; Larson and Shevchenko 2019; Murray 2010, 2019; Pu 2019; Renshon 2017; Volgy et al. 2011; Wohlforth 2009). Significantly, Renshon (2017) shows that a state's search for higher international status may not just reflect some ir-rational psychological impulse; this behavior can also be instrumental in con-tributing to its improved position in the world. Pu (2019), moreover, provides a more nuanced view on China's status-seeking behavior, suggesting that this be-havior is not driven by just "one gear" always pushing others to acknowledge its self-perceived importance. Beijing can also be "multivocal" (to use a term from Goddard 2018b), trying to persuade others that China is still a developing country and thus to allay others' concerns about its growing power and to iden-tify itself with the developing world. Finally, and as noted earlier in passing, the search for status does not apply only to rising states. Krickovic and Zhang (2020) emphasize this point, arguing that declining states may be even more anxious about their international status and thus may be more sensitive to and insistent on the maintenance of their status.

This growing attention to states' status-seeking behavior naturally raises questions about the extent to which the existing international order is open to admitting new members to the select club of great powers, the most salient fea-ture of status achievement. According to Ikenberry (2008: 24), the post-1945 liberal international order fostered and supported by the West and especially the United States has the qualities of being "open, integrated and rule-based." It is, in his view, an order that is hard for latecomers like China to resist and easy for them to join. Recent events, however, suggest that the United States under the Trump administration began to abandon those multilateral institutions and arrangements that have characterized this postwar liberal international order (e.g., Ikenberry 2017a; Ikenberry and Nexon 2019). From the perspective of Beijing and Moscow, the West has included among its criteria for admission to the select club of great powers conditions such as a regime's record on human rights and its acceptance of democratic institutions—demands which they see as an infringement on their sovereignty and an attempt to alter their domestic politics. Thus, as several scholars have observed (e.g., Mastanduno 2019; Mearsheimer 2019), the liberal order has been bounded geographically and ideologically in its membership and it has not been truly global. In Nye's (2019: 71) words, this "order was never global and not always very liberal." It has moreover failed to restrain the exercise of US power when Washington felt its important interests were at stake (Schweller 2001). The idea of liberal international order has also been questioned on other grounds (e.g., Allison 2018; Glaser 2019). We have mentioned earlier that China's values, institutions, and identity are significantly discrepant from those held by other countries, leading Allan et al. (2018: 841) to conclude that "the [prevailing] democratic and neoliberal hegemonic ideology effectively excludes China with its authoritarian national identity from full membership in the present order."

China and Russia face "civilizational" barriers to being admitted to the ranks of great powers (such as the G7 or G8), and the criteria for their admission to the select club of established powers are similar to the obstacle encountered by Turkey thus far in attempting to join the European Union and are reminiscent of the racist resistance Japan had met in an earlier era. Whether Western demands for human rights and democratic reform are sincere and genuine, or whether they are code words for "you are just not one of us," is critical in determining whether China and Russia perceive the existing international order to be open or closed. Washington's support for allies such as Taiwan and South Korea of course has predated their democratic transformation, and the United States continues to support countries such as Saudi Arabia which can hardly be described as democratic or respectful of human rights. The Black Lives Matter movement and persistent racial inequalities raise further questions about its own performance on human rights. Beijing and Moscow's perceptions will of course influence their strategies to achieve recognition and upward mobility. Their views will also in part depend on their judgment about how their domestic reforms thus far have been received by the West.

Surely, China's relations with the United States in the 1970s and 1980s during the Nixon, Ford, and Carter administrations were more cordial than today, even though the government in Beijing has become less authoritarian and Chinese society has become more open since that time. The other major change in this relationship is that China has in the interim gained more relative power and has narrowed the gap separating it from the United States. These trends suggest that the latter rather than the former consideration has been more decisive in affecting the evolution of Sino-American relations. In other words, contrary to Washington's professed commitment to human rights and democratic reform, concern about balance of power has been a more important factor influencing these countries' bilateral relationship. Such a conclusion would in turn throw into doubt the extent to which insistence on human rights and democratic reform as a condition for status recognition is sincere, and it would lend support instead to the perception that such professed concerns have been contrived to deny recognition.

As for Russia, Mikhail Gorbachev and his immediate successors had made significant concessions to Western demands to end the Cold War. Moscow had dissolved the Warsaw Pact and even the Soviet Union and its Communist Party, accepted a capitalist economy, downsized its military, and ceased support for insurgency movements abroad. It had also introduced multi-party elections. Ironically, and as in the case of China, it has found itself supporting incumbent governments such as those in Syria and Venezuela, whereas in an ironic twist of role reversal, the United States and other Western countries have been the ones supporting rebel groups seeking to overthrow these governments. "From Moscow's perspective, Russia for successive years made a series of concessions to the West, including accommodating NATO expansion, reacting with restraint to democratic revolutions in its 'near abroad,' and facilitating strategic access for the United States in Central Asia and Afghanistan" (Kupchan 2010: 397). Yet in the opinion of many Russians, including Vladimir Putin, these concessions have not been reciprocated and have in fact led to even greater Western pressure and encroachment seeking to marginalize their country (for an exchange of opinion on Russia's problems with Ukraine, see Massie 2014; McFaul, Sestanovich, and Mearsheimer 2014). Such perception would naturally provide the ingredients for the rise of revisionism. As Shifrinson (2018: 2) observes, the United States has been relentless in exploiting Moscow's weaknesses, "initially pressing for asymmetric diplomatic and military concessions before eventually facilitating the demise of the Soviet alliance network and hindering Soviet economic recovery." The West's pledge not to extend NATO to Central and Eastern Europe is but one prominent example of promises unkept (Shifrinson 2018: 147). Third parties would naturally pay attention to Russia's experience. Beijing would presumably conclude that weakness and concessions would not necessarily produce Western (including US) goodwill.

Conclusion

There is not any necessary association between a country's growing power and its tendency to become a revisionist state. In Thies and Nieman's (2017: 127) words, the view that "the growth in material power over time . . . should give rise to revisionist NRC [national role conception] is contradicted by the evidence: as

Chinese power grows, its self-conceived identity becomes more peaceful and system-supportive." This conclusion is also supported by these colleagues' examination of the words and deeds of the other BRICS countries. Medeiros (2009: 203) has reached a similar conclusion about China, stating that

> China has been largely working within the current international system to accomplish its foreign policy objectives. China is not trying to tear down or significantly revise the current constellation of global rules, norms, and institutions on economic and security affairs. Rather, on balance, it is seeking to master them to advance its international interests—an approach that has proven quite productive for Beijing.

He continues, "there are more instances of China gradually accepting international rules than objecting to and then trying to revise them" (Medeiros 2009: 204). Other more recent commentators have reached the same conclusion. Weiss (2019: 94) remarks that "China is a disgruntled and increasingly ambitious stakeholder in [the US-led international order], but not an implacable enemy of it." Similarly, Johnston (2019: 12) states succinctly, "China is not challenging the so-called liberal international order as many people think."

A state can change its foreign policy motivation. Its revisionism is not a fixed attribute. Thus, Japan joined World War I on the side of ostensibly "status-quo" powers but turned into a "revisionist" state in the interwar years. Similarly, Germany's foreign policy showed a sharp break between the Weimar Republic and the Third Reich. There was also a dramatic transformation in the Soviet Union's foreign policy orientation from the days of Stalin to the days of Gorbachev, and from Gorbachev to Putin. We have seen China similarly transformed since the Maoist years. And as we have argued, the United States took a decisive turn to revisionism during the so-called (George W.) Bush revolution in foreign policy.

We can also conclude from the preceding discussion that revisionism is a product of both foreign and domestic conditions, although the relative influence exercised by these two sources can be quite different depending on whether a country enjoys a position of preponderant power in the international system. Revisionism could stem from domestic sources, as when those dedicated to the overthrow of monarchial order, communists with a revolutionary ideology of proletarian internationalism, or national socialists committed to a vision of world domination by a master race came to power. International pressures could exacerbate the intensity of feelings on the part of those holding these views. At the same time, a state's overwhelming power can also create an opportunity for it to promote and propagate its vision of a new international order. Relative deprivation caused by a discrepancy between a state's achievements and the recognition accorded to it by other states seems to be a common factor causing grievance and resentment to demand the redistribution of resources and benefits and, if these demands encounter persistent resistance, challenges to the existing international order are likely to ensue. Perceived national humiliation and indignity can also be a powerful source of anger. Yet even in the absence of such perceived humiliation and indignity, a country can be motivated by a messianic impulse and missionary zeal to make the world more congenial to its values and interests, as the United States has done after the Cold War and the 9/11 terrorist attack. We do not offer any formulaic proposition about the emergence of revisionism, although we see such development resulting from a combination of both domestic and foreign conditions. Domestic politics in the pertinent country must provide fertile ground for nurturing and empowering those who hold revisionist views, and the international environment must somehow lend legitimacy and credibility to them. We can perhaps hypothesize that the greater the power advantage a country enjoys over other countries, the more important will be its domestic politics in deciding the nature of its foreign policy orientation.

The preceding discussion suggests that revisionism reflects a rising state's *experience* with how its demand for redistribution and recognition has been received by the established powers. This perspective points to the social and political interactions among states, and it points to some seriously problematic aspects of the prevailing debate in the United States and the West more generally about how to respond to a rising China, a debate that is typically dichotomized between whether to contain or engage this country. Yet, as power-transition theory makes quite clear, a country's growth trajectory is determined primarily by its domestic conditions (Organski and Kugler 1980; Tammen et al. 2000). Therefore, foreign attempts to influence China's future growth will be relatively ineffective according to this theory. As for engagement, this policy approach focuses on socialization to integrate China into the current US-dominated international order, and to induce the Chinese to join this order because of the attractiveness of its material rewards (Ikenberry 2008). This perspective therefore seeks China's conversion—defining a "responsible stakeholder" as one that plays according to the rules set by Washington. In other words, "responsibility" is treated as the same thing as "supporting and enforcing US interests" (Murray 2019: 216). The problem with this approach is of course that it insists on China making all the necessary adjustments, and it overlooks or dismisses China's own sense of its identity and its own understanding of its role in international relations. Yet, "to satisfy its recognition demands, the established powers must engage the rising power *on its own terms* and not structure its interactions with the goal of identity change [by the rising power]" (Murray 2019: 206; emphasis in original).

There is another sense in which the prevailing US views on "socializing" China can be one-sided. Given recent events showing Washington's decisions to abandon and even reject various international institutions and accords, can one speak of "un-socializing"? What can account for this process whereby a long-standing advocate and even a founding sponsor of the post-1945 international order becomes alienated from it? One should seek to explain not only Beijing's changing conduct, but also Washington's, to avoid the risk of giving idiosyncratic accounts. What general explanation can account for their divergent behavior that we will document in the next chapter?

Finally, it should be obvious by now that the label "revisionist" or "revisionism" can be a source of significant confusion and even controversy. This term has been often deployed pejoratively in social and political construction, rather than being used as an analytic concept for scholarly inquiry. As we have already argued, when a state is revisionist, the new norms, rules, and institutions it seeks to introduce and propagate may or may not receive our personal approval. But this consideration should not prevent us from using the concept in an analytic and, hopefully, objective manner.

3

Meaning of International Order and Evidence on Revisionism

In this chapter we turn to an attempt to monitor and track the extent of a country's revisionism. We limit our attention to the great powers (especially the United States and China) because these countries are most likely to have the power assets to pursue a revisionist agenda. It takes both "willingness" (a revisionist motivation) and "opportunity" (the necessary capabilities) for a revisionist power to change an existing international order. Small and weak countries, such as El Salvador and Honduras, will not be able to produce this change, even if they have a desire to alter the existing international order. As DiCicco (2017) has remarked, dissatisfaction is not the same thing as revisionism. He and other colleagues (e.g., Danilovic and Clare 2007; Kang and Gibler 2013; Sample 2018) have also pointed out that these concepts have been heretofore under-theorized and under-studied.

The Problems with Existing Studies

There have been previous empirical attempts to determine whether China is a revisionist state (e.g., Chan 2004b; Feng 2009; Johnston 2003; Kastner and Saunders 2012). These studies, however, tend to focus their attention exclusively on China. Therefore, they do not compare China's words and deeds with those of other countries such as the United States. Moreover, to the extent that these studies provide only a snapshot of Chinese foreign policy at one time, they do not tell us how Beijing's status-quo or revisionist orientation has evolved over time. Yet it is important for us to explore this possibility. Both offensive realism and power-transition theory suggest that as a rising state gains more power, it can/will become more aggressive and revisionist. Is there any evidence to support this proposition? Western analysts have generally overlooked the alternative possibility that a declining but still dominant hegemon can become more inclined to demand changes to the international order that it has helped to establish and to threaten to abandon this order unless its rules are revised to further accommodate or advance its interests.

As mentioned in Chapter 1, the existing literature tends to assume that a reigning hegemon, even when it suffers relative decline, will continue to be committed to the defense of the international order, whereas a rising power is seen to be motivated by a revisionist desire even though its upward mobility should have given it a larger stake in the existing international order. Thus, as pointed out earlier, there is a tendency for analysts to shuttle their logic—attributing a status-quo commitment to the reigning hegemon because it is supposed to have the largest stake in the existing international order, and a revisionist motivation to an upstart because it has gained more power to challenge and alter this order. Is it possible for a declining hegemon to become more revisionist because it now has a smaller stake in the international order? Given this smaller stake, it should have a smaller incentive to defend this order and a greater incentive to agitate for its change. Moreover, even in the context of its relative decline, the hegemon still has more power than other countries to alter this order to its further advantage. Conversely, can a rising upstart become more committed to this order because it now has a larger stake in this order and, as a result, it has less incentive to use its increased power to upend the rules of the game that have enabled its ascent thus far? In commenting on the behavior of rising powers, existing theories of offensive realism and power transition tend to emphasize the competitive dynamics in interstate relations, and they usually do not give enough attention to the influence of socialization that can transform a rising upstart's views, interests, and even its self-identity because of its deeper and more extensive engagement with international society. At the same time, existing accounts do not give enough attention to how an incumbent hegemon may become disenchanted with and alienated from the international order that it has played a leading role in shaping and fostering.

Naturally, our view suggests that the foreign policy motivation or intention of a state is not fixed. In contrast, the dominant tendency of the existing literature is to assume, rather than to demonstrate empirically, that simply because of a state's status as the preponderant power, it will remain steadfast in its defense of and commitment to the international order. Thus, Tammen et al. (2000: 9) state, "By definition, the dominant power is satisfied . . . [and therefore] is the defender of the status quo. After all, it creates and maintains the global or regional hierarchy from which it accrues substantial benefits."

In contrast, we argue that the foreign policy motivation or intention of states is subject to change, and it cannot be inferred simply from their relative power position in the interstate system or concluded as a matter of definitional fiat. As Xiang (2001: 9) has remarked as early as 2001, "it is hardly obvious . . . just who is defending the status quo." Writing before Donald Trump became the US president, he questioned the conventional wisdom that the United States was a status-quo power. He presented a contrarian argument, stating, "The irony today is that it is precisely America's Edwardian mind-set—simultaneously self-righteous and frustrated—that gives the impression that Washington is the opposite of a status quo power. Indeed, recent American diplomacy is causing alarm among its allies, friends and foes alike, raising a simple question: who is defending the status quo—China or the United States?" (Xiang 2001: 9). In our view, this question can only be settled by examining systematic evidence. As Ikenberry and Nexon (2019: 397) have indicated, the existing literature has ignored "the possibility, highlighted by Trump's foreign-policy dispositions, that a hegemonic power may actively aim to undermine the very order that it constituted."

We have also emphasized that international order is always in flux and is being contested and renegotiated—meaning that there is a constant tension and struggle between the promotion of new rules, norms, and institutions and the preservation of the established ones. States also have different preferences about which of these rules, norms, and institutions need to be retained, reformed, or rejected, and under what circumstances. Therefore, in our view it is too facile and even downright misleading to assign states to dichotomous categories of "revisionist" and "status-quo" countries. In our view, this is hardly a matter of "all or nothing."

Moreover, we are troubled by the fact that the existing literature tends to be content to end its inquiry after making attributions of states' "revisionist" or "status-quo" orientations, implying that it should be obvious what strategies or courses of action will be undertaken by states so labeled. For example, with some major exceptions (e.g., Ikenberry and Lim 2017; Kastner et al. 2016), most scholars do not usually address the question of *how* China will act if it is a revisionist state (He and Feng 2020). But, as we have mentioned earlier and as we will discuss further in the next chapter, it is far from obvious that all revisionist states can be expected to use the same approach to pursue their agenda. In other words, it is not enough to assign this label. We need to go further to investigate the likely strategy or policy that a supposed revisionist state is likely to adopt. We cannot leap to the conclusion that just because a state is considered revisionist, it will necessarily resort to military violence. Thus, to pursue the example just mentioned, Beijing's revisionist impulses may incline it to seek institutional reform in the regional forums and in the economic realm without, however, causing it to mount a military or ideological challenge to the global primacy commanded by Washington (He and Feng 2020). It has thus far not sought to match the United States in armament, nor has it tried to establish security alliances or challenged US dominance in regions that Washington considers to be its spheres of influence (e.g., the Western Hemisphere, the Middle East, and Western Europe).

We recognize that it is very challenging to infer a state's future motivations or intentions. At the same time, we contend that there is no alternative to accepting this challenge. The determination of leaders' motivations or intentions is at the core of international relations discourse (e.g., Edelstein 2002; Brooks 1997; Jervis 1978; Kydd 2000, 2005; Rosato 2014/2015; Yoder and Haynes 2015). The relevant empirical and theoretical debates hinge not so much on the relative capabilities of states (or the balance of power among them), but rather concerns how the pertinent leaders will use the power at their disposal. As mentioned in Chapter 1, this was the key idea behind the theory of "balance of threat" advanced by Walt (1987) to explain why most major states had supported the United States (the stronger country) rather than the Soviet Union during the Cold War in an apparent contradiction to the expectation of balance-of-power theory (this theory's logic has led Waltz [1979] to predict that other states should support the weaker side in a bilateral contest). Whether a state is revisionist or is committed to the existing international order of course pertains directly to this and other similar questions. Instead of skirting such questions by definitional fiat, we would rather undertake an empirical effort to gauge the relative revisionist disposition of states.

We do not have a magical solution to the problem of uncertainty about the motivations or intentions of a state, but we argue that an approach relying on multiple empirical indicators should give us more confidence in our inferences. To the extent that different indicators drawn from different sources and reflecting different aspects of statecraft converge to suggest the same conclusion, we gain more confidence in this conclusion. Moreover, when states undertake costly policies that are difficult to reverse for political or economic reasons, their conduct provides more persuasive evidence of their motivations or intentions. Such costly policies can entail heavy investments in one's tangible or intangible assets, described by Fearon (1997) as "sinking costs" and "tying hands," respectively, for example in making visible military preparations or deliberately engaging a leader's personal and her country's reputation to an announced course of action. When states' words and deeds correspond—when they not just talk the talk, but also walk the walk—this correspondence also lends greater credence to disclosing their true character. Goddard (2018b) argues that even "cheap talk" can disclose a state's intention or character because the rhetoric it deploys to legitimate its policies can reassure or alarm other states.

Before introducing our empirical indicators and evidence, we turn to a more extended discussion of the meaning and nature of "international order." As we have argued before, the debate about whether a country has a revisionist or status-quo intention focuses on whether its leaders will observe the existing "rules of the game." These rules are captured by the concept of international order, consisting of widely shared norms and expectations about how states ought to conduct themselves in international relations. International institutions are also a constituent part of this order as they are formed by states to coordinate their cooperation by lowering information and transaction costs, establish common protocols and procedures, and legitimate and propagate emergent consensus.

The Meaning of International Order

Discourse on "international order" has been confusing because scholars have not always been clear in their usage of this term. Some do not even bother to define it, assuming that its meaning should be self-evident to their audience. Others adopt and apply different conceptions of this term (He and Feng 2020). Some, especially those with a realist perspective, tend to use it to refer to the interstate distribution of power and resources (especially military capabilities). This tendency inclines them to treat "international order" and the "status quo" synonymously, disposing them to view any disturbance to the existing interstate balance of power, and especially any power shift that reduces a hegemon's dominance, to be ipso facto an indication of a revisionist attempt to undermine the "international order." This view therefore conflates international order and hegemony, and it has the obvious effect of depicting any rising state attempting to improve its relative power position or its share of resources as a troublemaker that destabilizes the "international order." This tendency accordingly depicts the "revisionist" state in question to be in opposition to not just the dominant power, but also the entire international community.

As we have indicated in Chapter 1, we disagree with this conception. Clearly, a state can have a dispute with another state—including the hegemon—without, however, necessarily wishing to upend the norms, rules, and institutions regulating interstate conduct. Note also that from the perspective of power-transition theory, when international order is used as a synonym for the existing balance of power, the two independent variables suggested by this theory to explain the occurrence of systemic war—namely, a power shift to the relative advantage of a latecomer and this latecomer's revisionist agenda—become redundant and duplicative. There is then a tautology that makes such a power shift, by definition, to mean a revisionist intention on the part of the rising latecomer. Moreover, as suggested by the quote from Tammen et al. (2000) cited earlier, the hegemon is not and cannot, by definition, be revisionist regardless of what it says or does.

In contrast to some with a realist bent, scholars adopting a liberal or constructivist perspective tend to see international order primarily in terms of the prevailing international norms, rules, and institutions, reflecting the shared expectations and aspirations of states and their customary conduct or routine practice. Representing the liberal perspective, for Ikenberry (2017b: 59), "International order refers to the organizing rules and institutions of world politics. It is the governing arrangements that define and guide the relations among states." As a constructivist, Alagappa (2003: 39) gives more importance to norms and ideas; he refers to international order as "a formal or informal arrangement that sustains rule-based interaction among sovereign states in their pursuit of individual and collective goals." In a similar vein and speaking from the English school's tradition, Goh (2013: 7) describes international order "as rule-based interactions among states in which shared norms, rules, and expectations constitute, regulate, and make predictable international life." Naturally, as these quotes suggest, there is a great deal of overlap between these conceptions of international order. As the reader must have surmised by now, we follow in this book these liberal/constructivist conceptions of international order and distinguish this concept from the interstate distribution of power or resources. For us, international order means "a normative or institutional arrangement among sovereign states that governs their interactions in the power-based international system" (He and Feng 2020: 12).

Common expectations and regular observance enable states to make mutual adjustment and accommodation, thereby strengthening the basis for interstate stability and cooperation. Their collective understanding about what constitutes proper and legitimate conduct—or, if you will, "the rules of the game"—makes interstate relations more predictable and orderly. Such understanding helps to regulate though not necessarily eliminate interstate violence and warfare. When it is widely held and deeply entrenched, we can refer to the existence of a *community* of states or an international *society*, as emphasized by scholars from the English school (e.g., Bull 1977; Buzan 2010; Clark 2005; Hurrell 2007). According to this perspective, even hegemony has a basis in social recognition and consensual legitimacy (Clark 2009). Kissinger's quote introduced in Chapter 1 suggests that such a community or society can coexist with an interstate system characterized by the competitive logic of power politics. By discouraging the unbridled pursuit of power, the norms, rules, and institutions of international order mitigate the anarchical nature of the interstate system engendered by the relentless competition for power among autonomous, self-regarding states. This effect can have its source in the officials' own self-restraint, such as when they eschew certain actions because they believe that these actions are wrong or illegitimate, or when they are concerned about the "shadow of the future" (Axelrod 1984) because other states may respond to their action by undertaking similar actions (due to imitation, reciprocation, or retaliation). Or this effect may simply stem from the relevant officials' routinized practice reflecting entrenched customs, habitual conduct, and even moral conviction. In contrast to this self-restraint, traditional realpolitik emphasizes external deterrence relying on the application of countervailing power or the threat of violence as a basis for and a means to achieve order and stability in interstate relations. Whereas the logic of appropriateness tends to dominate in norm- or rule-based international society, the logic of consequences prevails in the power-based interstate system (March and Olsen 1998, 2004; Risse 2002).

As just mentioned, we can conceive of international order to consist mainly of two dimensions, based respectively on norms and rules/institutions (He and Feng 2020). A norm-based conception directs our attention to basic and long-standing ordering principles, such as the sovereignty of states, respect for their territorial integrity, and non-interference in their domestic affairs. These norms and principles present the foundation for international order. They represent what Buzan (2010: 6) considers to be the "primary institutions" or "organic institutions" of international order that provide the basis for developing "secondary institutions" constituting the power relations among states and their rules, laws, and organizations. We often have these norms and principles in mind when we refer to the basic "rules of the game" in international relations: norms and principles that give rise to the common understanding and shared expectations that regulate and stabilize these relations. In contrast, a rule- or institution-based conception gives more consideration to international order as represented by the organizations and accords that states formally join. The United Nations, the World Trade Organization (WTO), the Universal Declaration of Human Rights, the Geneva Conventions, and the Paris climate accord are examples of this rule- or institution-based aspect of international order. Such international organizations and accords serve the important purposes of providing forums for states to coordinate their policies, and of representing the collective voices of the global community and expressing its agreements and aspirations. Accordingly, a state's membership in international organizations and its voting record in these organizations can indicate the extent to which it participates in this rule- or institution-based international order and the extent to which its preferences are aligned with the rest of the world. Similarly, its record of signing and ratifying important international treaties can show the extent to which it is willing to bind itself to existing international consensus.

We introduce three kinds of analysis to discern a country's possible revisionist orientation: evidence pertaining to norm-based international order; evidence pertaining to rule-/institution-based international order; and other relational and behavioral patterns in international dealings (see Table 3.1). We want to emphasize that our evidence is suggestive, and it is difficult to make definitive conclusions about a state's future intentions and its leaders' policy thinking. Moreover, there is not any clear-cut delineation on the measurement of a state's behavior in different domains of international order. In our view, these domains are not mutually exclusive. Some of the fundamental norms have already been enshrined and institutionalized into international treaties and taken up by international organizations and protocols, while others are characterized by a lesser extent of institutionalization and operationalization.

Table 3.1 Measurement of Revisionist Tendency

Domains of International Order	Behavioral and Measurement Indicators
Norm-Based International Order: fundamental principles and basic "rules of the game" of international relations	To what extent does a country respect and observe the basic norms? • Principle of sovereignty • Sovereign states as principal actors in international relations • Sovereign independence and equality • Primacy of territorial states • Respect for international borders and territorial inviolability of states • Restraint from interfering in another state's domestic affairs • Mutual recognition of the legitimacy of ruling regimes and states' respective traditional spheres of influence • Right of "self-defense" • Peaceful settlement of international disputes • The use of force as the last resort
Rule-/Institution-Based International Order: participation in international organizations, conventions/treaties, and protocols	To what extent does a country participate in international organizations and observe international treaty obligations? • Membership in international organizations • Scope and intensity of participating in multilateral diplomacy • Commitment to existing international treaty obligations • Contribution to the management and operation of existing international organizations • Voting records on major international issues (with the majority or not) • Contribution to new international conventions, accords, and treaties • Constraining domestic jurisdictions from overruling international treaty obligations
Other relational and behavioral patterns in international relations	How does a country interact and socialize with other countries in its international dealings? • Alliance portfolios • Arms sales • Leaders' visits • International networks • Economic relations (trade and investment) • Peer associations • Rhetoric on international issues

Norm-Based International Order

Although reasonable people can have different opinions on whether sovereignty has become an obsolescent idea and needs to be modified in the modern era, it has surely been the most important ordering principle for international relations since the Treaty of Westphalia (1648). It has been an enduring legitimating device, regulating and guiding these relations (Krasner 1999), even though there are other conceptions of sovereignty that compete with the Westphalian version (Paris 2020). In addition to the principle of sovereignty, the primacy of the territorial state has been another enduring ordering principle of the modern international order. Although there are many non-state actors in international political economy, states as politically organized units based on territory and delimited by physical boundaries have remained the principal actors, despite frequent predictions of their imminent demise (Herz 1957, 1968). Respect for international borders and the territorial inviolability of states are another enduring principle of international order, especially since wars have often stemmed from disputes over contested territory.

As an extension of the principle of sovereignty, international order has embodied the norm of mutual recognition of the legitimacy of ruling elites, and reciprocal restraint from interfering in another state's domestic affairs. As remarked earlier, revolutionary France's republicanism and communism's call for the dictatorship of an international proletariat can be considered revisionist ideologies because they challenged the legitimacy of the then-prevailing orders of monarchical and bourgeois rule, respectively. Still another part of norm-based international order pertains to widely shared views on the requirements for resorting to armed force (Walzer 1977). Traditional invocations of "just war" and contemporary views on the right of "self-defense," as embodied in the UN Charter, are pertinent here. Finally, norm-based international order includes mutual recognition by the great powers of their respective spheres of influence (Bull 1977; Etzioni 2015; Hast 2014; Keal 1983). To the extent that these countries can delineate the geographic boundaries of their competition, a more restrictive international order ensues and the danger of conflict among these countries declines (Kegley and Raymond 1994).

Even a casual observer of Chinese and US foreign policy would notice the dramatic changes that have occurred in the past seventy years since the establishment of the People's Republic of China. In the 1950s and 1960s, Beijing was vocal in supporting insurgency movements seeking to overthrow bourgeois regimes, and it advocated a worldwide campaign of armed struggle to achieve this goal. When Moscow demurred and sought peaceful coexistence with the West, Beijing accused it of having abandoned orthodox Marxist doctrines. During this period, Beijing denounced international agreements to control arms and rejected international organizations such as the United Nations as a tool of Western capitalist countries. It even fought the US-led UN forces in the Korean War. During much of the first three decades of the People's Republic, China was economically isolated, and after its split with the Soviet Union, diplomatically isolated as well, until it joined the United Nations in October 1971. Beijing did not start its economic reforms to open to the rest of the world until the late 1970s, when Deng Xiaoping returned to power. Since then, however, it has rapidly increased its presence in international organizations so that its level of participation in these organizations has now reached a level comparable to that of its peers. It has also now become deeply enmeshed in the global economy, being connected to it by dense, interlocking networks of production and finance. Equally important, we have seen a U-turn in its attitudes that now recognize the legitimacy of foreign ruling elites and profess non-interference in others' domestic affairs to be a cornerstone of its foreign policy. It has reversed its former support of insurgency movements, and it has ironically been criticized in the Western media now for supporting incumbent governments (e.g., in Sudan, Burma, Serbia, Syria, and Venezuela) that practice authoritarian rule and suppress domestic dissent and for providing foreign assistance without conditions that the recipient governments improve their governance practices and treatment of their citizens' human rights. Changing its previous stance on arms control agreements and UN peacekeeping missions (Fung 2019), China has now become an active participant in these arrangements. It is, for example, a party to the multinational deal to curb Iran's nuclear program and has been active in efforts to persuade North Korea to give up its nuclear weapons. Among the Security Council's permanent members, it is now also the largest contributor of personnel to UN peacekeeping missions.

In the decades immediately after World War II, the United States has been the most important source of support for incumbent governments trying to turn back armed insurgencies, especially leftist or communist insurrections seeking to overthrow regimes sympathetic to the West. From Greece to Korea to Vietnam, Washington provided massive financial aid and, in some cases, direct combat support to defeat these "anti-status-quo" groups. In the Korean War, Washington rallied international support under the UN "Uniting for Peace" resolution to legitimate its intervention. As many observers have pointed out, it has been an indispensable force for creating the post-1945 liberal economic order by establishing the Bretton Woods regime and other accords. It has also established an extensive alliance network, most notably the North Atlantic Treaty Organization, in a multilateral effort to contain the spread of communism.

More recently, however, we have seen major changes in US foreign policy, suggesting a reversal of its traditional stances no less significant than the ones characterizing the transformation of Chinese foreign policy. Since the Cold War's end, Washington has openly advocated regime change as a goal of its foreign policy toward governments that it finds repugnant. It has actively intervened, sometimes directly and militarily, in efforts to overthrow or destabilize incumbent regimes in Grenada, Panama, Iraq, Afghanistan, Iran, Libya, Serbia, Syria, and Venezuela. It sometimes invokes "responsibility to protect" or "humanitarian intervention" as a justification for its actions, although this justification is asserted only selectively (as shown by its inaction in the face of humanitarian tragedies in Rwanda and Haiti, and its withdrawal from Somalia). Significantly, just as China has become more insistent on non-interference in other countries' domestic affairs, Washington's policy has moved in the opposite direction. We encounter the odd phenomenon in the existing literature that despite these countries' respective positions on whether to respect or challenge the traditional principle of sovereignty and the legitimacy of ruling elites, China is often described by US scholars as a "revisionist" power and the United States is characterized as a "status-quo" power. This tendency obviously reverses the customary meaning of these terms.

The last war involving China was in 1979, when it fought Vietnam. Since then there has not been any large-scale combat involving the People's Liberation Army, even though there have been frequent episodes of "militarized interstate disputes" involving China—that is, disputes that have been accompanied by some form of military display, such as in cases of Beijing's contested sovereignty with Japan and the Southeast Asian countries in the East China Sea and the South China Sea, respectively. There have also been occasional escalations of military tension across the Taiwan Strait, such as in 1995–1996, when China fired missiles targeting waters near this island prior to its presidential election. Compared to the years since 1979 with those preceding it, however, the incidence and severity of military conflict involving China have clearly gone down. In contrast, the United States has been involved in many more episodes involving the use (or show) of force, and these episodes have involved much more violence, especially in Afghanistan and Iraq. If we accept the logic that disputes and conflicts fought closer to a country's homeland are likely to suggest a more defensive motivation and, conversely, those located in the "far abroad" are likely to indicate a more offensive motivation, there is again a large difference between China and the United States on this dimension. The frequency, scale, and location of these episodes, however, are less relevant to norm-based international order than their effects on the existing understanding shared by most countries regarding the legitimacy and legality of actions undertaken by Washington.

The US justification for waging a preventive war in invading Iraq in 2003 stretched the meaning of self-defense, and its allegation that Saddam Hussein had weapons of mass destruction and connections with Al Qaeda turned out to be false. The established view of international legalists emphasizes the "imminence" of being attacked as a necessary condition for resorting to force in self-defense. This traditional view has been ironically propagated and enshrined in an episode (1837) involving the US steamboat *Caroline* which was seized and burned by the British because it was rendering aid to Canadian rebels fighting British authority. In protesting against this British action, US Secretary of State Daniel Webster argued that a state's preemptive use of force could only be justified when the necessity of self-defense was "instant, overwhelming, leaving no choice of means, and no moment for deliberation." Washington's unilateral assertion of a right to wage preventive war challenged customary international law and, in Hurd's (2007: 199) words, "was profoundly revisionist."

Although Washington did not choose to offer extensive legal justification for its other undertakings in its war against terrorism—such as extra-legal "rendition" to kidnap and detain suspected terrorists abroad and even extra-judicial killings such as by drone attacks (including a foreign government's leader in a third country, when assassinating Iran's General Qasem Soleimani in Baghdad in January 2020), these actions suggest a sharp break from existing international norms. Rules about the treatment of civilians and enemy combatants have of course had a long, established tradition, including the Geneva Conventions. Beyond formal legal agreements to protect civilians and enemy combatants, there is an emergent consensus concerning the use of certain weapons such as land mines and chemical, biological, and nuclear weapons. We discuss later international treaties to prohibit certain types of weapons and conventions to prosecute and punish war criminals when we turn to discuss the rule- or institution-based conception of international order.

Military "intervention without some effort to gain [UN Security Council's] approval is now virtually obsolete, a remarkable feature of contemporary international relations that merits both theoretical and policy attention" (Thompson 2006: 2). This emergent principle has of course encountered subsequent reversals in the wake of NATO's military actions against Serbia, Libya, and Syria. When the United States and its Western allies realized that they could not gain the Security Council's approval to use force, they decided to bypass it and to attack these countries under NATO auspice instead. These decisions represent "forum shopping" to legitimate actions already decided upon. They point to significant "backsliding," in view of Thompson's statement just quoted. They also suggest how much change has occurred since 1950, when these same countries sought UN approval for their "police action" in Korea (the Uniting for Peace resolution was passed by the General Assembly in order to circumvent Soviet veto in the Security Council where, incidentally, with Washington's help China's seat was taken up by Kuomintang's government in Taiwan).

Rule- or Institution-Based International Order

Scholars such as Walt (2002) have argued that institutions such as the United Nations contribute to legitimating US power. In the same vein, we have argued that membership in international organizations indicates a state's prima facie disposition to participate in multilateral diplomacy and to follow these organizations' established procedures to arrive at decisions on collective action. Thus, when a state joins an international organization, it indicates at least some willingness to be bound by this organization's rules and procedures and to forfeit some of its discretion and autonomy to act unilaterally (Chan 2004b). Conversely, when a state declines membership in an international organization, it indicates its disdain for or distrust of this organization, such as when the United States refused to join the League of Nations (Rathbun 2012). Existing research shows that when two states share membership in many international organizations, they are less likely to become embroiled in militarized interstate disputes (Russett and Oneal 2001; Russett et al. 1998). Moreover, the larger the number of international organizations a state belongs to, the more it is committed to the existing international order. When a state leaves an international organization like the League of Nations (e.g., Germany, Italy, and Japan), it is likely to be embarked on a war path. Table 3.2 provides a list of major international organizations that China and the United States belong to. As already mentioned, although Beijing was extremely isolated in the earlier years after the founding of the People's Republic (belonging literally to only a handful of international organizations), its involvement in various international organizations is now at a level comparable to that of other major states.

In addition to international organizations, rule- or institution-based international order consists of international conventions, accords, and treaties that communicate agreements reached by states and convey the relevant states' commitments and obligations to carry out certain actions. These conventions, accords, and treaties can also express the international community's aspirations. Whether a state decides to join and continue these formal commitments can disclose important information about its intentions. When it accedes to an international agreement, its action announces to the world that it is at least predisposed to comply with the agreement's terms and that it shares the goals and objectives expressed by this agreement. By taking on this public commitment, this state distinguishes itself from other states that do not have the same intention or even the same aspiration. Contrary to the view that such commitment is meaningless because states are always free to renege in the future, there is a reputation cost if a state fails to discharge its legal responsibility. In addition to the "screening" effect disclosed by a state's decision to join or not join an international accord, the very act of joining may have a separate "constraining" effect so that having joined an

Table 3.2 Comparing China and the United States' Participation in International Organizations

Name of International Organization	China	United States
ADB (Asia Development Bank)	✓	✓
AfDB (African Development Bank) (non-regional member)	✓	✓
AIIB (Asian Infrastructure Investment Bank)	✓	
ANZUS (Australia, New Zealand, United States Security Treaty)		✓
APEC (Asia Pacific Economic Cooperation)	✓	✓
Arctic Council (China participates as observer)	✓	✓
ARF (ASEAN Regional Forum)	✓	✓
ASEM (Asia-Europe Meeting)	✓	
ASEAN plus dialogue partnership (dialogue partner)	✓	✓
Australia Group		✓
BIS (Bank for International Settlements)	✓	✓
BRICS (Brazil, Russia, India, China, and South Africa)	✓	
BSCE (Organization of the Black Sea Economic) (observer)		✓
CBSS (Council of the Baltic Sea States) (observer)		✓
CCPCJ (Commission on Crime Prevention and Criminal Justice)	✓	✓
CDB (Caribbean Development Bank)	✓	
CE (Council of Europe) (observer)		✓
CERN (European Organization for Nuclear Research)		✓
CICA (Conference on Interaction and Confidence-Building Measures in Asia) (United States participates as observer)	✓	✓
CoD (Community of Democracies)		✓
CP (Colombo Plan)		✓
CSW (Commission on the Status of Women)	✓	✓
EAPC (Euro-Atlantic Partnership Council)		✓
EAS (East Asia Summit)	✓	✓
EBRD (European Bank for Reconstruction and Development)		✓
FAO (Food and Agriculture Organization)	✓	✓

Continued

Table 3.2 *Continued*

Name of International Organization	China	United States
FATF (Financial Action Task Force)	✓	✓
G-7 (Group-7)		✓
G-20 (Group-20)	✓	✓
G-24 (Group-24)	✓	
Group-77	✓	
IAEA (International Atomic Energy Agency)	✓	✓
IBRD (International Bank for Reconstruction and Development	✓	✓
ICAO (International Civil Aviation Organization)	✓	✓
ICC (International Chamber of Commerce)	✓	✓
IDA (International Development Association)	✓	✓
IDB (Inter-American Development Bank)	✓	✓
IFAD (International Fund for Agricultural Development)	✓	✓
IFC (International Financial Corporation)	✓	✓
IFRC (International Federation of Red Cross and Red Crescent Societies)	✓	✓
IGC (International Grains Council)		✓
IHO (International Hydrographic Organization)	✓	✓
ILO (International Labor Organization)	✓	✓
IMF (International Monetary Fund)	✓	✓
IMO (International Maritime Organization)	✓	✓
IMSO (International Mobile Satellite Organization)	✓	✓
Interpol (International Criminal Police Organization)	✓	✓
IOC (International Olympic Committee)	✓	✓
IOM (International Organization for Migration)	✓	✓
IPU (Inter-Parliamentary Union)	✓	
ISO (International Organization for Standardization)	✓	✓
ITSO (International Telecommunications Satellite Organization)	✓	✓
ITU (International Telecommunication Union)	✓	✓
ITUC (International Trade Union Confederation)		✓

Table 3.2 *Continued*

Name of International Organization	China	United States
LAIA (Latin American Integration Association) (observer)	✓	✓
MIGA (Multilateral Investment Guarantee Agency)	✓	✓
MINUJUSTH (UN Mission for Justice Support in Haiti)		✓
MINURSO (UN Mission for the Referendum in Western Sahara)	✓	
MINUSMA (UN Multidimensional Integrated Stabilization Mission in Mali)	✓	
MONUC (UN Mission in Democratic Republic of the Congo)	✓	
NAM (Non-Aligned Movement) (observer)	✓	
NATO (North Atlantic Treaty Organization)		✓
NEA (Nuclear Energy Agency)		✓
NSG (Nuclear Suppliers Group)	✓	✓
OAS (Organization of American States) (China participates as observer)	✓	✓
OECD (Organization for Economic Co-operation and Development)		✓
OPCW (Organization for the Prohibition of Chemical Weapons)	✓	✓
OSCE (Organization for Security and Cooperation in Europe)		✓
Pacific Alliance (observer)	✓	✓
Pacific Islands Forum (dialogue partner)	✓	✓
PBC (Peacebuilding Commission)	✓	✓
PCA (Permanent Court of Arbitration)	✓	✓
SAARC (South Asian Association for Regional Cooperation) (observer)	✓	✓
SCO (Shanghai Cooperation Organization)	✓	
SECI (Southeast European Cooperative Initiative) (observer)		✓
SICA (Central American Integration System) (observer)		✓
SPC (Pacific Community)		✓
UNAMID (UN-African Union Hybrid Operation in Darfur)	✓	

Continued

Table 3.2 *Continued*

Name of International Organization	China	United States
UNCTAD (United Nations Conference on Trade and Development)	✓	✓
UNESCO (United Nations Educational, Scientific and Cultural Organization)	✓	
UNFICYP (UN Peacekeeping Force in Cyprus)	✓	
UNHCR (United Nations High Commissioner for Refugees)	✓	✓
UNHRC (United Nations Human Rights Council)	✓	
UNIDO (United Nations Industrial Development Organization)	✓	✓
UNIFIL (UN Interim Force In Lebanon)	✓	
United Nations	✓	✓
United Nations Security Council (permanent member)	✓	✓
UNMIL (UN Mission in Liberia)	✓	
UNMISS (UN Mission in South Sudan)	✓	
UNOCI (UN Operation in Côte d'Ivoire)	✓	
UNRWA (UN Relief and Works Agency for Palestine Refugees in the Near East)		✓
UNTSO (United Nations Truce Supervision Organization)	✓	✓
UNWTO (World Tourism Organization)	✓	
UPU (Universal Postal Union)	✓	✓
WCO (World Customs Organization)	✓	✓
WHO (World Health Organization)	✓	✓
WIPO (World Intellectual Property Organization)	✓	✓
WMO (World Meteorological Organization)	✓	✓
WOSM (World Organization of the Scout Movement)		✓
WTO (World Trade Organization)	✓	✓
WVF (World Veterans Federation)		✓
Zangger Committee	✓	✓

Sources:

https://www.cia.gov/library/publications/the-world-factbook/fields/317.html;

https://www.fmprc.gov.cn/web/wjb_673085/zzjg_673183/gjs_673893/gjzz_673897/.

accord, a state may act differently than if it had not joined, out of a sense of moral or legal obligation or out of a concern for possible negative domestic and international political fallout if it were to fail to discharge its treaty obligations (Kelley 2007; Mattes and Vonnahme 2010; Simmons 2000; Simmons and Hopkins 2005; Von Stein 2005).

Donald Trump declared, "I am absolutely a nationalist" (https://www.cnn.com/videos/politics/2018/10/23/donald-trump-nationalist-sot-oval-office-lead-vpx.cnn), and he pledged in his inaugural speech, "From this day forward, it's going to be only America first—America first" (https://www.theguardian.com/world/video/2017/jan/20/donald-trump-inauguration-speech-full-video). He later withdrew the United States from the multilateral agreement on Iran's nuclear program (the Joint Comprehensive Plan of Action or JCPA), the Intermediate-Range Nuclear Forces Treaty (INF), the United Nations Human Rights Council (UNHRC), the United Nations Educational, Scientific and Cultural Organization (UNESCO), the Paris climate agreement (a decision subsequently reversed by Biden), and the Trans-Pacific Partnership (TPP). As mentioned earlier, he moreover pulled the United States out of the Arms Trade Treaty, the United Nations Global Compact for Migration, the Open Skies Treaty, and the World Health Organization (WHO, another decision reversed by Biden). He insisted on renegotiating the North American Free Trade Agreement (NAFTA) in order to gain more favorable terms for the United States (the renegotiated pact is called the US-Mexico-Canada Agreement, or USMCA, and it went into force in July 2020). He also pressured South Korea to renegotiate its free trade agreement with the United States (KORUS), and a new deal was signed in September 2018.

Although much of the media coverage has focused on the ongoing US-Chinese trade conflict and the Trump administration's efforts to revamp NAFTA, Washington began an aggressive war on the WTO. The Trump administration consistently criticized this global trading system as unfair to US interests. In an interview with *Bloomberg News* on August 31, 2018, President Trump said: "if they don't shape up, I would withdraw from the WTO" ("Trump Threatens to Pull US out of World Trade Organization," https://www.bbc.com/news/world-us-canada-45364150). In his speech to the UN General Assembly in September 2019, he said the WTO needs "drastic change" to counter Chinese cheating, claiming that "for years these abuses were tolerated, ignored or even encouraged." He vowed not to accept a bad trade deal with China (quoted in Macias and Pramuk 2019). In a similar vein, US Trade Representative Ambassador Robert Lighthizer complained, "The WTO is completely inadequate to stop China's harmful technology practices," and averred that "the United States must be allowed to defend itself against unfair trade practices, and the Trump Administration will not let China use the WTO to take advantage of American workers, businesses, farmers, and ranchers" (quoted in Macias 2020: n.p.).

Over the last three years, the Trump administration targeted the WTO's Appellate Body and blocked the appointment of its judges in a deliberate effort to sabotage this organization's core institution. It exploited WTO weaknesses and began a policy of "aggressive unilateralism" to paralyze its dispute-settlement mechanism. Ambassador Robert Lighthizer called for a "broad reset" of WTO's tariffs in its latest conflict with the global trade organization ("Top Trade Official Says US Will Seek 'Broader Reset' of WTO Tariffs," https://www.ft.com/content/00cdebfa-e364-4914-a629-29f1fdd290ff). Washington's attempt to disempower the WTO's Appellate Body and call for an overhaul of the global trade system could mark a real turning point in US global trading policy.

How Washington responds to a recent ruling by WTO's three-person panel against its imposition of tariffs on Chinese goods would be especially instructive (Baschuk 2020). Washington has resorted to Section 301 of the 1974 Trade Act, claiming that these tariffs were necessary to retaliate against China's violations of intellectual property rights. In September 2020, the WTO panel ruled that the United States violated international rules when it imposed US$400 billion on Chinese goods in 2018. This ruling responds to China's complaint that the US tariffs violated WTO's process requiring Washington to first go through its dispute-settlement mechanism to seek recourse before taking unilateral retaliation. In the WTO panel's view, the US tariffs had singled out Chinese products for retaliation, thus agreeing with China's claim that it had violated the WTO's most-favored-nation provision because the US tariffs had not given the same treatment to all WTO members.

Although the Trump administration's actions appear more extreme and blatant, in the history of US diplomacy they are not unique; its predecessors also declined to join important international organizations like the League of Nations and the International Trade Organization, or refused to accede to international accords such as the Comprehensive Test Ban, the Treaty to Ban Landmines, the International Criminal Court, the Basel Convention to regulate transborder shipment of hazardous waste, the Kyoto protocol to reduce the emission of greenhouse gas, the United Nations Convention on the Law of the Sea (UNCLOS), the International Covenant on Economic, Social and Cultural Rights, the Convention on the Elimination of All Forms of Discrimination against Women, the Convention on Biological Diversity, the Convention on the Rights of Persons with Disabilities, and the Convention on the Rights of the Child. George W. Bush also withdrew the United States from the Anti-Ballistic Missiles (ABM) Treaty. In an earlier era, as noted earlier, the United States had declined to join the League of Nations and the International Trade Organization. Signs indicating Washington's exercise of "muscular" policies and its pursuit of assertive unilateralism were also evident during George W. Bush's administration (e.g., Buzan 2004a; Daalder and Lindsay 2005).

Buzan (2004a: 184–185) observes that the US turn toward unilateralism, Manicheanism, and hyper-securitization had even preceded the Bush (George W.) administration whose foreign policy "was nothing less than an assault on the international social structure built mainly by the US over the previous half-century, and therefore a seismic shift in US grand strategy." This shift reflected in part changes in the international arena, reflecting the US ascendance to an undisputed and indeed unprecedented position of unipolar preponderance, but it was also motivated and driven by domestic impulses. Paradoxically, as we have mentioned earlier, China's rise and thus a US loss of power relative to that country can also incline Washington to seek changes in the norms, rules, and institutions of international order. This remark in turn suggests that power shifts do not in themselves determine whether a country would become revisionist. Other variables, such as domestic incentives, also have to be considered.

Bacevich (2002: 90) has remarked that "American statecraft is not, in the first instance, about 'them'; it is about 'us.'" Indeed, it is the combination of international and domestic circumstances that produced this shift in US foreign policy: the greater the preponderance enjoyed by a country, the less it is constrained by foreign considerations and the more it will be motivated by domestic considerations, instincts, and impulses.

Still, given the significant extent to which the Trump administration has gone to abandon multilateral diplomacy and disengage from international institutions, we may well expect a possible "reversion to the mean." Thus, as already mentioned, the Biden administration has decided to return the United States to the WHO and the Paris climate accord. Time will tell the extent to which the Trump administration's actions represent an aberration. In this book's Appendix, we provide a list of those international treaties pending ratification by Beijing and Washington. We have also collected data reporting all international treaties that China and the United States have joined since 1949. We do not report this information here because of space limitation, but those interested in it can access this link: https://fss.um.edu.mo/wp-content/uploads/2021/03/Multilateral-treaties-comparing-China-and-the-US.pdf.

Although China has also declined to become a party to international agreements to establish the International Criminal Court, to ban landmines, and to ratify the International Covenant on Civil and Political Rights, it has joined and ratified other international treaties, such as UNCLOS, the Basel accord, and the Paris climate agreement. To our knowledge, Beijing has thus far not withdrawn from any significant international organization or accord. Although joining an international organization or international convention does not necessarily mean that a country is a "responsible stakeholder" or a "status-quo" country, its membership record does say something about its disposition to engage in multilateralism and to be part of important international institutions.

As we have emphasized previously, the direction and momentum of a country's changing record are important considerations. Whereas China has clearly become more integrated into the international community, the United States has been on an opposite path. Moreover, when judged in a comparative light, China has become less revisionist, according to our interpretation of this evidence, and the United States more so.

Washington's declining interest in multilateral institutions (including some for which it had played a leading role in creating) is very telling in how US policymakers see the benefits and costs of conducting foreign policy through multilateral institutions. In an increasingly globalized world, the boundary between domestic and foreign affairs has become blurred and permeable. More and more members of both the US elite and public feel that their country has been taken advantage of by others in international trade and military alliances, or that it has sacrificed too much of its national interests for others or for the sake of international causes and world peace. In recent years, Washington has reduced its membership fees to the United Nations and even NATO's operations. According to UN figures, the United States owes $674 million for 2019, and $381 million from previous budgets (https://www.npr.org/2019/10/10/769095931/u-n-warns-of-budget-crisis-if-nations-dont-pay-1-3-billion-in-dues-they-owe). The Trump administration had stopped payments altogether to the UN Relief and Works Agency (UNRWA) in 2018. It had moreover suspended payments to the WHO in 2019 before finally announcing its decision to withdraw from this organization in late May while a global pandemic was still raging (the Biden administration later rejoined this organization in January 2021). Washington also began to reconsider its participation in the postwar multilateral trade regime, switching its emphasis from multilateralism to bilateralism. On some sensitive international issues, such as pursuing sanctions against Russia, it has shown an increasing tendency to extend its domestic jurisdiction to foreign countries.

In the final analysis, international order is what states make of it. The views and preferences of most states aggregate to present their collective sense about those values, norms, and principles that should inform and guide proper conduct and confer legitimate rights in interstate interactions. This is the reason for us to consider voting patterns in the United Nations as one of our empirical indicators to gauge the extent to which a country finds itself inside or outside of international consensus. Are this country's policies increasingly out of step with the rest of the world, or are they becoming more aligned with other countries?

As we reported in Chan et al. (2019), China has been consistently in the voting majority in the General Assembly, whereas the United States has become increasingly isolated. During roughly the first forty-four years of its presence in the United Nations (1971–2015), Beijing voted "yes" in 78.8% and "no" in only 3.3% of the ballots it had cast—compared to the United States voting "yes" only 21.9%

of the time and "no" in 54.2% during the same period. These figures can be compared to the following benchmark: of all the ballots that were cast in the General Assembly during those years, 75.1% were in the affirmative and only 4.7% were in the negative, with abstentions (10.8%) and absences (9.3%) comprising the remainder (Voeten 2004, 2013; Voeten et al. 2009). If we treat this body as the most representative and authoritative voice of the international community, these comparative statistics show rather conclusively that the United States has been much more outside of this community's consensus than China. By this measure, the United States is more out of step with the rest of UN members than the other permanent members of the Security Council. "Yes" votes constituted 72.5%, 43.8%, and 42.3%, respectively, of the ballots cast by the Soviet Union/Russia, France, and Britain, whereas their "no" votes were 9.7%, 20.9%, and 25.8%, respectively. Since the early days of the United Nations, when the United States and its Western allies commanded a supermajority in this organization, they have increasingly become a minority voice. Washington's positions on many policy issues have become less popular over time, and it finds itself increasingly isolated. It is an outlier in the General Assembly's roll call votes, compared to China as well as the other great powers (Johnston 2019: 18).

Even though its policy preference is unpopular, a permanent member of the Security Council has a veto power to frustrate or thwart the majority's preference. The exercise of veto power is a public act of defiance to block the passage of a resolution preferred by other states. We can assess the extent to which a country is out of step with international consensus and the extent to which it is willing to openly oppose this consensus by examining the frequency of its resort to veto power (Chan 2016). In the early days of the United Nations, the Soviet Union frequently used its veto. More recently, the United States has become the leading country to resort to this power (http://research.un.org/en/docs/sc/quick/veto). Between October 1971 (when China joined the United Nations) and December 2019, China has cast a veto on fourteen occasions, France on fourteen occasions, Britain on twenty-four occasions, the Soviet Union/Russia on thirty-seven occasions, and the United States on eighty-two occasions. These figures again leave little doubt about which country is more out of step with the majority view of the international community. This said, there has also been a noticeable increase in China and Russia's resort to vetoes in more recent years.

It is important to acknowledge that the views and preferences of most UN members can seek to promote changes in the norms, rules, and principles that have heretofore defined the rules of the game (just as the Western countries have propounded the novel principle of "responsibility to protect" and the United States has tried to justify its doctrine of "preventive war"). For instance, this majority has for some years advocated its vision of a "new international economic order" and has offered an agenda to reach this vision. This advocacy, however, has encountered varying degrees of objection and resistance from Western countries—which, in this instance, find themselves in the role of defenders of the old norms. The United States and Britain had also tried to dampen resolutions supported by most countries condemning South Africa and Rhodesia's racist regimes. These examples again remind us that states can often find themselves engaged in a constant struggle to change some elements of international order while defending others. Those who agitate for change are of course revisionists by definition, and those who want to maintain business as usual are defenders of the status quo. As already stated, these descriptors should not be used pejoratively to communicate an analyst's personal approval or disapproval of the state or policy in question, as people can have different opinions about whether certain change or stasis should be accepted or rejected.

Other Relational and Behavioral Indicators

Some scholars have used other indicators, such as states' alliance portfolios and arms buildups, to infer their revisionist or status-quo disposition and their commitment to change or maintain the existing international order (e.g., Kim 1991, 1992; Lemke and Werner 1996; Werner and Kugler 1996). The extent of power disparity between two states has also been used to make this inference under the assumption that being stronger or more dominant inclines a state to be more "satisfied" with the "status quo," and conversely, weakness translates to being "dissatisfied" and "revisionist" (e.g., Kim 2002). Still another approach has been to use a state's regime type (such as democracy or autocracy) to infer its policy orientation, based on the assumption that the world's hegemons have been democracies and have been committed to the "status quo," and therefore other democracies should also have this inclination (Lemke and Reed 1996). As yet another example, Chinese leaders' foreign trips have been used to discern Beijing's revisionist disposition (Kastner and Saunders 2012). This research is based on the reasoning that these leaders are more likely to visit and therefore lend support to "rogue" states opposing the United States and the West generally if they have a revisionist agenda. More recent attempts to operationalize the concept of dissatisfaction have introduced considerations such as the rate of increase in per capita income, involvement in territorial disputes, and the cost of borrowing money, and some of them have sought to differentiate between a state's specific unhappiness with another state in a regional context and its general discontent with the international system (e.g., Danilovic and Clare 2007; Kang and Gibler 2013; Sample 2018). As mentioned already and as cautioned by DiCicco (2017), dissatisfaction is not the same thing as revisionism, which indicates a desire or intention to alter the existing rules of the game. A country can be dissatisfied with its relations with another state without being revisionist in wanting to overthrow or upend the existing international order.

The assumption that the dominant power must be a defender of the "status quo" and its allies and associates must therefore also be "status-quo" powers can be easily extended to other kinds of data analysis. For example, given the logic of this reasoning, how these other states have voted in the United Nations and with whom they trade most heavily can be used to make inferences similar to those just reported, based again on the assumption that because the dominant state must be a "status-quo" power, other states that have close associations with this dominant power must also have a similar "status-quo" motivation. One may also consider Beijing and Washington's diplomatic presence abroad, such as the number and location of their respective embassies and consulates, to infer the relative importance they attach to other countries (e.g., Bley 2019). Naturally, given our disagreement with the assumption that the dominant power must necessarily be a "status-quo" power, inferences based on this logic are problematic, in our view.

Still, we can employ data such as those mentioned in the preceding paragraphs to make other kinds of observations and inferences. For instance, what can Chinese leaders' foreign travels tell us about Beijing's networks of friends, associates, and significant others? Are there any signs that Beijing has been trying to establish a formal alliance or even an informal coalition designed to compete with the United States? If so, in which geographic region? Similarly, is there any evidence that Beijing has been trying to create a trading bloc? To what extent has it been able to establish a political or economic sphere of influence in its neighborhood? The answers to these questions are potentially germane to the two determinants suggested by Goddard (2018a) to influence a revisionist state's choice of its strategy. These two variables pertain to the extent to which the country in question has general access to international institutions, and the extent to which it occupies a bridging position connecting it to a group of close, like-minded associates. An example of a country that lacks extensive access to international institutions but enjoying a bridging position to its own network of associates would be the Soviet Union during the Cold War, when it abstained from extensive engagement with the capitalist world order but maintained close ties with its Eastern and Central European ideological partners. In contrast, and as our data show, China today has become very deeply and extensively enmeshed in the global political economy and international governing institutions, and it has also established close networks of trade, aid, and political contact with regions such as Sub-Saharan Africa and Southeast Asia.

As just mentioned, these observations are meaningful in the context of Goddard's (2018a) typology of different strategies that are likely to be pursued by different revisionist states. Her typology and analysis, based on network theory, suggest that when a revisionist state has high access to international institutions and when it also enjoys an important position linking it to subgroups of close associates, it will likely pursue a nonviolent strategy to seek rule-based institutional reforms. She sees this type of revisionist behavior as reflecting a "bridging" or "broker" role in international relations, as exemplified by Prussia's statecraft during the 1880s. This characterization corresponds with and supports our discussion in the next chapter, addressing China's pursuit of "soft" revisionist strategies to promote institutional changes.

It is also important to note what our evidence does not show: China has refrained from seeking foreign alliances and military installations. It is true that Beijing has close political ties with, has sold weapons to, or has gained some access to maritime facilities in Pakistan, Burma, Bangladesh, Sri Lanka, and Djibouti. But this profile is significantly different from the alliance networks and military assets that the United States has established abroad or, for that matter, that the Soviet Union had maintained or sought during the Cold War. This is an important difference distinguishing China's foreign presence and posture from these two countries. Beijing's overseas involvement has been primarily commercial and economic in nature, and it has thus far eschewed the pursuit of military allies, client states, and foreign outposts reminiscent of the traditional statecraft of "strategic states" (as distinct from the "trading states" described by Rosecrance 1986).

We present in Table 3.3 the profiles of overseas trips made by leading Chinese officials (Foreign Ministers Yang Yiechi and Wang Yi, Premier Li Keqiang, and President Xi Jinping) during 2013–2017. Most of these trips were made to China's immediate neighbors, especially those in Southeast Asia. Another distinctive feature is the large number of trips made by these top leaders to Sub-Saharan Africa. The United States and other G-7 countries were also the destination of a relatively large number of these trips, and Russia stood out as an especially frequent host country for these Chinese officials. Except for Burma (a contiguous neighbor located in Southeast Asia), travel by top Chinese officials to the so-called pariah states (such as Sudan and Iran) did not appear to support the hypothesis that Beijing has been trying to build an anti-US coalition with them. The other remarkable features of Table 3.3 point to the relatively high frequency of official Chinese trips to Central Asia and Latin America/the Caribbean. The general picture conveyed by this table suggests that Beijing has established an extensive global diplomatic network, focusing especially on Southeast Asia and Sub-Saharan Africa. Thus, China's diplomacy has both a global reach and a regional focus.

How much change do we see in the top Chinese officials' profiles of foreign travel? Table 3.4 shows the pertinent data from the previous Chinese administration under Hu Jintao and Wen Jiabao. The most significant difference between

Table 3.3 Foreign Visits by Chinese Foreign Minister, Premier, and President: February 2013–November 2017 (Xi-Li period)

	Yang and Wang	Li	Xi	Combined
Southeast Asia	19	7	7	33
Koreas, Mongolia	2	2	2	6
Central Asia	10	3	8	21
Mideast	14	0	3	17
Latin America and Caribbean	11	5	10	26
United States	3	0	1	4
Other G-7 (includes Japan)	5	7	4	16
Other Western Europe	3	5	4	12
Eastern Europe	4	4	4	12
Sub-Saharan Africa	26	4	4	34
Oceania	4	2	3	9
South Asia	10	2	4	16
Russia	4	2	3	7

Trips to "Pariah States": Cuba (2), Venezuela (2), Sudan (1), Iran (2), Burma (4).

Sources:

https://www.fmprc.gov.cn/web/wjdt_674879/wsrc_674883/default.shtml.

China Foreign Affairs Annual (中国外交年鉴), volumes 2012 to 2018, which document Chinese leaders' overseas trips in each year, Beijing: World Affairs Press 世界知识出版社, 2012–2018.

this period and the administration under Xi Jinping is the increased frequency of foreign visits made by top Beijing officials in more recent years. In other words, Chinese diplomacy has become more active in recent years. Southeast Asia and Sub-Saharan Africa have especially seen a substantial jump in hosting Chinese officials in the Xi administration. Conversely, travel undertaken by top Chinese officials to the Middle East declined slightly in this administration. Overall, foreign travel by these officials shows a significant increase over time, and this travel shows a worldwide reach, with an emphasis on Southeast Asia and Sub-Saharan Africa, as already remarked. This proclivity conforms to the view that Beijing sees itself both as a leader in its home region and as a champion of the developing world (Pu 2019). It has seemingly established itself in a pivotal intermediary or broker position with respect to the two geographic areas just mentioned. There was even less evidence in the travel records of Chinese officials during Hu's

Table 3.4 Foreign Visits by Chinese Foreign Minister, Premier, and
President: January 2009–December 2012 (Hu-Wen period)

	Yang	Wen	Hu	Combined
Southeast Asia	6	7	2	15
Koreas, Mongolia	3	3	0	6
Central Asia	2	2	5	9
Mideast	14	6	1	20
Latin America and Caribbean	5	4	1	10
United States	2	0	1	3
Other G-7 (includes Japan)	4	5	3	12
Other Western Europe	5	7	3	15
Eastern Europe	4	2	3	9
Sub-Saharan Africa	17	0	4	21
Oceania	0	0	0	0
South Asia	2	3	0	5
Russia	2	2	2	6

Trips to "Pariah States": Syria (1), Burma (1), Cuba (1), Sudan (1).

Sources:

https://www.fmprc.gov.cn/web/wjdt_674879/wsrc_674883/default.shtml.

China Foreign Affairs Annual (中国外交年鉴), volumes 2008 to 2013, which document
Chinese leaders' overseas trips in each year, Beijing: World Affairs Press 世界知识出版社,
2008–2013.

administration that Beijing was seeking to establish strong liaisons with the so-
called pariah states in an anti-US coalition.

Table 3.5 provides comparable data on foreign visits made by US secretaries of
state and presidents during the Obama and Trump administrations. Compared
to China, US leaders clearly gave more emphasis to the Middle East, the other G-
7 countries, and Western Europe. They also did not give nearly as much attention
to Sub-Saharan Africa as the Chinese leaders. The Trump administration also
appeared to give much less emphasis to Latin America/the Caribbean, a region
that is generally seen as the United States' "backyard."

To complement the data on leaders' foreign travels as an indicator of a
country's allocation of its diplomatic attention and the intensity of its international links, we have also collected data on export trade and foreign investment

Table 3.5 Foreign Visits by US Secretary of State and President: March
2013–December 2017 vs. January–December 2017

	Kerry	Obama	Tillerson	Trump
Southeast Asia	16	1	4	2
Koreas, Mongolia	4	0	1	1
Central Asia	7	0	0	0
Mideast	86	5	10	3
Latin America and Caribbean	17	0	1	0
China	8	1	2	1
Other G-7 (includes Japan)	81	4	6	6
Other Western Europe	49	2	4	1
Eastern Europe	11	1	1	0
Sub-Saharan Africa	13	0	0	0
Oceania	3	0	2	1
South Asia	13	0	3	0
Russia	5	0	1	0

Trips to "Pariah States": Burma (3), Cuba (2).

Sources:

https://history.state.gov/departmenthistory/travels;

https://history.state.gov/departmenthistory/travels/president/trump-donald-j

https://history.state.gov/departmenthistory/travels/secretary/tillerson-rex-wayne.

made by China and the United States to gain an appreciation of their respective external economic orientation and emphasis. Tables 3.6 and 3.7 report, respectively, free trade agreements (FTAs) and bilateral investment treaties (BITs) that these countries have signed with others. The pertinent data show similar patterns whereby both countries' FTAs appear to have had more of a regional focus, with China favoring the Asia Pacific area and the United States giving more emphasis to its neighbors in the Western Hemisphere. In contrast, the BITs signed by both China and the United States demonstrate a more global orientation, encompassing a much larger number of countries, as well as a more diverse group of partners. China has been a much larger exporter of goods to the rest of the world than has the United States. It has therefore created stronger trade links with other countries by this measure of access (see also Table 3.8). Moreover, if BITs can be taken to show another type of access that a country has to the rest

Table 3.6 Comparing China and the United States' Free Trade Agreements (FTAs) (as of December 2020)

China	United States
ASEAN (including upgrade)	Australia
Australia	Bahrain
Chile (including upgrade)	Canada
Cambodia	Chile
Costa Rica	Colombia
Georgia	Costa Rica
Iceland	Dominican Republic
Korea, Republic of	El Salvador
Mainland and Hong Kong Closer Economic	Guatemala
Partnership Agreement (CEPA HK)	Honduras
Mainland and Macao Closer Economic	Israel
Partnership Arrangement (CEPA Macao)	Jordan
Maldives	Korea, Republic of
Mauritius	Mexico
New Zealand	Morocco
Pakistan (including 2nd phase)	Nicaragua
Peru	Oman
Regional Comprehensive Economic	Panama
Partnership (RCEP)	Peru
Singapore (including upgrade)	Singapore
Switzerland	United States-Mexico-Canada Agreement

Sources:
https://ustr.gov/trade-agreements/free-trade-agreements;
https://www.trade.gov/fta/;
http://fta.mofcom.gov.cn/english/fta_qianshu.shtml;
http://tfs.mofcom.gov.cn/article/Nocategory/201111/20111107819474.shtml.

of the world, China has clearly demonstrated this connection as well. Indeed, Beijing has established a more extensive set of investment ties than Washington, given the larger number of countries with which it has signed BITs.

Figure 3.1 introduces several plots showing the geographic distribution and changes over time in Chinese and US foreign direct investments (FDI). Although the amount of Chinese FDI has lagged behind that of the United States, it has shown more rapid increases in recent years from a lower base. Unsurprisingly, these countries' FDIs have shown different regional preferences. An overwhelming proportion (69.5% in 2017) of China's FDI has gone to its home region (Asia), whereas the top destination of US FDI has been Europe (59.1%, again in 2017). The leading recipients of China's Asian FDI in 2017 were, in descending order, Singapore, Kazakhstan, Malaysia, Indonesia, and Laos. Surprisingly, Latin America follows Asia in a distant second position

Table 3.7 Comparing China and the United States' Bilateral Investment Treaties (BITs)

China	United States
Albania	Albania
Algeria	Argentina
Argentina	Armenia
Armenia	Azerbaijan
Australia	Bahrain
Austria	Bangladesh
Azerbaijan	Bolivia
Bahrain	Bulgaria
Barbados	Cameroon
Belarus	Congo, Democratic Republic of (Kinshasa)
Belgium	Congo, Republic of (Brazzaville)
Bolivia	Croatia
Bulgaria	Czech Republic
Cambodia	Ecuador
Canada	Egypt
Cape Verde	Estonia
Chile	Georgia
Congo	Grenada
Croatia	Honduras
Cuba	Jamaica
Cyprus	Jordan
Czech	Kazakhstan
Denmark	Kyrgyzstan
Ecuador	Latvia
Egypt	Lithuania
Equatorial Guinea	Moldova
Estonia	Mongolia
Ethiopia	Morocco
Finland	Mozambique
France	Panama
Gabon	Poland
Georgia	Poland Business and Economic Relations Treaty
Germany	
Ghana	Romania
Greece	Rwanda
Guyana	Senegal
Hungary	Slovakia
Iceland	Sri Lanka
India	Trinidad and Tobago
Indonesia	Tunisia
Iran	Turkey
Israel	Ukraine
Italy	Uruguay
Jamaica	
Japan	

Continued

Table 3.7 *Continued*

China	United States
Katar	
Kazakhstan	
Kuwait	
Kyrgyzstan	
Laos	
Lebanese	
Lithuania	
Luxembourg	
Macedonia	
Madagascar	
Malaysia	
Mali	
Malta	
Mauritius	
Moldova	
Mongolia	
Morocco	
Myanmar	
New Zealand	
Nigeria	
North Korea	
Norway	
Oman	
Pakistan	
Papua New Guinea	
Peru	
Poland	
Portugal	
Romania	
Russia	
Saudi Arabia	
Singapore	
Slovakia	
Slovenia	
South Africa	
South Korea	
Spain	
Sri Lanka	
Sudan	
Sweden	
Switzerland	
Syria	

Table 3.7 *Continued*

China	United States
Tajikistan	
Tanzania	
Thailand	
The Netherlands	
The Philippines	
Trinidad and Tobago	
Tunis	
Turkey	
Turkmenistan	
UAE	
Ukraine	
Uruguay	
Uzbekistan	
Vietnam	
Yemen	
Zimbabwe	

Sources:

https://www.trade.gov/fta/;

https://tcc.export.gov/Trade_Agreements/Bilateral_Investment_Treaties/index.asp;

http://fta.mofcom.gov.cn/english/index.shtml;

http://tfs.mofcom.gov.cn/article/Nocategory/201111/20111107819474.shtml.

as a regional destination for China's FDI, exceeding the amount received by the more developed countries in Europe, North America, and Oceania. This phenomenon could reflect closer trade relations due in part to greater Chinese demand in recent years for Latin America's agricultural and mineral goods. Africa has received less Chinese FDI in both absolute and relative terms compared to the other regions. But compared to the geographic distribution of US FDI, this region has received more attention from Chinese investors. Europe has been by far the favorite destination of US FDI, followed by Latin America and the Asia Pacific, and then Canada.

Figure 3.2 introduces additional information on foreign trade that contributes further to clarifying China and the United States' global economic presence and orientation. Not surprisingly, Asia has been the top regional destination for China's export of goods, followed by North America and Europe. Significantly, China has now established strong trade relations with all regions of the world. Comparing the export profiles of China and the United States, the most remarkable difference between them has been the relatively greater role assumed by Africa in the Chinese case. In 2017, as a proportion of their total exports, China sold about 4.3 times more to Sub-Saharan Africa than did the United States

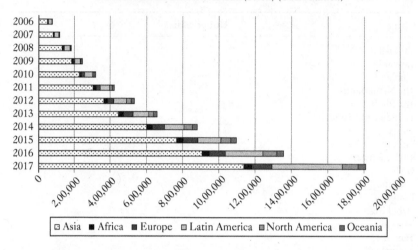

China Direct Investment Abroad (Stock) (USD: million)

□ Asia ■ Africa ■ Europe □ Latin America ■ North America ■ Oceania

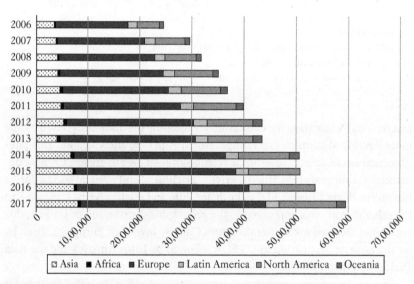

US Direct Investment Abroad Position on a historical basis (USD: million)

□ Asia ■ Africa ■ Europe □ Latin America ■ North America ■ Oceania

Figure 3.1 Comparing China's and the United States' foreign direct investment (FDI).

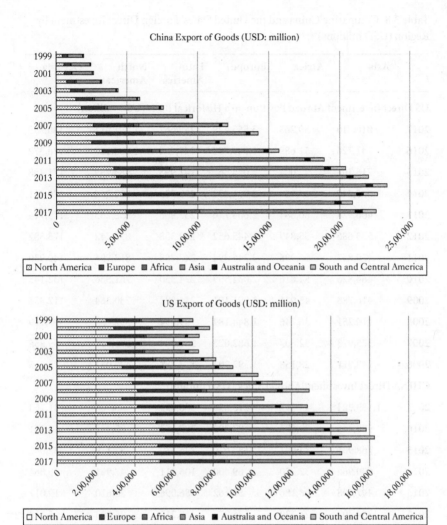

Figure 3.2 Comparing China's and the United States' export of goods (1999–2017).

Table 3.8 Comparing China and the United States' Foreign Direct Investment by Region (USD millions)

	Asia	Africa	Europe	Latin America	North America	Oceania
US Direct Investment Abroad Position on a Historical Basis (USD million)						
2017	816,710	50,285	3,553,429	255,667	1,091,911	180,793
2016	741,726	51,689	3,309,782	247,404	1,008,160	178,378
2015	716,208	52,004	3,075,567	241,993	983,799	171,488
2014	675,240	69,029	2,901,039	250,323	972,366	186,431
2013	406,974	60,884	2,604,776	237,966	858,263	175,714
2012	533,686	55,849	2,445,652	262,338	877,242	173,582
2011	479,857	56,996	2,246,394	247,788	813,996	140,930
2010	464,826	54,816	2,034,559	234,350	761,366	132,145
2009	416,788	43,941	1,991,191	216,892	730,364	112,353
2008	410,251	36,746	1,844,182	199,894	592,288	97,119
2007	375,973	32,607	1,682,023	207,204	571,027	89,858
2006	348,911	28,158	1,397,704	172,288	429,051	73,565
CHINA Direct Investment Abroad Stock (USD million)						
2017	1,139,324	43,297	110,855	386,892	86,906	41,763
2016	909,445	39,877	87,202	207,153	75,472	38,241
2015	768,901	34,694	83,679	126,319	52,179	32,092
2014	600,966	32,350	69,400	106,111	47,951	25,864
2013	447,408	26,186	53,162	86,096	28,610	19,017
2012	364,407	21,730	36,975	68,212	25,503	15,114
2011	303,435	16,244	24,450	55,172	13,472	12,007
2010	228,146	13,042	15,710	43,876	7,829	8,607
2009	185,547	9,332	8,677	30,595	5,185	6,419
2008	131,317	7,804	5,134	32,240	3,660	3,816
2007	79,218	4,462	4,459	24,701	3,241	1,830
2006	47,978	2,557	2,270	19,694	1,587	939

Sources:

https://www.ceicdata.com/en/united-states/direct-investment-abroad-by-country;

https://www.bea.gov/international/di1usdbal;

https://www.ceicdata.com/zh-hans/china/outward-direct-investment-by-country;

http://hzs.mofcom.gov.cn/article/date/201512/20151201223578.shtml;
中国对外直接投资统计公报.

(US$94.7 billion for China, compared to US$22.0 billion for the United States; see Table 3.9). These figures reinforce the picture conveyed by the data on foreign visits made by these countries' top leaders and the destination of their respective FDI. In addition to China's looming diplomatic and economic presence in its immediate neighborhood in Asia, Sub-Saharan Africa appears to be a region where Beijing has also begun to establish a substantial intermediary or broker role in its foreign relations.

Several conclusions leap from the tables and figures we have presented. The patterns shown by them reinforce our earlier remarks. Clearly, China has become more integrated in the global community—both politically and economically. We can reach this conclusion even if we only examine evidence from the more recent years since the start of the twenty-first century (as opposed to comparing these recent data with China's situation in 1949 when the People's Republic was founded). Moreover, our data suggest that China is no less embedded in the global community than the United States. Indeed, relatively speaking and in some respects such as in foreign commerce and investment, China's economy has opened to the rest of the world more than has the United States, and it has engaged the rest of the world more extensively than has the United States. It would be interesting to see whether recent trade tensions between the United States and China would affect supply and production chains and cross-border investments in ways that alter or reinforce the patterns just reported. As already mentioned, we have collected information on international treaties that the United States and China have joined, as well as those from which the United States has withdrawn and those pending ratification in Washington and Beijing. This additional information again supports the conclusion that while China has become more engaged in multilateral diplomacy and international institutions, the United States has moved in the opposite direction. Judging from this information, we cannot conclude that Beijing is more outside the international order or is a more revisionist state than Washington.

Finally, there are obvious and clear differences in these two countries' allocation of attention to different parts of the world. For instance, whereas China's foreign direct investment has gone mainly to Asia, this investment from the United States has largely favored Europe. In terms of these countries' exports, their respective neighborhood (Asia and North America) has been again their largest market. Compared to the United States, Sub-Saharan Africa has received more of China's political and economic attention. The broad conclusions reached by our ensemble of different kinds of data are important and pertinent because they indicate that China has established extensive links to global institutions, and it has become deeply integrated into the international community both politically and economically. It has also established a pivotal broker relationship with two clusters of countries located in its immediate (Asian) neighborhood and in

Table 3.9 Comparing China and the United States' Export of Goods by Region (USD millions)

	Total		North America		Europe		Africa		Asia		Australia and Oceania		South and Central America	
	US	China	US	China	US	China	US	China	US	China	US	China	US	China
2017	1,546,463	2,263,354	525,980	497,146	332,758	428,975	22,065	94,718	485,791	1,096,340	29,501	51,264	150,367	94,911
2016	1,451,454	2,097,631	496,963	445,208	317,710	389,917	22,274	92,272	452,093	1,041,117	26,498	47,549	135,915	81,569
2015	1,503,320	2,273,468	517,315	472,793	319,590	403,241	27,123	108,541	457,391	1,140,100	29,322	50,489	152,579	98,305
2014	1,621,861	2,342,293	553,824	458,512	333,464	438,825	38,090	106,035	480,977	1,188,381	31,661	46,572	183,845	103,968
2013	1,578,318	2,209,004	526,709	426,781	326,497	405,744	35,280	92,799	475,378	1,134,070	30,038	44,615	184,415	104,995
2012	1,545,630	2,048,714	508,526	407,626	329,183	396,399	32,726	85,311	456,566	1,006,812	35,445	44,868	183,184	107,700
2011	1,482,275	1,898,381	479,580	374,051	329,471	413,571	32,883	73,083	439,241	899,038	32,088	40,894	169,012	97,743
2010	1,278,110	1,577,754	412,921	323,715	285,592	355,188	28,340	59,954	387,361	731,955	25,320	33,017	138,577	73,925
2009	1,055,802	1,201,612	333,550	250,850	258,062	264,651	24,329	47,735	307,897	568,651	22,415	24,927	109,549	44,798
2008	1,287,224	1,430,693	412,370	288,139	324,997	343,422	28,393	51,240	359,151	664,119	25,367	25,878	136,946	57,896
2007	1,147,753	1,217,776	384,806	263,821	283,069	287,849	23,426	37,298	327,286	567,874	22,386	21,101	106,780	39,833
2006	1,025,840	968,936	364,378	227,937	242,994	215,370	18,583	26,688	290,765	455,727	20,741	16,009	88,380	27,204
2005	900,859	761,953	332,146	180,206	209,928	165,628	15,310	18,682	252,498	366,408	18,653	12,887	72,324	18,143
2004	814,647	593,326	300,611	138,203	191,790	122,386	13,202	13,813	231,292	295,487	16,372	10,171	61,380	13,265
2003	724,582	438,228	267,336	101,398	173,063	88,168	10,613	10,182	206,392	222,580	15,233	7,290	51,946	8,610

2002	692,911	325,589	258,393	77,133	163,626	58,278	10,663	6,961	193,494	171,303	15,184	5,289	51,551	6,625
2001	728,833	266,155	264,721	59,431	181,529	49,239	12,119	6,007	198,930	140,957	13,379	4,074	58,156	6,446
2000	781,607	249,201	290,290	56,609	187,448	45,482	10,966	5,042	218,795	132,308	14,825	3,910	59,283	5,850
1999	695,420	194,931	253,509	45,181	171,834	35,482	9,880	4,115	190,881	102,563	14,163	3,113	55,153	4,478

Sources:
http://data.stats.gov.cn/easyquery.htm?cn=C01;
https://www.census.gov/foreign-trade/balance/index.html.

Sub-Saharan Africa. Other analysts studying trade patterns and congruity in UN voting patterns have reached similar conclusions (e.g., Pang 2014).

Conclusion

Discourse on power transition typically attributes states' revisionist or status-quo motivations by definitional fiat or categorical assertion. It assumes that the meaning of *the* international order is commonly understood and uncontroversial, rather than treating it as an ongoing process of constant contestation and renegotiation. It also overlooks the fact that states can be norm entrepreneurs seeking to introduce some new ideas and principles—such as crimes against peace and humanity, humanitarian intervention, regime change, and preventive war—while seeking concurrently to protect and sustain some other old ideas and principles.

We have applied in this chapter the English school's perspective on international society, emphasizing that international order is not the same thing as the existing distribution of interstate power. We have also introduced a norm-based understanding of international order, as well as a rule- or institution-based understanding of this order. In discussing both perspectives, we show that Chinese foreign policy has undergone a sea change over time, so that compared to this policy during the earlier decades of the People's Republic, it can hardly be described as revisionist today. Beijing has professed to support the dominant international norms, especially the principle of state sovereignty and noninterference in others' domestic affairs. It has abandoned its earlier support for insurgency movements and has joined rather than shunned the world's international organizations. It has also become an active participant in multilateral efforts to keep peace and discourage nuclear proliferation. Its leaders' foreign travels support this view of an increasingly active Chinese foreign policy, one that has a global orientation, albeit also a regional emphasis. It has, moreover, signed and ratified most recent international accords. Its positions on various resolutions voted on by the UN General Assembly and Security Council have been generally aligned with those of the other member states. In sharp contrast to its earlier days of political and economic isolation and its rejection of international organizations and institutions, it has now become an active and contributing member of the global community. Its diplomacy has now established a global presence, and its foreign trade and investment have enmeshed it deeply in the global economy. This global reach is important for our discussion of a revisionist state's possible strategies. Goddard (2018a) hypothesizes that another factor influencing this state's choice of strategy is whether it has developed a "broker" position with respect to some cluster of other states. In combination, these two factors are likely in her view to incline a revisionist state to seek peaceful, rule-based change of international order.

In contrast, recent US policies—especially under the administrations of George W. Bush and Donald Trump—have moved in the opposite direction. Although Washington was mainly responsible for the creation of the post-1945 liberal international economic order and multilateral institutions, it has now professed a palpable sense of discontent with, even disdain for them. It has withdrawn from some important international organizations and treaties, and it has decided not to join others in the first place. It has also propagated doctrines such as regime change and preventive war that are clearly contrary to established international norms and rules. Moreover, as shown by its voting records in the United Nations, the United States has increasingly found itself outside of emerging international consensus on various issues. Indeed, in many ways, Washington has been undermining the very institutions and norms that it has tried to foster and promote in earlier years.

A state's actions can disclose its revisionist intentions. But its words also matter. Recent ideational challenges to the liberal international order have emanated more from Washington than from Beijing. Donald Trump's "America First" rhetoric with respect to the global political economy offers a sharp contrast to Xi Jinping's speech given at the 2017 Davos World Economic Forum defending and supporting globalization. Trump's statements in early June 2020, calling for the use of "overwhelming force," even threatening to dispatch military forces, to "dominate" demonstrators (whom he called "terrorists") protesting police brutality undercut the moral authority of the United States condemning Beijing for curtailing the rights of people in Hong Kong to engage in similar activities (https://www.cnn.com/2020/06/01/politics/wh-governors-call-protests/index. html). His harsh words about women, immigrants, foreigners, racial minorities, and the "liberal" media point to blatant efforts to secure his domestic political base. Drezner (2019: 529) reminds us that Susan Strange (1987) has argued some time ago that "American domestic politics was far the likelier cause of global volatility than waning US hegemony." More recently, Nye (2019: 80) has echoed this concern, remarking that "America's place in the world may be threatened more by the rise of populist politics at home than the rise of other powers abroad." Musgrave (2019) concurs that domestic political partisanship, not external challenges, poses a greater threat to the US-centered international order.

As we have acknowledged, reasonable people can disagree with the meaning we have given to specific pieces of data introduced in this chapter. They can also point to specific flaws in the data we have presented. However, the collective import of the entire ensemble of evidence seems to us quite incontrovertible. Moreover, the changes over time in the direction of Chinese and US policies are also unmistakable to us. The main conclusion to be drawn from this evidence is that while

China has become less revisionist over time, the United States has become more so. Thus, a rising state does not necessarily have to become more inclined to challenge the existing international order as it gains more power. Conversely, a dominant state is not inevitably committed to this order whether it is gaining or losing relative power. In other words, revisionism and status-quo commitment are not inherent in states' relative power positions. These remarks naturally raise important questions about the validity of prevailing theories, especially power-transition theory, that have been offered to explain international peace and conflict.

We feel relatively confident in offering the preceding observations, although it is of course possible that future US presidents may reverse the recent policies of the Trump administration. This said, the Trump administration's policy orientation was not entirely new. The increasing discrepancy between US preferences and those of other countries, as shown by their voting positions in the United Nations, could be discerned from at least the Clinton administration. The advocacy of regime change and endorsement of preventive war had also occurred during the administration of George W. Bush. In other words, the process of increasing US disassociation from the rest of the world started some time ago, and it only accelerated during the Trump era.

Still, we return to an important point introduced earlier. Hegemonic rule is not based just on the dominant power's coercive capabilities, but it also rather requires and is sustained by widespread consent, a sense of legitimacy, and social recognition by the subordinate states (Cox 1987; Clark 2005, 2009; Lake 2009). China's values, institutions, and model of governance do not resonate with the elites and mass publics of other countries. They cannot compete effectively with those of the United States, an advantage that has generally been described as America's "soft power" (Nye 2004). The United States is more popular than China in the rest of the world, and not just in countries such as Japan, Germany, and Britain that are traditional US allies. This more positive image of the United States is held by people in neutral and developing countries, including some in China's traditional political and cultural orbits. India, Kenya, Nigeria, the Philippines, and Vietnam are some examples. China's inability to reach out and appeal to people outside its effective jurisdiction is most vividly demonstrated by its continued problems with efforts to reunify with Taiwan and, of course, to reassure the people of Hong Kong who have participated in massive protests in the recent past. This inability suggests even dimmer prospects that Beijing will be able to displace the current international order dominated by the United States, even though the policies of the Trump administration have caused alienation and alarm abroad. Before Beijing can install its own vision to become a new international order, it must be able to delegitimize the current order, but this will be very difficult for it to accomplish because, as Allan et al. (2018) show, the values, identities, and institutions promoted by the United States, such as liberal democracy and market economy, continue to be very attractive to and popular in the rest of the world (which is not to say that there are no dissident voices questioning especially the institutions of capitalism).

Foreigners' negative views of China reached new heights during the Covid-19 pandemic, with many people expressing the belief that Beijing had mismanaged this disease. In 2020, those who held negative views of China outnumbered those with positive views generally by a margin of three to one in the fourteen countries surveyed by the Pew Research Center (Silver et al. 2020). In some countries, this margin was larger. For example, in Japan only 9% of the respondents had favorable views of China compared to 86% with unfavorable views, and the corresponding figures were 15% and 81% for Australians and 14% and 85% for Swedes. In eight of the fourteen countries surveyed, the increase in those expressing negative views of China jumped more than ten percentage points in just one year. This change was especially dramatic in Australia where people having negative views of China increased from 57% to 81%. This increase was also rather significant in Britain, Sweden, Germany, and the Netherlands. There was a similar increase in the number of respondents expressing no confidence in the leadership of Chinese President Xi Jinping, with the United States and Canada leading the pack with a rise of 27 and 24 percentage points in just one year from 2019 to 2020. Significantly, there was a large majority (70% or more of the respondents) indicating no confidence in Xi in all the fourteen countries surveyed.

Table 3.10 combines this survey with another one conducted also by the Pew Research Center, one that focused on the United States (Wike et al. 2020). This latter survey covered thirteen countries, all except Sweden are traditional US allies (other countries typically included in Pew surveys, such as India, Kenya, and the Philippines, were not included this time because of logistical issues created by the pandemic; these countries usually give the United States high marks). This survey focusing on the United States organized its data report differently from the one focusing on China, even though they covered a similar topic. Thus, whereas changes between 2019 and 2020 reported for China (the top part of Table 3.10) refer to *unfavorable* views of this country and *non-confidence* in Xi Jinping, the changes reported for the United States (the bottom part of the table) refer to *favorable* views of this country and *confidence* in Donald Trump.

Table 3.10 shows that confidence in Trump, even in countries traditionally allied with the United States, was low (16%, median for thirteen countries), compared to Russia's Vladimir Putin at 23% and China's Xi Jinping at 19% (Wike et al. 2020). In several European countries, Trump received even higher levels of no confidence than Xi. The publics in all thirteen countries gave the United States the lowest ranking on its handling of the coronavirus among the countries surveyed. Only 15% (the median for all thirteen countries) thought that its handling of the coronavirus was "very/somewhat good," compared to 57% for the European Union and 37% for China. As shown in Table 3.10, these publics also had rather low levels of favorable views of the United States, and these positive views of the

United States were exceeded by large margins by unfavorable views. The disparities between those who had confidence in Trump and their counterparts expressing no confidence in him were even more significant. For both survey questions, foreigners' opinions of the United States and its president have experienced substantial decline in just a short time between 2019 and 2020.

This said, the percentages of people having favorable views of the United States were consistently higher than the corresponding figures for China among the countries covered by the two Pew surveys, in some cases by a substantial margin. This result supports our suggestion that China has an image problem abroad, and its values and identity do not resonate with the people of many other countries. At the same time, one may ask whether the United States should have

Table 3.10 Foreigners' Perceptions of China and the United States, 2020

	Views on China				Views on Xi	
	Favorable (percent)	Unfavorable (percent)	2019–2020 Change in Unfavorable	No Confidence in 2019	No Confidence 2020	2019–2020 Change in No Confidence
Canada	23	73	+6	60	74	+14
United States	22	73	+13	50	77	+27
Italy	38	62	+5	54	75	+21
United Kingdom	22	74	+19	60	76	+16
Spain	36	63	+10	66	75	+9
Denmark	—	—	—	—	82	—
Sweden	14	85	+15	67	82	+15
France	26	70	+8	69	80	+11
Netherlands	25	73	+15	53	70	+17
Germany	25	71	+15	61	78	+17
Belgium	—	—	—	—	73	—
South Korea	24	75	+12	74	83	+9
Japan	9	86	+1	81	84	+3
Australia	15	81	+24	54	79	+25
14–Country Median	24	73				

Source: Silver et al. 2020.

Table 3.10 *Continued*

	Views on the United States			Views on Trump		
	Favorable (percent)	Unfavorable (percent)	2019–2020 Change in Favorable	Confidence	No Confidence	2019–2020 Change in Confidence
Canada	35	62	−16	20	80	−8
Italy	45	55	−17	16	84	−16
United Kingdom	41	56	−16	19	81	−13
Spain	40	58	−12	16	83	−5
Denmark	34	65	—	10	90	—
Sweden	33	65	−12	15	85	−3
France	33	67	−17	11	88	−9
Netherlands	30	69	−16	18	82	−7
Germany	26	70	−13	10	89	−3
Belgium	24	75	—	9	90	—
Median	33	65		15	85	
South Korea	59	39	−18	17	82	−29
Japan	41	54	−27	25	68	−11
Australia	33	64	−17	23	76	−12
13-Country Median	34	64		16	83	

Source: Wike et al. 2020.

received higher positive ratings because they were given by respondents in allied countries (except Sweden).

Foreigners (even Americans) may show considerable ambivalence, skepticism, and doubts about the United States, such as due to its ineffective containment of the Covid-19 pandemic, its mistreatment of racial minorities (as shown by the Black Lives Matter movement), and its mismanagement of the economy (such as the Great Recession of 2008). This phenomenon, however, does not suggest that China will be by default able to step into a void to replace the United States and to rewrite the rules of the current international order. The former does not necessarily entail the latter. Perceptions of ineffectiveness and illegitimacy can of course erode foreigners' consent to and support for Washington's hegemonic order. This process can take a long time before its effects destabilize this order (if then, because other countries can still support this order even if US legitimacy or power declines). It may resemble the description of punctuated equilibrium offered by paleontologists who study biological evolution, whereby protracted periods of small, incremental, and barely visible changes are followed by large and abrupt transformations (e.g., Baumgartner and Jones 1993; Cioffi-Revilla 1998; Hu 2012).

4

Revisionist States' Strategies and Encounters with Their Counterparts

As mentioned in previous chapters, revisionism is not an inherent attribute of rising powers. Any state, including a ruling state or a hegemon, can turn to revisionism if it is not satisfied with arrangements in the international order. In this discussion, we highlight the significance of the normative and institutional features of international order which, in addition to the distribution of power in the international system, can affect the stability of international relations. We argue that the rise and fall of great powers is a natural outcome resulting from the different rates of economic growth among states. Thus, when a state manages to enhance its economic and military capabilities relative to others, this development can alter the power distribution in the international system. This state's mere quest for power, however, cannot be counted as revisionist behavior because it is normal and natural for all states to jockey for more wealth and security in a competitive international system.

The question, then, is how revisionist behavior should look if states' competitive pursuit of power does not count as such. We argue that revisionist behavior reflects an intention to challenge two key components of international order: institutional arrangements and normative foundations. Institutional arrangements are broadly defined from territorial demarcations among states to key configurations of intergovernmental organizations, treaties, and regimes. Normative foundations, on the other hand, refer to the fundamental ideas and norms defining the nature of, as well as the interactions among, states. The distinction between institutional arrangements and normative foundations is similar to that between secondary institutions and primary institutions in the English school of international relations theory, according to which primary institutions are close to normative foundations, and secondary institutions refer to institutional arrangements (Buzan 2004b, 2018). Later we will discuss in more detail the difference between primary institutions and secondary institutions in shaping a state's revisionist strategies.

There are basically two types of revisionist behavior. One is what we term "hard revisionist" behavior, which refers to using military means to challenge the existing institutional order, including both its primary institutions and secondary institutions. If a state only increases its power but does not challenge the existing norms and intergovernmental arrangements, it is not a revisionist state. However, if it seeks to change the prevailing institutional order after increasing its power by, for example, changing the existing territorial boundaries with its neighbors or challenging the sovereignty norm among states, then it has a revisionist agenda. In other words, the mere occurrence of power shifts in international relations does not necessarily lead to revisionism. A state's use of its power to change the primary or secondary institutions of international order indicates that it is revisionist. We should, however, recognize that there are different degrees and forms of revisionism, meaning that we should eschew treating this concept as a binary category as emphasized earlier. Using military power to revise the existing international order, whether its institutions, norms, or both, points to "hard" revisionist behavior (the focus of Chapters 1 and 2). It is important to distinguish this "hard" form of revisionism from the "soft" form seeking institutional change and the various strategies available for seeking such institutional change (the focus of this chapter).

Power, especially military capability, is by no means the only way to challenge the existing institutional order. Buzan (2018: 461), for example, acknowledges that there can be "reformist revisionists" who seek peaceful institutional change rather than violent overthrow of an existing international order. Drawing from He et al. (forthcoming), we argue that states can use non-military means to pursue "soft" revisionist strategies, including "institutional reform," "institutional obstruction," "institutional exit," and "institutional competition." We hypothesize that a state will consider two factors in selecting its soft revisionist strategy: its perceived benefits (relative to its costs) from the existing institution, and its comparative advantage in the institution-related issue area. The interplay of these two factors will shape its policy choice. Other states will have to decide how to cope with the demands from a revisionist state adopting soft strategies. They can choose either to accommodate or to reject demands from this revisionist state, and if to reject, by either peaceful or violent means. The outcome of these states' interactions naturally depends on not only the revisionist state's demands and actions, but also how others choose to respond to it.

There are four sections in this chapter. First, we discuss two hard revisionist strategies, military conquest and military subversion, which states can use to overthrow the existing international order. We argue that nuclear deterrence, especially mutual assured destruction (MAD), will make hard revisionist strategies costlier and riskier for states to pursue. Moreover, economic interdependence in the age of globalization and the advent of nationalism should further diminish the attractiveness of resorting to military conquest. Parenthetically, possession of nuclear weapons should also make accommodation and retrenchment easier for a declining great power because it should reassure this country's leaders about its continued survival (because any attempt by another country seeking to conquer it militarily will have to face the threat of nuclear retaliation). Second, we introduce an "institutional revisionism model" to show how the interplay between the perceived benefits from institutions and comparative advantage in the institution-related issue area shapes a state's policy choice among the four soft revisionist strategies mentioned earlier. Third, we undertake brief case studies to illustrate the theoretical utility of our model of institutional revisionism. Last, we argue that the bargaining and negotiation processes between revisionist states and their counterparts shape how possible future transition of international order may unfold peacefully by consent.

Hard Revisionist Strategies—Military All the Way Down

The rise and fall of great powers in history are sometimes accompanied by military conflicts or systemic wars. According to Kennedy (1987), the decline of a great power normally starts from its strategic overstretching. During the process of its decline, this state's economic power becomes increasingly insufficient and incapable of sustaining its overseas commitments and imperial ambitions. If a systemic or power-transition war occurs, it can alter the identity of the dominant power and can change the nature of international order (conventional history in the West argues that the power transition between Britain and the United States was peaceful and did not rewrite the rules of international order). Gilpin (1981: 15) reflects this view when he suggests, "the principal mechanism of change throughout history has been war, or what we shall call hegemonic war (i.e., a war that determines which state or states will be dominant and will govern the system)." Although it is debatable which party, a rising state or a ruling state, has been usually responsible for initiating past wars and conflicts, conventional history prevailing in the West tells us about many episodes where military force was allegedly applied to challenge or defend international order (Copeland 2000; Organski 1958; Organski and Kugler 1981; Taliaferro 2004). This is an irony because in the one case of undisputed post-1815 power transition between the world's top two countries, namely, Britain and the United States, the same historical accounts argue that the international order has endured without war (supposedly because the United States was a "status-quo" power). Parenthetically, although there were wars and rivalries before the Napoleonic Wars (such as the Anglo-Dutch dyad and the Habsburg-France dyad), it is not clear to us how the outcomes of these conflicts had altered (or would have altered) the nature of the international system. In contrast, we can more easily imagine how a victory by republican France would have changed Europe's then system of monarchical rule.

There are two kinds of hard revisionist strategies: military conquest and military subversion. The aim of a revisionist state is to change the existing institutional order, including both its normative foundations and intergovern-mental arrangements. Since states are self-regarding actors, they face constant threats from other states in a competitive international system (albeit not one that is entirely anarchical, as suggested by the very notion of international order and the idea of an international society governed by some basic understanding and sharing of rules and norms among these same self-regarding states, as these rules and norms can serve their common interests) in which no overarching au-thority can guarantee their security (of course, power-transition theory, among others, sees the world as hierarchical and ruled by an order imposed by the most powerful country). Power, in both military and economic forms, becomes the only reliable way to ensure a state's survival, according to realists' perception of states having to operate in a Hobbesian world (Mearsheimer 2001; Morgenthau 1948). Military conquest used to be understood as a normal strategy for a state to apply in its effort to maximize its economic wealth, as well as its coercive ca-pability in the international system. Consequently, military means was taken to be the most direct way for a state to change the existing international order, espe-cially its institutional arrangements reflecting their base in either norms or rules.

The two world wars in the twentieth century have shown the tragic consequences when states relied on military means to resolve their revisionist dissatisfactions and resentments. States pursuing this military means of seeking physical conquest and aggrandizement have been described as "strategic states" that share a vision of power in terms of territorial expansion, military alliances, and political patronage. Rosecrance (1986) has been the most prominent scholar arguing that this vision of power has become increasingly obsolescent in the con-temporary world, and that states seeking to promote their commercial competi-tiveness (e.g., Japan, Germany) have been more successful than their "strategic" counterparts (e.g., the United States, the Soviet Union) in the recent past.

Another hard revisionist strategy is military subversion, as distinct from overt military invasion or conquest by one country targeting another one. However, a state can militarily sponsor and support an opposition party or armed groups in a foreign country so that the target government can be overthrown by force. During the Cold War, this strategy of military subversion was employed by both camps to maximize their ideological and military influence in the Third World. For example, Mao's support for communist revolutions in the Southeast Asian countries represented a policy of military subversion. Although a state may not be directly involved in military conflict with another country, its behavior is still revisionist because it seeks to change another country's existing govern-ance structure, violating both the non-intervention principle and the sover-eignty norm that have provided the foundation of international order since the Treaty of Westphalia in 1648. This behavior also reflected an ideological antag-onism between communism and capitalism during the Cold War, when the two competing camps waged a contest to change the political nature and governing norm of the other side. During those years, the United States had supported or had been implicated in military coups or subversions to overthrow regimes perceived to be unfriendly to its interests, such as in Iran (Mohammad Mossadegh), Chile (Salvador Allende), Guatemala (Jacobo Arbenz), and, unsuccessfully, Cuba (Fidel Castro).

The Western countries' democratic crusade by covert and overt action (such as their policy of regime change aimed at Iraq, Libya, Syria, and Venezuela) in the post–Cold War era can also be seen as revisionist behavior, because it violated the sovereign rights of the target state and challenged the prevailing international norm of non-intervention in other countries' internal affairs (Finnemore 2003). The non-intervention norm is by no means static and unchangeable, as we can see from the emergence of the idea of responsibility to protect (R2P) in the United Nations (Bellamy 2009). However, if a state uses military means to subvert a foreign government, this kind of intervention, rooted in ideological differences and not based on a consensus of the international community, represents revisionist behavior following a hard strategy.

It is worth noting that both military conquest and military subversion have lost much of their appeal and popularity in contemporary world politics for three reasons. First, military conquest does not always pay economically and politically due to the potential target countries' resistance, reflecting especially the advent of nationalism (Liberman 1993, 1996). Compared to previous eras of Western domination, state and non-state local actors that used to be relatively easy targets of foreign predation have now acquired resources and capabilities that enable them to put up more effective resistance (Gause 2019). While the costs of military conquest have thus gone up, globalization has concomitantly and significantly decreased its economic rewards (Brooks 1999). Second, widely shared international norms, such as Westphalian sovereignty, non-intervention, and territorial integrity, have recognized the right of survival for even the small and weak states that are most vulnerable to foreign predation, and this recognition has protected them to some extent against the unbridled exercise of brute force by the strong states (Gause 2019; Zacher 2001). The strong states may possess the necessary power to engage in aggression and aggrandizement, but their use of power may be restrained by public opinion both abroad and at home.

That territorial conquest has become unpopular in today's world politics is shown by the reaction to Russia's annexation of Crimea. This action was considered a violation of international norms, especially the international legal order (Allison 2017). Similarly, overt use of force, such as by the United States in a "preventive war" against Iraq, has been widely viewed to represent a violation of the existing international consensus on the use of force in the name of self-defense, and it has consequently been politically (not to mention militarily and economically as well) costly to Washington.

Last, but not least, nuclear deterrence among those great powers that have these weapons and their close allies and associates, especially confidence in the effectiveness of nuclear deterrence based on the doctrine of MAD between the United States and the Soviet Union during the Cold War, has led many people to argue that old-fashioned hegemonic war has now become obsolete and unthinkable (Morgan 2003).

All of this does not mean that states have foregone the military option to challenge international order, especially in their relations with those that are weaker and more vulnerable. Although military means, whether involving invasion or subversion, have relatively high risks, the benefits of this hard revisionist strategy may sometimes also appear substantial. However, as we have noted earlier, no single country, no matter how powerful, can unilaterally impose international rules and norms on other countries without their voluntary support and compliance, even though this support and compliance may be partial, reluctant, and always contingent. The post-1945 international order, including the designation of UN Security Council's permanent members, has been mainly decided and underwritten by the winning side of World War II, although significantly, some "winners" (Britain and France) had become exhausted by the war and their international status suffered greatly relative to other "winners" (the United States and the Soviet Union) whose continued rise after the war was further assisted by their allies' exhaustion. Nevertheless, nuclear deterrence, as well as technological advances in developing other weapons of mass destruction, has changed the likely way in which future order transition will be introduced and instituted. Contemporary states need to consider how to address their dissatisfactions and resentments regarding some specific components of the international order without having to wage a systemic war, one that may very well destroy their rivals as well as themselves at the same time. Indeed, recent research on contemporary Chinese foreign policy shows that Beijing can pursue a variety of strategies contingent on specific issues and circumstances. For example, Wuthnow et al. (2012) show that Beijing's behavior toward different international institutions can vary in "watching, engaging, circumventing, and shaping" them. It would therefore be wrong to be obsessively focused on military means to alter international order while overlooking the much more common phenomenon of non-military means to achieve the same end in today's world. A country's conduct can be much more nuanced and multifaceted than is sometimes depicted (that they have only one gear and no "reverse" in the repertoire "driving" their foreign policy).

Institutional Benefit, Comparative Advantage, and Soft Revisionist Strategies

If a systemic war fought among the world's great powers is unlikely and even unthinkable in the era of nuclear weapons and globalization, how can a revisionist state challenge the international order in a peaceful way? As mentioned earlier, institutional order entails both primary institutions and secondary institutions. As Buzan (2004b) suggests, the primary institutions are the "durable and recognized patterns of shared practices rooted in values held commonly by the members of interstate societies, and embodying a mix of norms, rules, and principles." Buzan (2004b: 182) further distinguishes "master primary institutions" from "derivative primary institutions," such that the latter are nested within the former. For example, sovereignty is a primary institution, while nonintervention is a derivative primary institution stemming from and being nested in the idea of sovereignty. In a similar vein, diplomacy is a primary institution, while multilateralism is a derivative primary institution rooted in diplomacy (Buzan 2014: 184).

Besides primary institutions, there are secondary institutions which include intergovernmental organizations, treaties, and regimes related to both master primary institutions and derivative primary institutions. For instance, the United Nations and the International Court of Justice (ICJ) are secondary institutions related to sovereignty (a master primary institution) and non-intervention (a derivative primary institution) because both the United Nations and the ICJ are established to ensure and protect the primary institutions. In other words, these secondary institutions are created on the basis of the primary institutions.

The distinction between primary and secondary institutions is only one of several available classifications. Other scholars have introduced different typologies of institutions, such as Mayall's (2000) distinction between institutions and principles, Reus-Smit's (1997) discussion of constitutional structures and fundamental institutions, and Ruggie's (1998) remarks on regulative and constitutive rules. In this discussion, we use Buzan's typology of primary versus secondary institutions for two reasons. First, this typology highlights the difference in the durability of primary institutions compared to secondary institutions, calling attention to the former's stronger resilience (or their greater resistance to change) relative to the latter. Second, a revisionist state will have greater difficulty mounting a challenge to the primary institutions in the short run, especially if certain strategies, such as outright overt application of military coercion, are infeasible or highly costly.

As Buzan (2004b: 181) points out, "[primary institutions] will typically undergo a historical pattern of rise, evolution and decline that is long by the standards of a human lifetime." This remark implies that even when a preponderant power resorts to its enormous physical force, it will have great difficulty in attempting to revise or fundamentally change the primary institutions. Instead, it will take a long time for the primary institutions to be changed or revised. This change—as we have emphasized before—requires the co-optation and cooperation of subordinate states and cannot be simply imposed by the dominant state. Therefore, how primary institutions will be changed or revised is beyond any single state's capability, especially in view of the various costs of and obstacles to the use of military coercion discussed earlier. Therefore, we consider unlikely any attempt by a revisionist state seeking to alter fundamentally the existing international order by resorting unilaterally to massive, overt military conquest and coercion. Given China's geostrategic situation (in contrast to the United States, it lives in a congested neighborhood with several other great powers and significant secondary states located nearby) and the formidable counter-coalition that can be mobilized against it if Beijing were to resort to this attempt, this prospect is still more unlikely. This said, our main focus in this chapter, as it should have become evident by now, is to examine a revisionist state's strategy to change and alter the secondary institutions of international order, that is, the intergovernmental organizations, treaties, and regimes embedded within the primary institutions. This focus acknowledges Drezner's (2019) argument that an optimal revisionist strategy would be to first challenge the existing hegemonic economic order and the ideational foundation of this order before attacking its various material dimensions. We argue instead that revisionist behavior in today's world is most likely to involve attempts to influence the secondary institutions.

Significantly, even though they tend to be durable and persistent, the primary institutions of international order are not permanent or fixed. They are susceptible to gradual change, starting from the secondary institutions related to them. As mentioned before, the United Nations is the main secondary institution created to protect and ensure the primary institutions of sovereignty and territorial integrity in the postwar era. If only a few states violate the UN charter by engaging in military aggression against other countries, the primary institutions of sovereignty and territorial integrity can still endure, so long as an overwhelming majority of this organization's other members continue to observe and uphold its charter. However, if many states invade others without suffering any consequences, the United Nations as an institution will collapse. If such a situation should develop, we would conclude that the primary institutions of sovereignty and territoriality no longer constitute the core foundation of international order. In other words, primary institutions are challenged and undermined by assaults on the secondary institutions. Although our research focuses on a state's strategies seeking to revise the secondary institutions, it illuminates such paths of challenging and undermining the primary institutions in world politics.

Four Strategies to Deal with Secondary Institutions

Many scholars have examined how a revisionist state can challenge the existing international order, and particularly an incumbent hegemon, through non-military means. Some, for example, introduce the idea of soft balancing, arguing that secondary states can use non-military means to undermine the dominant power's legitimacy or hinder its effectiveness in a unipolar world (Brooks and Wohlforth 2005; He and Feng 2008; Lieber and Alexander 2005; Pape 2005; Paul 2005, 2018). Although soft balancing seems to be an ad hoc strategy used by secondary states to impede or constrain a hegemon's unilateralist tendency, scholars have gradually enriched our understanding of this kind of statecraft so that it is no longer a unique phenomenon to be expected only in circumstances described to be unipolar (e.g., He and Feng 2008; Friedman and Long 2015; Pempel 2016; Saltzman 2012). Paul (2018) has shown soft balancing to be a ubiquitous phenomenon that can be observed in a variety of circumstances ranging from the times of ancient empires to the modern era of globalization. One potential problem with the concept of soft balancing, however, lies in its ambiguity pertaining to what it does not cover (see, however, Tessman and Wolf 2011). Non-military means of statecraft can encompass an enormous variety of state behavior, and this category is too broad to describe meaningfully the specific strategy that a revisionist state can employ to influence and alter the existing institutional order.

He (2008, 2009) develops a theory showing how states can engage in soft balancing by adopting two institutional strategies: inclusive institutional balancing and exclusive institutional balancing to constrain their rivals (in this case, in the Asia Pacific after the Cold War). Inclusive institutional balancing refers to a strategy to include, or engage and enmesh, a potential competitor or adversary in an institution, and efforts seeking to constrain the target state by relying on the rules and norms of the institution in question and, of course, the other members' collective influence. Exclusive institutional balancing, as its name suggests, attempts to bar the target state from an institution and to use the cohesion of this institution's members to exert pressures on it. He's ideas of institutional balancing encourages us to think about how states can respond to threats or countervailing pressures from others through institutional means. However, how a revisionist state can seek to influence the existing institutional order seems to be beyond the scope of his argument.

Goddard (2018a) has proposed an approach based on network theory to examine how institutional settings can shape revisionist behavior and strategy. She argues that depending on two factors—access and brokerage—regarding a state's position within the existing networks of international institutions, there are four ideal types of revisionist strategies: integrated revisionists who are more likely to pursue institutional engagement; bridging revisionists, who will seek rule-based change through reform; isolated revisionists, who prefer an "exit" strategy; and rogue revisionists, who are more likely to wage a war against the existing international order. Goddard's study indeed sheds considerable light on different revisionist strategies. We will build on her work, although we exclude the path taken by rogue states leading eventually to a war, which is not strictly speaking an institutional strategy.

Focusing on a variety of Chinese conduct in global governance, Kastner et al. (2016, 2018) argue that a rising power can adopt three types of strategy toward the existing arrangements in global governance: to free ride and passively "accept" the arrangements of existing regimes; to "hold up" and change some rules of existing institutions; or to "invest" and actively engage in existing as well as new regimes. They argue that the strategic setting of specific issue areas—outside options and indispensability—will shape a rising power's policy choices toward the existing regimes. In a similar vein, Lipscy (2017) highlights the importance of "outside options" in determining a state's negotiation leverage in international institutions. Kastner et al. assume that only a rising power can be revisionist. Their theory does not consider that established powers, and even those that continue to gain power after reaching their hegemonic status, can also turn to revisionism if they are not satisfied with the existing arrangements of specific secondary institutions. Although in this respect our model differs from theirs, in other respects it also complements theirs, as we show in the following.

Based on social identity theory, Larson and Shevchenko (2010, 2019) examine how states can seek to join a higher-status group through three strategies. The first is social mobility, in which a state can emulate the values and practices of the group that it aspires to join. The second strategy is social competition. In this approach, the aspiring state challenges members of the higher-status group in an area in which it has an advantage and can claim to be superior. The third strategy is called social creativity, whereby the state aspiring for a higher status reframes a negative attribute as positive or tries to excel in a different domain, one that is not stressed by the higher-status club. Larson and Shevchenko (2010, 2019) call attention to states' desire for a higher status, as well as the importance of hierarchy in separating states of different status rank, in world politics. Their study focuses on states outside a status club seeking admission to it, with special attention to Russia and China. Although international institutions are implicitly used to indicate the existence of status clubs, how the nature of an institution can affect the strategic choices of an aspiring or revisionist state is less clear, especially if this state is already inside the relevant institution.

Building on the existing literature reviewed earlier, we propose four institutional strategies that a revisionist state can employ to influence or challenge existing institutions: institutional reform, institutional obstruction, institutional exit, and institutional competition. While the first two strategies can be considered an approach that states can use to influence institutions from inside, the second two strategies are ones through which states can challenge the existing institutions from outside.

Institutional reform is similar to the "voice" option described by Hirschman (1970) some time ago, as well as the "institutional engagement" path described in Goddard's (2018a) network-based theory. The purpose of institutional reform is not to overthrow the existing institutional arrangements. Instead, it is to revise their rules, procedures, leadership, and agenda so that the newly reformed institutions will be able to better meet the revisionist state's interests and reflect its values than before. For instance, the quota revision by the International Monetary Fund (IMF) represents an effort at institutional reform driven by the emerging economies, which believe that their voting power in that institution should recognize their increased economic importance.

Institutional obstruction is another strategy that a state can use to challenge existing institutions from inside these institutions. It refers to a strategy when a state that is dissatisfied with some rules or arrangements of the pertinent institutions chooses non-cooperation by obstruction to show its displeasure. Moscow's conduct in the earlier years of the United Nations is reminiscent of this strategy. This relatively passive behavior will not necessarily succeed in bringing about changes in the rules and procedures of the institutions in question. However, this state's actions will hinder and impede the progress and even the daily operations of these institutions. The ineffectiveness, decline, and even perhaps eventual collapse of the institutions may be the objective behind a revisionist state pursuing this strategy.

Another example of institutional obstruction can be drawn from the failure of the "Six Party Talks" among North Korea, South Korea, the United States, China, Japan, and Russia to address Pyongyang's program to develop nuclear weapons in the early 2000s. There are many reasons for this failure. One key reason is the spoiler role that North Korea played in these negotiations, through which it was able to skillfully impede any meaningful progress (Niksch 2006). Eventually, the negotiations ended when North Korea withdrew from them in 2009 and after it undertook a series of provocations.

Institutional exit is an "external" strategy for a state to challenge existing institutions, whereby it voluntarily withdraws from an institution. This strategy reflects Hirschman's (1970) "exit" option when a member has experienced disappointments with the organizations to which it belongs. In the same vein, Goddard suggests that an isolated revisionist state can choose an "exit" strategy to express its dissatisfaction with the institution in which it used to be a part.

The purpose of an "institutional exit" strategy can be twofold. On the one hand, it may reflect a deliberate attempt to undermine the legitimacy of the existing institution. The US decision to withdraw from the World Health Organization (WHO) illustrates this intent. Similarly, Germany, Italy, and Japan's decisions to withdraw from the League of Nations suggest this motivation. Such withdrawal or disengagement may be a precursor to even more aggressive behavior to follow. On the other hand, and often concomitantly, this strategy may be pursued because it can provide more freedom of action to the state in question, liberating it from the constraints imposed by the rules of the institution and the preferences of a majority of its members. The vigorous opposition mounted by some senators against the United States joining the League of Nations offered an instance suggesting a desire to avoid foreign commitments or constraints on the part of isolationists and unilateralists. Japan's withdrawal from the League of Nations after the Assembly adopted a report criticizing it for invading Manchuria and recent US decisions to leave the Trans-Pacific Partnership and the Iran nuclear deal tell us that the exit strategy may be exercised by a rising as well as a ruling state that is dissatisfied with its international situation. This exit strategy naturally undermines the legitimacy of the institution in question, and if enough important states decline to join it or to abide by its rules, protocols, and decisions, both its effectiveness and survival will come into serious doubt.

The fourth and final strategy a state can use to revise existing institutions is institutional competition. A state applying this strategy creates a new institution to directly compete with and to even challenge the very existence of the old institution. By creating competing forums, this strategy presents the most direct and serious action challenging the existing institution from outside. Whereas institutional reform aims to revise some rules or even the leadership of the existing institution from inside, the goal of institutional competition is to use an alternative institution to undermine the relevance and legitimacy of the existing one and even to replace it.

The establishment of the United Nations is a successful institutional replacement of the League of Nations. Similarly, the creation of the Bretton Woods institutions, such as the World Bank and the IMF, can be considered an institutional replacement of the gold standard, a regime led by Britain in global financial governance. However, institutional competition does not mean that the alternative institution must replace the old one. For example, the East Asia Summit (EAS) established in 2005 is widely seen as an alternative framework of Asian regionalism that challenges the ASEAN Plus Three (the Association of Southeast Nations Plus Three, or APT) forum founded after the Asian financial crisis in 1998 (He 2009). Although replacement may be the ultimate outcome desired by the relevant revisionist states, the main purpose of a strategy of institutional competition is to diminish and undermine the importance and relevance of the existing institution in a specific issue area.

Three points are worth noting regarding these four "soft" revisionist strategies. First, a state can adopt different strategies toward different institutions. Institutions, especially secondary institutions, are mainly issue-based in nature. For example, NATO is a multilateral security organization—a military alliance—dealing with security threats in Europe. APEC (Asian Pacific Economic Cooperation), however, is an intergovernmental institution aimed at boosting economic cooperation among countries in the Asia Pacific region. Although the United States is a member state of both NATO and APEC, its institutional strategies toward them will likely be different because security and economics are two different issue areas.

Second, these four strategies can be adopted by any state, whether it is a hegemon or a rising power, so long as this state is not satisfied with the existing institution and has some capability to influence it. All states may want to see some existing norms, rules, and institutions made more congenial to their values and interests, but the extent of this desired change and the method used to pursue it can be critically different. Any state, not just a rising power, can apply these different institutional strategies to change the existing institutional order. A weak state may not have enough capability to mount a strategy of institutional competition by itself, but it can join other disaffected states and stronger ones in this effort. Naturally, a strategy of passive resistance, obstructionism, and non-cooperation (by, for example, deliberate foot-dragging or absenteeism) is available to weak as well as strong countries.

Third, the four strategies just presented are obviously ideal types and, moreover, states can pursue different strategies in different issue areas, as just mentioned. For instance, Beijing can try to create new institutions such as the Asian Infrastructure Investment Bank and, at the same time, participate in and even voice support for other existing institutions such as ASEAN and the United Nations. Thus, although we have sketched the four institutional strategies as mutually exclusive, states can operate in a gray zone whereby they can pursue "loyalty, voice, exit" and even outright opposition in some combination at the same time. The purpose of presenting the ideal types, however, is naturally to clarify the central tendency or the main thrust of a state's statecraft, even though realizing that in reality states rarely adopt one strategy to the exclusion of others, especially when their status, role, and situation in international relations are in the midst of a transition process and when they face cross pressures from multiple fronts and issues—as in the case of today's China. This said, how and under what conditions will a state give primacy to a specific strategy to mount an institutional challenge? What we seek to highlight is a matter of relative emphasis in the relevant state's statecraft and signs of important shifts in its policy orientation. Mind you also that challenge in this context does not necessarily imply a violent, overt, or wholesale overthrow of the existing rules, norms, or arrangements. It can involve incremental, consensual, and peaceful reform.

Comparative Advantage and Institutional Benefit

We propose a rationalist model of institutional revisionism to explain the variations in a state's institutional strategies. A state will naturally consider the associated costs and benefits when deciding to alter the existing institutional order. The benefits include prospective material and non-material gains from the existing institution. The material gains refer to the distributional benefits, such as economic privilege and trade quota, from institutions. For example, the IMF voting power is set unequally among its member states, a feature which reflects the different distributional benefits for different members. The non-material gains from institutions can be recognition and status that institutions can legitimate for states. For instance, the World Trade Organization (WTO) is not only a global trade regime for states to lower tariffs and enjoy material benefits from trade, but also an international institution that can recognize and legitimate the social status of a state in the international society. This is why both China and Russia, as well as many developing countries, were eager to join the WTO after the Cold War, despite the fact that it entails stringent conditions and commitments during the process of accession (Lardy 2004).

According to rationalist institutionalism, states form institutions to reduce transaction and coordination costs and to foster cooperation with one another by increasing the shadow of the future and reducing the danger of defection. A hegemon or a ruling state plays a key role in establishing multilateral institutions, which mainly reflect its interests and ideology (Keohane 1984). In other words, this dominant state will take the lion's share of benefits, material and non-material, from the institution that it has played a leading role to initiate or establish. Indeed, proponents of power-transition theory and hegemonic-stability theory have argued that, in one way or another, global stability and prosperity depend on the provision of public goods which only a preponderant state has both the capability and the incentive to provide. In this light, some have asked whether a rising China will "step up" and assume the role of a provider of public goods (e.g., Nye 2017).

However, when the processes of diffusion of power and the economic law of diminishing returns set in, the benefits received by the ruling state from the institutions it has taken a leadership role in forming will decrease over time. Concomitantly, the costs of sustaining such institutions and the constraints they impose on the dominant power's freedom of action can increase over time. At the same time, rising powers that have recently joined these institutions and have gradually become familiar with their rules of the game may reap larger rewards without having to bear a proportionate burden of maintaining and supporting these institutions. The logic of this discussion suggests that a cost-benefit analysis may very well incline an existing dominant but declining power to re-examine its commitment to prevailing institutions, including those it has played a leading role in creating.

Conversely and contrary to the presentation usually found in the existing literature, a rising power may very well have an incentive to support or at least maintain those institutions that have enabled its ascent. Whether a state will seek to alter an existing institution will depend on its calculation of benefits and costs. If it expects less benefits and more costs from the existing arrangements, it will be motivated to alter them. Conversely, when it expects greater prospective benefits compared to costs, it will hesitate to undermine the institution, even if it is not entirely satisfied with it. Because officials are forward looking, we can try to tell their expectations about future benefits and costs by way of backward inference from the institutional strategies they have selected to pursue.

It is worth noting that institutional benefits are measured in relative terms. This means that although all states should gain some benefits from the institutions they join, the benefits they receive are not equally distributed. Much like the debate over "absolute gains versus relative gains" in international relations in the 1990s (Baldwin 1993; Grieco 1988, 1993; Powell 1991; Snidal 1991), states also care about their relative benefits from institutions, not only in comparing with others, but also in comparison with what they used to get previously. Therefore, the unequal as well as changing distributions of the benefits can lead to dissatisfaction by states toward an existing institution, such as shown by recent US disenchantment with the United Nations and its associated organizations. Although dissatisfaction is not the same thing as revisionism, it can be the source for revisionist motivation to alter existing norms, rules, or institutions.

Another factor that a state will consider is its capability to influence an existing institution. As mentioned before, institutions are inherently anchored in specific issue areas. A state's capability to revise an existing institution stems mainly from its comparative advantage in a certain issue area. This comparative advantage can be measured by this state's influence compared to its peers. This concept plays a similar role as the "movable property" in Hirschman's (1970) analysis of the exit option available to a company or individual in coping with discontent with an existing group or organization. The more movable property possessed by an actor, the more likely for this company or individual to choose the exit option, simply because this entity or person can survive without the existing group or organization.

Similarly, the greater the comparative advantage a state has over its peers, the more likely it is for this state to choose an "external" institutional strategy to cope with its dissatisfaction with an existing institution. As mentioned before, there are two possible strategies in this situation: institutional exit and institutional competition. Institutional exit does not necessarily lead to institutional competition against the existing institution. Similarly, institutional competition does not necessarily require a state to physically leave an existing institution. In other words, a state can create an alternative institution to compete with an existing one in which it is still a member—albeit a dissatisfied one. "Exit" can also mean inaction, non-participation, or other types of abstention from the organization's proceedings (institutional exit can in this sense become blurred with institutional obstruction). Naturally, the threat of exit can give a state additional leverage to seek changes in the existing institution to which it belongs.

The interplay of these two variables, comparative advantage and institutional benefits (relative to expected costs), will shape a state's policy choice regarding different institutional strategies. Table 4.1 illustrates the configuration of this model of institutional revisionism. Cell 1 refers to a situation when a state enjoys both high comparative advantage and high benefits from the existing institution. As mentioned before, institutional benefits are a relative term. Enjoying a high level of benefits does not necessarily mean that a state must therefore be satisfied with the existing rules and procedures of the institution. It can still feel aggrieved because it believes that it is entitled to even more benefits. If this state is dissatisfied with the existing institution, it is more likely to pursue a strategy of institutional reform to revise those rules and procedures that it does not like. In other words, it will be more likely to voice its dissatisfaction inside the institution to change it. Due to its comparative advantage, it is also highly likely that this state's demands for reform will be accommodated by the other members.

Table 4.1 Model of Institutional Revisionism

		Institutional Benefit	
		High	Low
Comparative Advantage	High	1. *Institutional Reform* (IMF Quota Reform)	2. *Institutional Competition* (EAS vs. APT)
	Low	3. *Institutional Obstruction* (North Korea's non-cooperation diplomacy in the Six Party Talks)	4. *Institutional Exit* (the US withdrawal from the TPP)

Cell 2 indicates a situation in which a state has a high level of comparative advantage in an issue area pertinent to an existing institution, but it perceives its level of benefits received from this institution to be low. This state's sense of relative deprivation inclines it to consider creating alternatives beyond the current institution. Its high comparative advantage provides the necessary asset for it to build a new institution that can compete with the existing one. Since it plays a leading and even pivotal role in establishing the new institution, this founding state can seek to maximize its material and non-material gains, improving the benefits it has heretofore received from the old institution.

Cell 3 refers to a situation in which a state enjoys a high level of benefits from the existing institution but has a low level of comparative advantage in the institution-related issue area. The high benefits from the existing institution will make the state in question hesitate to give up the institution despite its possible dissatisfaction or reservation with some aspects of its rules and procedures (recall that this possible dissatisfaction or reservation reflects this state's sense of entitlement, the feeling that it should have even more benefits from and influence in the institution in question). The low comparative advantage limits its options, as well as its willingness to mount a challenge to this institution from the outside. Therefore, this state is more likely to choose a passive "obstruction" strategy to stay in the institution but not to contribute to its development and operation. It can be a free-rider in the existing institution and can be expected to even veto initiatives from the institution's other members if it believes that these initiatives will harm its interests. In other words, it is more likely to play a spoiler role.

Cell 4 indicates a situation in which a state has both a low level of benefits from the institution and a low level of comparative advantage in the institution-related issue area. This state faces severe constraints to improve its lot, even though it is dissatisfied. The low benefits will encourage this state to leave the institution. However, its low comparative advantage in the relevant issue area prevents it from creating any alterative institution that can better suit its interests. Therefore, this state is more likely to choose an exit strategy by pulling out from the institution or, alternatively, taking a path of passive resistance (a posture that is equivalent to exit by abstention or non-cooperation). This behavior signifies its dissatisfaction, although it is not an overt posture of outright opposition and challenge. This state is likely to bide its time and wait for a countervailing coalition to the existing institution to develop before it jumps on its bandwagon. It is itself too weak to mobilize such a coalition or to sponsor an opposing institution. It must therefore wait for an opportunity created by other stronger, like-minded revisionist states.

Our model is built on the existing literature on revisionism. However, it makes three improvements. First, our model does not only apply to rising powers, as most previous discussions on revisionism have implied. The key assumption of our model is that any state can become dissatisfied with an existing institution. Depending on its comparative advantage in an institution-related issue area, as well as the current level of its benefits (relative to its costs) from the existing institution, it can choose different strategies to influence it. It should be noted that our model can apply to a situation in which a state is both inside and outside a given institution. Significantly, the benefits to be derived from an institution may not be tied to formal membership in it. So, for example, although Switzerland is not a member of NATO, it could still benefit from the public goods of peace, stability, and deterrence provided by this alliance. This remark, of course, brings up the idea of free-riding by some countries that benefit from an institution without, however, having contributed sufficiently or directly to its provision of public goods. This said, some institutions may be exclusive clubs whereby the benefits of belonging can be limited to only its members, as in some cases of trade agreements. In such cases, the excluded state can decide to seek admission to the institution, to remain outside, and/or to create (or join) a competing institution. As this last remark suggests, the strategies we have sketched can be pursued concurrently by a state toward different institutions and can shift over time.

Second, our model can subsume and simplify the existing literature on institutional strategies. For example, the four proposed institutional strategies are rooted in the scholarship on soft balancing. However, they speak more specifically to institutional behavior, rather than non-military strategies of opposition and resistance in general. In addition, our four strategies can subsume Goddard's typology of institutional strategies, such as "institutional engagement," "bridging brokerage," and "institutional isolation." The strategies of institutional engagement and institutional revolution in Goddard's typology correspond to the strategies of institutional reform and institutional competition in our model. Institutional isolation in Goddard's typology is a kind of exit strategy suggested by our model.

We argue, however, that merely accepting the existing rules (i.e., institutional engagement) is not a revisionist strategy because it does not challenge the existing institutions. In fact, such behavior is the hallmark of a "status-quo" state. In addition, our model does not include Goddard's "rogue revisionist" strategy of relying on military means to change the existing institutional order. Naturally, this strategy is possible, as shown by Nazi Germany's policies. It is addressed in our discussion of hard revisionism of military conquest and subversion. But as we have argued earlier, outright application of military means to alter the international order has become increasingly costly, unrewarding, and thus self-defeating and unlikely in today's world. This strategy has become unthinkable, especially pertaining to the relations among contemporary great powers, for reasons we have articulated earlier. Therefore, we have left out military means in our model focusing on *institutional* revisionism.

Although we agree that a state can use military means—hard revisionist strategies—to challenge the existing institutional order, we see this contingency to be the least likely development, although should we be proven wrong, such a development would also have the most devastating consequences for the world. Some readers can surely disagree with us, and they may emphasize the danger of Thucydides's Trap in auguring a direct military clash between the United States and China. Thus far, Beijing has refrained from hard balancing strategies, such as seeking military allies and political clients abroad to compete for influence with the United States, or engaging in a direct, overt armament race with the United States (after all, the United States has outspent China militarily by a vast margin, exceeding the amount of military spending by the next eleven highest countries *combined* in 2019 (Stockholm International Peace Research Institute 2020).

Our model can also subsume the argument of strategic multilateralism featuring the alternatives of "accept," "hold-up," and "invest," discussed by Kastner et al. (2018). Their idea of "hold-up" is similar to our presentation of institutional obstruction, and their idea of "invest" is close to our views on institutional competition. However, as already mentioned, in our view, to accept the existing rules is not a revisionist strategy, even though a state can acquiesce to these rules for the time being in order to wait for a better opportunity to alter or revise them later. In addition, Kastner et al. seem to define the "invest" strategy broadly because a state can invest from both inside and outside of an institution. We argue that institutional reform is different from institutional competition, because the former is a revisionist strategy seeking gradual, incremental change from inside and largely by means of following the established rules and procedures of the existing institution, whereas the latter is a revisionist strategy undertaken from the outside and is typically associated in the existing literature with challenges mounted by revisionists to fundamentally alter the existing international order.

Last but not least, our model of revisionism considers factors both internal and external to institutions in shaping a state's revisionist strategies. Internally, a state will consider both the material and non-material benefits it gains from an existing institution (relative to its costs in participating in the pertinent institution). Externally, it will calculate its comparative advantage in the institution-related issue area (which of course means its capability relative to that of its rivals). Kastner et al. (2018) and Lipscy (2017) discuss a state's possible "outside option," and Goddard introduces a "brokerage" variable in their respective analyses of strategies available to a revisionist state. However, we suggest that a state's comparative advantage is the key to influencing its outside option, as well as its brokerage position in institutional networks. Naturally, when a state plays the role of a pivotal broker in its relationship with a particular set of other countries or when a state enjoys dense and intense relations with many other states (that is, in Goddard's terminology, when it enjoys strong institutional connections to

a subset of countries and a high access to global networks of institutions generally), these assets confer a comparative advantage to it. With a high comparative
advantage, a state will have "outside options" and is in a better position to consolidate and secure its pivotal intermediary position in multiple networks. In contrast, a state without a comparative advantage in an institution-related issue area
will have fewer outside options and will thus be in a weaker brokerage position
and have more limited access to interlocking networks of global and regional
institutions.

The United States, China, and Institutional Revisionism

In this section, we conduct some short case studies to illustrate the explanatory
utility of our model of institutional revisionism. We focus mainly on the institutional behavior of the United States and China, although our model has the
potential to be generalized to other cases as well.

Institutional Reform

The first case is about US and Chinese behavior to reform institutions. Since the
Cold War's end, the United States has become the sole superpower in the international system. It enjoys an unparalleled comparative advantage relative to
other states in the issue area of military security. Additionally, the United States
draws its military preponderance from its extensive alliances, especially after
these alliances expanded after the Cold War. In the Asia Pacific, the United States
has maintained bilateral alliances with South Korea, Japan, the Philippines, and
Australia. This situation, however, does not mean that Washington is necessarily
satisfied with its relations with its allies.

Since President Trump came to power, he repeatedly stated publicly that
NATO allies, as well as Japan and South Korea, should share more of the financial costs in their respective military alliance with the United States. Washington
enjoys a high comparative advantage in the area of defense security, and it has
also benefited greatly from its extensive alliance networks, including its bilateral
treaties with various Asia Pacific countries and informal ties with others such as
Taiwan. However, Trump did not feel satisfied with the existing burden-sharing
arrangements with Washington's formal and informal allies. In the issue area of
defense security, the United States is well placed in cell 1 of our model of institutional revisionism. This model suggests that Washington is more likely to
pursue a strategy of institutional reform to change the rules and norms of the existing institution. In the alliance systems dominated by Washington, this attempt

at institutional reform refers to changing the burden-sharing arrangements between the United States and its allies. Consequently, Trump successfully pressured both South Korea and Japan to pay more for the security protection they receive from the United States. In Trump's words, "South Korea is a very wealthy nation that now feels an obligation to contribute to the military defense provided by the United States of America" (Nikkei Asian Review 2019). Moreover, Trump is also reported to have "gain[ed] leverage by linking security to trade in a broader strategy" when he negotiated a trade deal with Prime Minister Shinzo Abe during his visit to Japan in 2019 (Nikkei Asian Review 2019).

China has been one of the greatest beneficiaries of the current global financial system. It became the world's second largest economy in 2010. According to the World Economic Forum (2016), China may even surpass the United States and become the largest economy in the world by 2029. In the economic sphere, a rising China has enjoyed some comparative advantages over the United States—the declining hegemon—based on projections of these countries' respective growth trajectories in recent years. However, China is not entirely satisfied with the existing institutions, especially its voting power in the IMF. Despite being the second largest economy in 2010, China's voting power in this organization was still behind Japan, Britain, Germany, and France before the reform adopted in 2010. This situation places China in cell 1 of our model, which indicates that this country receives a high level of benefits from the current institution and that it has a high comparative advantage in the economic arena. Therefore, China has adopted a strategy of institutional reform to push the IMF to alter its voting system in the 2010 G20 meeting, with support from other emerging economies. Beijing did not seek to overthrow the IMF, despite its dissatisfaction and revisionist intention. Instead, it tried hard to work with other emerging economies to reform this institution's rules, especially its system of weighted votes. It adopted a typical strategy of institutional reform.

Institutional Competition

We expect a state to choose a strategy of institutional competition when it is placed in a situation with a high level of comparative advantage and a low level of benefits from an existing institution. As mentioned before, the United States has enjoyed a comparative advantage in the security-related arena due to its unrivaled military capabilities in the post–Cold War era. However, in the Asia Pacific, a multilateral security architecture was led not by the United States, but by ASEAN—a group of small and middle powers. The United States supported ASEAN to take the lead in establishing the ASEAN Regional Forum (ARF) in 1994, because it would serve as a mechanism for security dialogue for

Washington to further engage both traditional and non-traditional security issues after the Cold War (Goh 2004). More importantly, this forum has also played a role for inclusive institutional balancing in constraining and socializing China, such as in its territorial disputes in the South China Sea (Foot 1998; He 2009). For more than two decades, the coexistence of US-led bilateralism and ASEAN-led multilateralism has defined the distinctive nature of the Asia Pacific's security structure after the Cold War.

After the 2008 global finance crisis, the role of ARF has seemingly declined in constraining China's policy, especially in the South China Sea. Beijing's diplomacy is perceived by many to have turned in a more assertive direction, as shown by diplomatic crises between China and its neighbors, including an incident involving boat collision over the Diaoyu/Senkaku dispute in 2010, the crisis stemming from Japanese government's purchase of these small islands in 2012, as well as the standoff between China and the Philippines at Scarborough Shoal in 2012 (He and Feng 2012; Jerden 2014; Johnston 2013; Swaine 2010). Consequently, the United States started its "pivot" or "rebalance" toward Asia during Barack Obama's second term (Campbell 2016). On the one hand, Washington strengthened its bilateral alliances in the region. On the other, it initiated its mini-lateral security cooperation with Japan, India, and Australia in the framework of the Quadrilateral Security Dialogue (Quad) in 2008.

To a certain extent, the Quad was a strategy of institutional competition stemming from Washington's dissatisfaction with the ASEAN-led multilateral security architecture in constraining China's assertiveness. Due to Australia's unilateral withdrawal in 2009, the Quad was short-lived. However, after Trump came to power, Washington launched its Indo-Pacific Strategy, whereby it revived the Quad grouping in late 2017 with a clear purpose of dealing with China's increasing influence in the region. The rebirth of Quad 2.0 reflects a strategy of institutional competition adopted by Washington toward the existing multilateral security arrangements led by ARF, seeking to contain China's rise more effectively (Tow 2019).

China's comparative advantage relative to other states, including the United States, lies in its economic potential. Since 2013, China has become the largest trading state, overtaking the United States, in the world. Although the IMF instituted its quota and governance reforms in 2010, the US Congress intentionally delayed ratifying these proposed reforms until December 2015. The delayed IMF reforms frustrated China and other emerging economies. Due to China's comparative advantage in the economic arena, it started to move beyond the existing institution by adopting a strategy of institutional competition, as suggested by cell 2 of our model of institutional revisionism.

In 2013, China put forward the idea of establishing the Asian Infrastructure Investment Bank (AIIB). When the AIIB was officially formed in March

2015, fifty-seven states joined as founding members, including some developed economies such as Britain, Germany, France, Italy, Australia, and South Korea. On August 31, 2016, Canada officially applied to join the AIIB and became the first North American country to seek membership. To date, the United States and Japan continue to say "no" to the AIIB. As some scholars point out, China's initiation of the AIIB represented the start of its challenge to the US-led system of global economic governance, as well as the postwar international economic order (Huang 2015; McDowell 2015; Roach 2015; Wan 2015). Although the AIIB has thus far not presented an alternative financial institution that can potentially displace the IMF and the World Bank, it is the first time that China has competed with the United States in the domain of global financial governance (He and Feng 2019). No matter whether it will succeed or not in the future, this initiative has indeed embodied China's strategy of institutional competition to alter the existing institutional order, especially its financial institutions.

Institutional Obstruction

While both institutional reform and institutional competition are proactive strategies that a state can pursue to make some changes either inside or outside an existing institution, institutional obstruction provides a state with a less active and even negative way to undermine this institution's relevance and effectiveness. As mentioned before, the United States had blocked the IMF quota and governance reforms for five years. This blocking behavior can be considered as an attempt at institutional obstruction in dealing with pressures from the emerging economies to transform the IMF from inside this organization. The decline of the US economy after the 2008 global financial crisis and "the rise of the rest" in world politics have placed Washington in a situation of relatively low comparative advantage in the economic domain. However, the United States still benefits greatly from its leadership position in the current financial institutions, especially in the IMF and the World Bank. Therefore, it is situated in cell 3 of our model of institutional revisionism, suggesting that Washington is likely to adopt a strategy of institutional obstruction.

The United States has utilized its default veto power and the IMF's institutional procedures to block and delay this organization's quota and governance reforms. It is a rational decision from Washington's perspective for two reasons. On the one hand, according to the IMF's decision-making procedures, without Washington's approval the proposed reforms will not be valid. The United States thus has the power and right to block those reforms that it does not like. On the other hand, it also seems sensible for Washington to try to slow down the IMF's reform process so that it can further consolidate its leadership after its economy bounces back.

However, in the eyes of other states, Washington's obstruction hinders the IMF's progress and adaptation. It is a direct reason for China to seek an outside option by initiating the AIIB in 2013. Facing China's challenge, the United States employed another way of obstruction, seeking to delegitimate China's AIIB efforts inside the system of global financial governance (albeit outside the AIIB itself). As reported by the *New York Times*, Caroline Atkinson, the US deputy national security adviser for international economics, was a strong defender of the existing system and a major player who sought to influence the membership of the AIIB. In a series of high-level meetings, Atkinson and her colleagues tried to form a "containment strategy" directed against the AIIB (Perlez 2015).

In particular, "Australia and South Korea were discouraged from signing up, and G-7 countries were advised that the United States wanted a united front" (Perlez 2015). Washington's efforts at obstruction failed after Britain and other European powers registered their support for AIIB in 2015. Although Washington issued official denials that it had intended to sabotage China's AIIB initiative, it is an open secret that it took this initiative by Beijing seriously and that its refusal to join the AIIB sought to delegitimate China's potential leadership in the domain of global financial governance. As Roach et al. (2015) point out, "the US opposed the AIIB simply because it was a Chinese initiative, full stop."

The United States is not the only country employing a strategy of institutional obstruction to protect its interests. China did the same, though in a different issue area. Beijing signed the United Nations Convention on the Law of the Sea (UNCLOS) in 1982 and ratified it in 1996. However, when addressing territorial disputes in the South China Sea, it has insisted on its historical right, a claim that is ambiguously defined according to the UNCLOS. Since the South China Sea issue is related mainly to the security domain, China does not have a comparative advantage, especially after the US pivot toward Asia and its deepening involvement since 2010 with various other claimant states engaged in the South China Sea disputes. If we treat these disputes as a legal issue, China also lacks a comparative advantage in this area. It faces competing claims from other claimants, including Brunei, Malaysia, the Philippines, and Vietnam, in addition to Taiwan. That Beijing has signed the UNCLOS means that to a certain extent, its policy options have been constrained and limited by this treaty's requirements and stipulations. Yet Beijing does not want to leave the UNCLOS due possibly to a concern over its international reputation and/or a sense that some clauses contained in the UNCLOS may be useful to protect its maritime interests. Therefore, on the issue of South China Sea disputes, China finds itself in cell 3 of our model, where it is more likely to adopt a strategy of obstruction inside an existing institution.

In fact, China has employed this obstruction strategy toward the Philippines' efforts to seek arbitration in their competing claims of sovereignty in disputed areas in the South China Sea. In 2015, Manila challenged the legality of China's territorial assertion as demarcated by its so-called nine-dash line. It brought its competing claim to the Permanent Court of Arbitration. Beijing declared that it would not participate in the arbitration process. Nevertheless, the arbitral tribunal ruled that it had jurisdiction over the case in late 2016. After The Hague ruled in favor of the Philippines in 2016, China declared that it would neither accept nor recognize this ruling. China's behavior in the eyes of others represents institutional obstruction because it used the rules of the UNCLOS to reject the arbitration procedure as well as the arbitration ruling. It should be noted that China is not the only country that has opted out of the UNCLOS arbitration procedures. Other countries, such as Britain, Australia, and France, have also made the same declaration and, of course, the United States has declined to join the UNCLOS. As with the effort by US Congress to block the IMF reforms, Beijing has declined to participate in the arbitration case over contested sovereignty with Manila in their South China Sea dispute.

Another example of China's obstruction strategy can be drawn from its behavior in the UN Copenhagen Climate Change Conference. In negotiations concerning climate change, Beijing does not enjoy a strong comparative advantage because its emissions levels (driven by its rapid economic growth) were widely criticized by the international community. The UN climate conference, however, is the highest venue for the member states to discuss this issue. China derives significant influence and status from its position as a permanent member of the Security Council and as the largest developing economy in this UN gathering. Therefore, it is placed in cell 3 of our model, with a relatively weak comparative advantage but a high level of benefits at the 2009 UN climate conference in Copenhagen.

One key issue taken up at this conference is the negotiation over legally binding commitments for emissions reduction. China has a clear position, insisting on the so-called common but differentiated responsibility on the part of developing and developed countries to address the problem of climate change (*China Daily* 2015). In other words, China argues that developed countries should cut their emissions more than the developing countries. The key problem, however, is whether both developing and developed countries should set legally binding commitments for emissions reduction. While developed countries were generally disposed to make such a commitment, China and the developing countries expressed their deep concerns over how their economic development might be adversely affected by emissions reduction.

The Copenhagen conference ended eventually with a non-legally binding document because of the joint efforts by China and other developing countries at obstruction. Although there were legitimate and domestic reasons for China's behavior (Bodansky 2010), it appeared to developed countries as deliberate obstruction by it and the other developing countries to intentionally block progress on negotiating a concerted global effort to address the danger of climate change. As Hilton and Oliver (2017) point out, the US and European media largely blamed China's "diplomatic obstructionism" (Revkin and Broder 2009) and "accused China of sabotaging the negotiations and refusing to back higher ambition, even where it had no direct impact on its own obligations" (Lynas 2009).

However, from China's perspective, its obstruction strategy was a success because China utilized the existing rules and procedures at the Copenhagen conference to head off a legally binding proposal to reduce emissions, one that did not serve its economic interests. Again, we are not judging or criticizing China or other countries that employ a strategy of institutional obstruction. Instead, we suggest that their behavior reflects a seemingly rational choice for dissatisfied revisionists operating inside institutions.

Institutional Exit

As our model suggests, a state can choose a strategy of institutional exit when it perceives a low level of benefits from an existing institution and it has a low level of comparative advantage in the relevant issue area. The United States under Trump employed this strategy frequently after 2017. For example, Washington withdrew from the Trans-Pacific Partnership (TPP) as soon as he came to power. In addition, he announced that the United States would withdraw from the Paris climate accord as well as the Iran nuclear deal, despite outcries from Washington's European allies. His decisions to withdraw from various multilateral institutions may be motivated by both domestic and international reasons. Washington explained its decision to leave the United Nations Educational, Scientific and Cultural Organization and the United Nations Human Rights Council (UNHRC) in October 2017 and June 2018, respectively, because of their supposed anti-Israel policy. Yet this situation was not new, and its decisions cannot be easily explained without considering the Trump administration's political impulses and calculations.

Some of Trump's policies also followed the logic of a strategy of institutional exit that is driven by a low level of institutional benefits as well as a weak comparative advantage for the United States. For example, he believed that the United States would not benefit from the TPP grouping on trade, because this accord would not be based on "fair trade" and it would make American workers worse off. The huge trade deficits between the United States and Asian countries also placed Washington in a disadvantageous situation, at least according to Trump's beliefs about trade.

Therefore, from Trump's perspective it was rational to withdraw from the TPP because he saw the United States being placed in cell 4 of our model, that is, in a configuration of low benefits and weak comparative advantage. Trump also threatened to withdraw from the WTO, the world's principal institution on trade, which in his view has been "unfair" to the United States. Trump's exit decisions can again encompass multiple purposes. Due to Washington's unparalleled power, its departure would certainly undermine the relevance, effectiveness, and legitimacy of the target institution, as we can see from the TPP's declining status after Washington's withdrawal.

Naturally, the threat to adopt an exit strategy may also enhance Washington's leverage to renegotiate the terms of an agreement, as well as to revise the rules of the existing institution so that they are better aligned with its perceived interests. For example, the United States threatened to withdraw from the Universal Postal Union (UPU) due to the perceived "unfair" postage rate for packages arriving from other countries. After an "extraordinary congress," the UPU decided to compromise on the US proposal in September 2019 and, consequently, the United States decided to remain in the UPU. Washington also threatened to withdraw from the North American Free Trade Agreement (NAFTA). Canada and Mexico basically compromised on Trump's demands in subsequent rounds of renegotiation, and these three countries signed a new US-Mexico-Canada Agreement (USMCA), as an updated version of NAFTA, in September 2019. Therefore, Washington can use the threat of exit as a leverage to either force internal reforms by an existing institution or, alternatively, to undermine an existing institution that it finds objectionable.

Compared to the United States, China does not have the same leverage in exercising this strategy for two reasons. First, as a rising power and a latecomer on the institutional scene, it is still in the process of engaging or entering the existing institutions. Second, an exit strategy can be more costly to its reputation and influence. This strategy will likely be a last resort for China when it has exhausted other options. Russia, a re-emergent but dissatisfied power, however, has faced involuntary exit after the Crimean crisis in 2014, when it was forced out of the G8 and subjected to sanctions undertaken by the Western countries. In 2016, Russia officially withdrew from the International Criminal Court after it published a report describing the Russian annexation of Crimea as an occupation. Neither the United States nor China has joined this international institution.

Russia has threatened to withdraw from the Council of Europe if its voting power was not resumed. After the Council of Europe decided to resume Russia's voting rights in 2017, Moscow announced that it would after all remain in this body (France 24 2019). After the United States announced that it would withdraw from the Intermediate-Range Nuclear Forces Treaty, Russia also withdrew from it. It is another example of forced "exit" behavior. Clearly, not all states have the same leverage to employ a strategy of institutional exit. The more power a state has, the more leverage it enjoys and the more likely it is for this state to employ an effective exit strategy in the international system.

Conclusion

We have discussed both hard and soft strategies that a state can choose to pursue its revisionist agenda toward an existing international order. Militarily, a state can employ invasion or subversion to challenge existing institutional arrangements and norms, especially the principles of sovereignty and territorial integrity in world politics. As we have mentioned before, due to the very high costs of military conquest, as well as the risks of nuclear devastation, today's great powers are less likely to adopt hard revisionist strategies to challenge the existing international order than in previous eras. This generalization does not mean that military invasion has become completely obsolescent, as shown by the US invasion of Iraq and Afghanistan in the recent past, although we do see such action to be practically impossible in relations among the great powers. Altman (2020) reports that the incidence of conquest has not diminished significantly in recent years, but such episodes tend to involve small pieces of territory (rather than entire countries) that are sparsely populated and undefended and are thus unlikely to escalate to large wars. Moreover, military subversion, broadly defined to mean the application of physical force to purse regime change in weaker and smaller countries, continues to be practiced occasionally, as evidenced by US and NATO actions against Libya, Serbia, Syria, and Venezuela. We argue that soft revisionist strategies, including institutional reform, institutional competition, institutional obstruction, and institutional exit, are more likely to be chosen by revisionist states to influence the existing institutional order in the age of globalization and mutual nuclear deterrence.

In dealing with a revisionist state's challenge, other states have two policy options: counterbalancing and accommodation. For hard revisionism, hard counterbalancing strategies, especially both internal balancing (military buildup) and external balancing (alliance formation), have historically been the most direct responses. States have, however, also been known to sometimes choose a buck-passing strategy so that they avoid confronting a hard revisionist state and look to other states to do the "heavy lifting" for them in containing this threat. They have also sometimes "underbalanced" because their domestic constituents are unable to agree on the most appropriate strategy to deal with a rising threat (Schweller 2006). This lack of domestic consensus results in an incoherent and ineffective foreign policy, and yet this discord also reflects different assessments about another state's policy intentions (that is, its revisionist agenda) and the strategies that it is likely to pursue in its external relations.

The United Nations provides a platform for fostering security cooperation. It was successful in reversing Iraq's invasion of Kuwait, although it has been much less effective in restraining great powers when they resort to military force, as when the United States invaded Iraq, the United States and its Western allies attacked Libya and Serbia under NATO auspices, and Russia annexed Crimea. The real danger posed by hard revisionism toward world peace stems from the P-5 countries (the five permanent members of the UN Security Council) because they, more than other states, possess the greatest military capabilities to execute this agenda and they are more immune from the restraining influences of multilateral institutions. Nevertheless, nuclear deterrence offers a restraining influence to at least stabilize relations *among* the P-5 countries *themselves* when multilateral institutions are unable to do so.

Soft revisionism will become the most likely strategies for revisionist states to influence the international order. Some states can still choose hard counterbalancing strategies to deal with soft revisionist behavior. However, the economic and military costs of hard balancing will be extremely high for two reasons. On the one hand, military-based balancing will damage economic relations and increase hostilities among states. On the other hand, military means may not be effective in curbing soft revisionist challenges. For example, after the global financial crisis in 2008, emerging economies demanded that the IMF reform its quota and governance rules. It is a typical soft revisionist response based on changing economic realities and legitimate governance concerns. If the United States had used military means to oppose this demand, it would not only damage the IMF's legitimacy and Washington's leadership status in global financial governance, but also cause unnecessary military conflicts between it and other countries.

Therefore, in responding to soft revisionist challenges, soft balancing and accommodation will be the most effective, reasonable, and probable strategies that other states will consider. Soft balancing means to use non-military methods to counter soft revisionist requests, while accommodation means to meet the demands of revisionist states by institutional reform. Whether states adopt soft balancing in preference to accommodation depends on the bargaining process between the revisionist states and their counterparts. When states motivated by soft revisionism seek institutional change, possible future transitions in international order are likely to be more peaceful than in the past, when great powers were motivated by hard revisionism and adopted hard balancing in their statecraft.

5

A Peaceful Transition
of International Order?

For better or worse, the "rise of the rest" has become a reality of world politics in the twenty-first century (Zakaria 2008a, 2008b). Although the United States is still the most powerful country in the international system, economically and militarily, this situation does not exclude the possibility of a transition in international order (as this remark implies and as we have mentioned earlier, power transition need not produce an order transition; similarly, order transition can occur without a power transition in the hegemonic position of the leading state). Liberal scholars, such as Ikenberry (2008, 2011), believe that the liberal international order can be sustained despite the decline of US hegemony. Realists, such as scholars working in the tradition of power-transition theory and offensive realism, are worried about the so-called Thucydides's Trap, according to which rising and ruling states are likely to fight for power, security, and prestige (Allison 2017; Mearsheimer 2001, 2018). Constructivists seem to be uncertain about the future of the international order because ideas and ideologies can either clash with one another or coexist peacefully in the future (Allan et al. 2018; Buzan 2010; Kupchan 2014; Legro 2007).

Competition between the United States and China is likely and even occurring as these words are being written (as evidenced by the ongoing trade dispute between these two countries, and their contest over the next generation of technology such as 5-G communication and artificial intelligence). The 2017 US National Security Strategy (NSS) document labels China as a revisionist state, because it "challenge[s] American power, influence, and interests, attempting to erode American security and prosperity" (White House 2017: 2). In the 2020 US Strategic Approach to the People's Republic of China, the Trump administration reaffirmed the NSS's whole-of-government approach to protect American interests and advance American influence in order to counter Beijing (White House 2020: 12). Some Chinese scholars also see Sino-American competition as the reflection of a "structural contradiction," originating from the transformation of the international system due to China's rise and the decline of the United States (Yan 2014). Others regard it as the consequence of identity politics, underpinned by different political values and nationalism in both nations (Wang 2020).

Challenging prevailing theories of international relations, as well as popular premonitions about a looming conflict between the United States and China, we submit a more guarded view of probable future developments that are contingent on the bargaining and negotiation among states, especially between the United States as the ruling power and China as the rising power. Rather than simply asserting that China is a revisionist state and the United States is a status-quo state, we offer a more nuanced and complicated picture that addresses a large intermediate zone between optimism about the durability of the liberal international order, on the one hand, and pessimism regarding the danger of an impending hegemonic struggle, on the other.

International order has survived the one clear instance of power transition in the post-1815 world (that involving Britain and the United States). We can almost hear an immediate retort that in this instance, similar cultural heritage and shared democracy were responsible for the peaceful preservation of international order, despite a change in the identity of the ruling hegemon. In contrast, China and the United States have very different cultural values and political institutions, and hence there is a much greater danger of a clash between these countries. Yet, a closer look at the historical evidence suggests that Anglo-American relations were competitive and tumultuous during much of the nineteenth century, and these countries came close to fighting on several occasions (Chan 2020a; Layne 1994). Their relations did not turn to amity until Britain finally conceded regional hegemony of the Western Hemisphere to the United States after settling the border dispute between Venezuela and British Guiana in 1899. Although Britain and the United States featured liberal values and institutions in the nineteenth century, it would be a stretch to call them democracies, as universal suffrage (such as voting rights for women and minorities) and competitive elections were not introduced until much later. As for the argument of shared cultural heritage, such affinity did not stop the Austro-Prussian War and, more recently, the Korean and Vietnam Wars and tension across the Taiwan Strait. It also did not prevent the US Civil War. A moment's reflection reminds us that some of the most devastating wars were fought among Europeans who are supposed to belong to the same cultural family (Huntington 1996). Therefore, cultural affinity is clearly not a sufficient condition for amicable relations. It seems also not to be a necessary condition, such as evidenced by the close political and military ties between Japan and the United States today (as well as such "strange bedfellows" as the United States and its allies Pakistan and Saudi Arabia).

We have also seen other instances of peaceful power transition in the recent past if we are willing to consider such power shifts beyond just the two most powerful countries in the world. Both power-transition theorists and proponents of Thucydides's Trap in fact consider such cases in their analysis (e.g., Allison 2017; Organski and Kugler 1980). For instance, the two world wars—which they consider to be instances supporting their proposition—did not actually involve a change in the relative positions of the world's two most powerful states (namely, the United States and Britain), but rather pertained to Germany (which never caught up to the United States in its power) approaching Britain in only certain aspects of power measurement (Germany did not overtake Britain economically and certainly not the overall power of the British Empire). Allison (2017) includes among his case files an instance of peaceful power transition from the 1990s to "the present," citing the overtaking of Britain and France as ruling states by Germany as a rising state. Setting aside the question of whether Britain and France can still be considered ruling states as late as 2017, we can perhaps apply his logic to consider Japan's overtaking (economically at least) of these same countries, as well as Russia, as instances of peaceful power transition. Moreover, since China's more recent overtaking of Japan (as well as Britain, France, and Russia) to become the world's second largest economy, there are in fact quite a few instances of peaceful power transition which would weaken the claim of Thucydides's Trap.

In addition to these cases of peaceful power transition, we have also encountered episodes when states have resorted to war and military conquest to alter the existing international distribution of power. Germany and Japan's hegemonic bids were defeated in both world wars. Although the contest between the United States and the Soviet Union did not escalate to a hot war, it ended with the latter country's ignominious collapse and disintegration. Presumably, Chinese leaders and scholars are not oblivious to these countries' experiences and they will try to learn from them (Kirshner 2012). Although we do not deny the influence of structural forces in shaping and constraining officials' range of feasible policies, we also believe that it is important not to dismiss human agency and people's capacity to learn from the past and to avoid repeating the same mistakes that were committed by others. Officials are, after all, not automata simply responding to external pressures. Goddard (2020: 175) states that "given the cost of great power war, power shifts between the United States and China are unlikely to end in war (at least intentionally)." Structural forces do not determine that history will repeat itself. War occurrences are not decided by the alignment of stars, but by people's decisions. Thus, in the words of MacDonald and Parent (2020: 179), "Contra Allison, the United States and China are not trapped in the same old story of war and change; they remain coauthors of their future." Recent scholarship has shown rather compellingly that power transitions do not necessarily augur war (e.g., Chan 2020a, 2020b; Goddard 2018; Kang 2007, 2010; MacDonald and Parent 2018; Schake 2017; Shifrinson 2018).

In our view, Beijing has at least thus far avoided some of the traditional practices of "strategic states" (Rosecrance 1986), such as seeking military allies and protégés abroad, deploying troops and establishing military bases overseas, or competing for political influence in regions long dominated by the United States (Western Europe, the Middle East, and the Western Hemisphere). Although China's defense spending has increased rapidly in recent decades, it is still far behind that of the United States, which had outspent the combined military expenditures of the next eleven highest countries in 2019. Thus, we also do not see Beijing's defense spending as an attempt to engage the United States in an armament race; it rather represents more of an effort to hinder and impede US air and naval access to China's coast, where its economy is concentrated. Schwarz (2005: 27) remarks,

> Hardliners and moderates, Republicans and Democrats, agree that America is strategically dominant in East Asia and the eastern Pacific—China's backyard. They further agree that America should retain its dominance there. Thus U.S. military planners define as a threat Beijing's efforts to remedy its own weak position in the face of overwhelming superiority that they acknowledge the United States holds right up to the edge of the Asian mainland. This probably reveals more about our ambitions than it does about China's. Imagine if the situation is reversed, and China's air and naval power were a dominant and potentially menacing presence on the coastal shelf of North America. Wouldn't we want to offset that preponderance?

Although there has been much publicity on China's supposed turn to a more assertive foreign policy, we agree with those who question this proposition (Jerden 2014; Johnston 2013). In fact, Beijing has been rather restrained in its practice of military coercion (Fravel 2012; Li 2012), and as we have remarked earlier, it has avoided any war since 1979, in contrast to the much higher incidence of US involvement in wars and militarized disputes. There is also a huge qualitative difference between China's alleged new "assertiveness" in the South China Sea and outright US invasion and occupation of Afghanistan and Iraq, its "quarantine" of Cuba, its overt and covert attempts to engineer regime change abroad, and its drone attacks to kill alleged terrorists.

Naturally, there is a wide range between the two polar positions of high optimism and extreme pessimism, where states can engage in a variety of efforts to change or defend the institutional arrangements and normative foundations of international order. Seen in this light of initiatives, responses, and interactions involving soft balancing, revisionism is not an uncommon behavior or policy practice in world politics. All states can manifest some degree or form of revisionist preferences in the sense of seeking to promote changes in international norms, rules, and institutions that would be more congenial to their values and interests. Our analysis seeks to understand better such efforts of soft revisionism that are more common occurrences than devastating systemic wars, and that can produce institutional evolutions even though they do not necessarily produce headline news because they often involve gradual, diffused changes involving incremental adjustments over time (Drezner 2019). Strategic competition and soft revisionism, in our view, do not necessarily augur conflict and war. How to manage the US-China competition in which both countries can undertake various (not mutually exclusive) strategies of soft revisionism and soft balancing appears to us an area deserving more attention from scholars and officials alike.

The remainder of this chapter has five parts. First, we review our criticisms of the existing literature. We argue that the concept of revisionism should not be used normatively to suggest a negative connotation in referring to a state or policy, and it should not be applied as a fixed dichotomy to describe states' motivations. We also discuss more extensively the nature, origin, and evolution of revisionism in the history of several great powers. We embed this discussion in the context of recent studies of revisionism, and we seek insights from them for our policy recommendations (to be presented later in the chapter). Second, we review our attempt to discern states' revisionist or status-quo intentions (or motivations) empirically and systematically. This effort compares China's conduct with that of the United States, and it also tracks these countries' words and deeds over time. Although we acknowledge that it is always difficult and even controversial to make inferences about intentions (and especially when trying to infer future intentions) from observed behavior, we argue that our multi-indicator and comparative approach improves on previous studies. Our conclusion from this approach suggests that China and the United States have traveled on different paths, with China becoming less revisionist and the United States more so over time.

Third, we discuss strategies of soft revisionism that seek to alter international order by non-military means. This discussion underscores our point that revisionism is not an aberrant motivation and that all states can be expected to engage in some attempts to promote changes that would align the norms, rules, and institutions of international order closer to their own values and interests. Fourth, we discuss ongoing power shifts between the United States and China in the context of prospect theory. This theory proposes that people tend to take more risks when they are in a domain of loss, attempting to arrest or recover from their setback. In contrast, people tend to be motivated by risk-aversion when in a domain of gain, behaving conservatively to preserve the gains they have already made. Fifth and finally, we propose three policy recommendations on how to manage the strategic competition between two revisionist powers: (1) the United States and China should maintain a nuclear balance to assure mutual deterrence; (2) the United States needs to avoid risky behavior driven by its strategic fear in a domain of loss; and (3) China needs to reassure the United States and resist overconfidence and nationalism at home. In conclusion, we discuss two dangerous scenarios—a possible hot war and a new Cold War—which can happen between the United States and China if the two countries fail to manage their strategic competition. This said, institutionalized competition between these two countries may still produce a peaceful transition of international order in the twenty-first century.

The Nature, Origin, and Evolution of Revisionism

Although revisionism has been featured prominently in discourse on international relations, especially that which concerns itself with the question of war and peace among great powers, until recently there has been relatively little work undertaken to clarify it conceptually or to study it empirically. Attributions of a state's revisionist or status-quo motivation or agenda have often been asserted rhetorically as a sign of approval or disapproval, rather than as an observation based on systematic and comparative evidence. Revisionism has also often been used to refer to a lesser power's attempt to improve its relative international position—that is, to refer to efforts aimed at enhancing this country's relative power, even though it is not similarly used when an already dominant country tries to extend even further its already preponderant position. We argue that revisionism should not be used to refer to attempts to alter the existing distribution of international power, and it should instead focus on efforts motivated by a desire to alter the existing international order, as intended originally by Organski and Kugler (1980), who developed power-transition theory.

This view in turn begs the question of what constitutes the "international order," a topic many analysts using the concept of revisionism have failed to confront. Our discussion of international order draws on the English school, and we introduce a norm-based dimension and a rule- or institution-based dimension of international order. We present furthermore a variety of empirical indicators to track and compare the evolution of Chinese and US foreign policy, and we show that these countries have shown different trajectories over time. While China's foreign policy agenda has become less revisionist, the United States has become more so. The evidence presented by our ensemble of indicators converges in strong support of this conclusion.

Revisionism stems from a state's dissatisfaction or frustration, caused by its feeling that it has been denied adequate benefits (including intangible benefits such as status) in accordance with its international position or capabilities. The intensity of this dissatisfaction or frustration can vary, and the desire to alter the existing international order and the extent of change being sought can also vary. Relative deprivation (Gurr 1972) is the basic source behind revisionism. This view conforms to the thesis presented by earlier scholars who studied international power shifts or transitions (e.g., Gilpin 1981; Organski 1958; Organski and Kugler 1980). They acknowledge forthrightly that the existing rules, principles, and institutions of international order have been rigged by the established powers to benefit themselves disproportionately and that these established powers would not easily accommodate the demands for adjustment by newcomers.

When a rising power encounters repeated denial of or resistance to its demands to adjust the allocation of benefits (including status), it experiences "status immobility" (Ward 2017). The larger the discrepancy between its self-perceived allocation of benefits and its self-perceived power standing (or accomplishments), the greater is its sense of dissatisfaction and frustration (Renshon 2017). Accumulated grievances over repeated denial of or resistance to its redistributive demands intensify a state's revisionist motivation. As just suggested, the feeling that its aspirations have been frustrated does not need to be limited to efforts to deny material gains to the rising power (such as refusing to sell sensitive technologies to it or subjecting it to economic sanctions), but can also be more symbolic (such as obstructing its representation in the United Nations or G7/G8 summitries, blocking its bid to host the Olympics, and urging others not to join the Asian Infrastructure Investment Bank). The "barriers to entry" faced by a rising power (or a re-emergent one such as Russia) could be construed by it to reflect discrimination based on racial, ideological, or "civilizational" prejudices (such as Turkey's inability to gain membership in the European Union). This remark should not be construed to deny that from the perspective of the established powers, the admission of newcomers to their ranks may be costly or unacceptable because these rising powers feature values and institutions incompatible with their own identities (Allan et al. 2018).

The converse of the logic just described is also important. Barring gross errors in misperception and misjudgment, a rising state does not have any incentive to go to war if the difference between the distribution of benefits and the distribution of power is small or nonexistent (Powell 1999). Going to war will not enable a state to improve its share of benefits if this share already reflects accurately that which is warranted by its relative power. War is rational only when a prospective belligerent expects that the outcome of fighting will improve its share of benefits—meaning that only if it believes that its current share of benefits is less than what its relative power (as demonstrated by its performance on the battlefield) would entitle it to.

This discussion implies that revisionist states are not just insane states that have an unlimited appetite for aggrandizement. There are, of course, undeniably megalomaniacal personalities like Napoleon and Hitler who seemed to be incapable of restraining themselves from lashing out repeatedly against their neighbors, thereby turning all of them into their enemies. Powell's observation reported earlier, however, argues that most leaders are sensible and deliberate. Because wars are risky and costly (Fearon 1995), officials would rather reach a deal to get what they want peacefully without incurring the risks and costs of fighting. Although misperception and miscalculation are ever-present dangers in making foreign policy, formal game theoretic logic suggests that it would be rational for leaders of rising latecomers to let ongoing trends further improve their bargaining position to demand additional benefits from their counterparts. Why should they not postpone a conflict (so that the ongoing trend will enable them to achieve a peaceful overtaking), and avoid becoming the target of a dominant country's preventive strike (Copeland 2000; Levy 1987)? A rising state may instead become more aggressive when its growth starts to slow (relative to its counterparts) or even reverse, such as when German leaders before both world wars believed that a window of opportunity for them to secure their regional dominance had begun to close.

Existing accounts often overlook the role of dominant powers in wars. Significantly, the desire for "standing"—or a higher international status, prestige, or *gloire*—can motivate already dominant states to wage war. Lebow (2010: 18) finds this motive to be by far the most common source of war fought by great powers—even more so than their ostensible security concerns. He reports that the pursuit of standing was present as a primary or secondary motivation in 62 of 94 wars involving great powers since 1648. As suggested by the preceding discussion, revisionism is also not just an inherent character of rising powers; the established powers' reaction to and treatment of newcomers also matters. Murray (2019: 79) writes,

> By constructing the rising power as an innately revisionist state whose power must be contained at all costs, the established powers disavow their own role in producing this unstable relationship so that the rising power is made to bear a disproportionate burden in facilitating the conditions necessary for cooperation. In doing this, the established powers' own arming decisions are rendered unproblematic and inconsequential in bringing about the adversarial relationship.

Whereas the existing literature usually stresses the increasing demands of a rising state for recognition (often treating accommodation and appeasement synonymously), it tends to overlook the political, institutional, and psychological reasons that cause the established powers to resist these demands. These states often decline to adjust their roles in international relations and to make the necessary concessions to newcomers in the wake of their diminished power. Why do they often refuse to accommodate or recognize newcomers, or if they do offer adjustments, why are these concessions often seen as inadequate and tardy?

For example, US policies to ostracize and contain China before the 1970s (long before China's recent rise) surely had something to do with Mao's radical agenda to promote worldwide revolution to challenge the capitalist world order and his decision to "lean to one side." US intervention in the Korean War and China's counter-intervention also had a profound legacy in freezing these countries' relations before the 1970s. As another example, US support for expanding NATO membership to include former members of the Warsaw Pact, its promotion of various color revolutions in Russia's near abroad, and its armed interventions against Serbia are an integral part of the explanation for the reversal of Gorbachev's "new thinking" and the recent escalation of Russo-American antagonism. Moscow believes that it has been belittled, disrespected, and dismissed by Washington (Krickovic 2018; Larson and Shevchenko 2019). Thus, revisionism tends to be the result of a process of action and reaction between rising and established powers. The origins of this process for China and Russia can be traced to at least the days of their respective civil wars, when established powers (including the United States) intervened on behalf of their opponents—and long before anyone can claim that these countries posed a threat to the established powers or, for that matter, to the existing international order.

Prevailing discourse in the West tends to be one-sided because it does not usually consider this historical origin of the antagonism between the so-called ruling and rising powers. It attributes the cause of this antagonism primarily, even sometimes exclusively, to a rising state's greed and ambition, without asking about the role that ruling states have played in contributing to this antagonism. It also often insinuates any challenge to international order and resort to armed violence to be an exclusive monopoly of rising powers, without considering how current or previous ruling powers (e.g., Portugal, the Netherlands, Britain, and the United States) were also once rising powers and how these counties had acted in their foreign relations to attain their positions of dominance. Moreover, this discourse often overlooks the impermanence of international dominance, as numerous powerful empires and hegemons have risen and fallen in history. As recently as 1820, China had the world's largest economy, but we all know that the Qing dynasty fell on hard times due to both internal decay and external predation. China was then the dominant power—albeit one that was declining rapidly—and it was victimized by rising powers like Japan, the United States, and the European states.

When contemporary Western commentators warn about possible conflicts between rising and ruling states, they rarely realize the irony suggested by China's encounters with Japan and the West when the roles were reversed for the respective states from that which given by current discourse on power transition or Thucydides's Trap. Wars waged by Japanese and Western imperialist powers against China rarely make an appearance in the chronicles and case files pertaining to power-transition theory, suggesting a severe selection bias in ransacking history for supportive evidence. Alternatively, when such consideration is given, it tends to be presented only as China having a "chip on its shoulder" because it harbors historical grievances. These narratives therefore tend to conveniently dismiss and ignore as unimportant or irrelevant that China has thus far not taken war to Britain, France, Japan, or the United States, whereas these other countries had brought their colonial and imperialist wars, as well as various other military encounters, on Chinese soil. In contrast, to our knowledge no hostile Chinese soldier has ever set foot on these countries' soil. The major exception to this generalization is, of course, the Korean War, fought at China's doorstep. Few have, however, considered the case if the shoe were on the other foot. What would Trump or, for that matter, any US president have done if an invading Chinese army were reaching the Mexican side of the Rio Grande?

A rising state seeks to secure its identity by demanding the established states' recognition of its status, but this demand may threaten the latter's own self-identity. This phenomenon was aptly and tragically demonstrated in imperial China's many encounters with the West, when the Chinese court showed repeatedly its hubris, vanity, haughty arrogance, and supreme self-confidence as the center of the civilized world. Murray (2019) emphasizes revisionism to be part of international relations' identity politics (Rousseau 2006). It is a social construct based on the social interactions between rising and established states. The outcome of a rising state's struggle for recognition depends on the established states' willingness to accept or rebuff this demand. Thus, revisionism as a concept is more than just a product of these states' changing material capabilities or a reflection of a rising state's inherent ambitions. In Murray's (2019: 8) words, "Misrecognized rising powers are viewed as a threat and interpreted to have revisionist intentions. Misrecognition, in short, constructs the revisionism that creates instability during power transitions. In these instances, the established powers respond with military buildups of their own to contain the rising state's increasing power and to mitigate their own growing social and material insecurity."

When is an established power inclined to accommodate or, alternatively, to resist a newcomer, thus intensifying the latter country's revisionist motivations? Scholars (e.g., Paul 2016a; Rock 1989) have mentioned geographic distance, cultural affinity, economic interdependence, and the presence of other rising powers that can mount an even more threatening challenge as possible factors contributing to the peaceful Anglo-American transition. That the United States did not pursue hard revisionism (at least not in its relations with Britain, although Washington surely did seek to institute its own rules and norms in the Western Hemisphere) had also something to do with Britain's diplomacy, which made timely and ample concessions to a rising United States (e.g., Kennedy

2010), so that London could confront the closer threat coming from Wilhelmine Germany. This avoidance of hard revisionism needs to be qualified, however. Washington had engaged in hardball diplomacy, including threats to go to war against Britain and Germany if it did not get its way. Of course, it did fight Spain, Mexico, and indigenous peoples in its westward expansion.

In the wake of their country's increased power, the elite and mass public of a rising state are likely to experience a "revolution of rising expectations" about their country's proper role and place in world affairs. How effectively leaders of a rising state manage these expectations is also important in determining whether it adopts hard revisionism. Sometimes, these leaders—such as Russia's in the Crimean War—can overplay their hand, that is, demanding a role or status that exceeds their country's actual capabilities (e.g., Wohlforth 2009). Such overreach can be a cause for crisis and conflict, as can be a failure by the established states caught in relative decline to trim their overseas commitments and downsize their international profile (Kennedy 1987). Sometimes a rising state may respond to domestic pressure groups out of political expediency, such as Berlin's *Weltpolitik* and its decision to seek colonial expansion and build a *Hochseeflotten* (a "high sea" battlefleet) before 1914. These decisions caused a blowback from Britain, deepening these countries' mutual distrust and intensifying their rivalry. The influence of domestic politics in fueling international conflict is likely to be more important than power shifts among great powers. For example, Snyder (1993) has shown the role played by domestic political logrolling in imperial Germany and Japan in promoting these countries' expansionist policies, and Colaresi (2005) has studied how domestic partisan competition can encourage "scare politics" that appeal to people's nationalist impulses by confronting and even creating foreign enemies.

With China's recent rise, its leaders will almost certainly encounter more insistent demands from the mass public to undertake a more assertive foreign policy to redress this country's past humiliations and to restore its rightful place in the world. This remark suggests that democratization—or at least increasing popular input in the Chinese policy process—can in fact cause Beijing to become more bellicose. Concomitantly, China's rising power will inevitably cause concern and even worry among its neighbors and the United States. These two concurrent developments—rising aspirations on the part of a more influential domestic public *pushing* for more assertive policies, and increasing alarm on the part of other countries *pulling* China into more tense confrontations abroad—combine to reduce the policy space available to Chinese leaders. Note also that these two developments are not separate from each other; they can reinforce and feed on each other so that foreign pushback intensifies domestic demand for a more assertive foreign policy, which in turn causes more foreign resistance and opposition.

As just described in the preceding paragraphs, foreign and domestic pressures can interact to produce more crises and conflicts. Domestic politics in the established states, such as racist US legislations in the 1920s to limit Japanese immigration and to bar Japanese-Americans from owning land, can also affect political discourse in Japan and alter this discourse in a direction favoring advocates of hard revisionism (Ward 2017). The tendency to scapegoat foreigners and to blame China for the loss of American manufacturing jobs can similarly have a blowback effect in China, giving sustenance to Chinese hardliners who argue that the United States is seeking to block China's rise. In this way, nationalists in both countries can feed on the other side's rhetoric and conduct to create an echo chamber of increasing recrimination and hostility. Recently, Democrats and Republicans alike seem to have settled on "standing up against" China as a strategy to mobilize voters, even though they can agree on little else. Domestic partisan politics can thus push countries into foreign conflicts. At the same time, alliance commitments can pull them into these conflicts. In the lead-up to the Peloponnesian War and World War I, leaders of the belligerent countries believed that if they did not support their ally (e.g., Corinth for Sparta, Austria-Hungary for Germany, and Serbia for Russia), they would suffer irreparable damage to their reputation for resolve and an irreversible setback in their power position in interstate relations.

According to the prevailing discourse, some countries became revisionists (e.g., Germany, the Soviet Union), but others did not (the United States in the late 1800s and Japan and Germany in the late 1900s). What could account for these differences? As already mentioned, Britain's policy of accommodation appears to have made an important difference in the US case. But was there something inherent about US domestic politics and its foreign policy pursuits that would distinguish this country's foreign conduct from, say, Japanese and German conduct during the interwar years, when they supposedly turned increasingly to hard revisionism? All these countries were expansionist powers. So, what would qualify the United States as a status-quo state during the period between roughly the end of its civil war and the start of World War I? Significantly, even though isolationism has been used to describe its foreign policy during this period, Washington was far from inactive, as it had undertaken repeated military interventions in the Western Hemisphere, waged wars against Mexico and Spain, and sought to "open" Japan and China as well as to colonize the Philippines. In our view, such acts of aggrandizement and expansion do not necessarily indicate revisionism, which should instead refer to whether the conduct in question violated the prevailing "rules of the game" at the time. (Sovereignty or, for that matter, self-determination, such as enunciated by President Woodrow Wilson's Fourteen Points after World War I, did not apply to non-Europeans who were victimized during the age of colonialism and imperialism; armed conquest was routinely practiced by great powers before 1945.) As we have argued, ruling or established states have typically reached their position of dominance and privilege by resorting to such aggrandizement and expansion. These remarks, of course, do not mean that we condone such aggrandizement and expansion. As we have argued before, the nature of international order and thus "the rules of the game" are a matter of contestation and are always evolving. It is also true that there is a considerable amount of hypocrisy and double standards in the manner in which prevailing discourse presents the conduct of today's established powers.

If the source of a rising power's discontent and dissatisfaction stems from its belief that it has been denied its share of international benefits as befitting its power and accomplishments, the same logic can also be applied to the ruling hegemon. If this dominant power feels that it is under-appreciated or under-recognized, it can also seek to change the existing rules of the game. When this hegemon commands overwhelming power relative to the rest of the world, other countries are less able or unable to resist its demands. This observation in turn suggests that overwhelming power alone, and not necessarily any fear of or concern about a potential threat coming from a rising power, can interact with a dominant state's normative values and political impulses to motivate it to introduce new norms or rules. This happened, for example, when the United States took the leading role in instituting new standards of international conduct (with respect to crimes against peace and humanity) at the Nuremberg Trials. Another example is provided by the George W. Bush administration's propagation of the doctrine of preventive war to justify its invasion of Iraq in 2003. These examples naturally question the current literature's tendency to claim that the incumbent hegemon is *necessarily* a status-quo power committed to the defense of the existing "rules of the game" (Lind and Wohlforth 2019).

As just suggested, revisionism can emerge not only from pressures; it can also stem from opportunities, both domestically and internationally—or a combination of pressures and opportunities. When the United States became the world's only superpower after the Cold War, it sought to rewrite the rules and principles of international order, for example, with respect to military intervention to promote regime change abroad and to wage preventive war against alleged future threats. Such revisionism can be an opportunistic response to having gained more international power (such as after the demise of the Soviet Union) and domestic political support (such as popular approval of the Bush administration after the 9/11 terrorist attack).

Systematic Evidence to Track and Compare Revisionism

We have sought in this book not only to clarify the concept of revisionism and to analyze historical cases of revisionism, but also to engage in the search for systematic evidence to discern states' revisionist motivations and agendas. How can we recognize a status-quo country and distinguish it from a revisionist one before a conflict occurs, rather than making this designation only after we have learned the peaceful or violent outcome of a power transition? We would want to avoid post hoc rationalization and revisionist history based on our knowledge of who fought whom and the identity of winners and losers in systemic wars. Comparing Japanese, German, and US behavior before World War I, one would be hard pressed to argue that the United States was more committed to the international order (or, for that matter, the existing international distribution of power) than the other two countries. Ironically, if anything, Japanese leaders from the time of Meiji Restoration had tried to imitate Western customs and copy Western institutions so that their country could/would be accepted among the ranks of "civilized" nations. Moreover, and ironically, Wilhelmine Germany was once held by many Americans—including President Woodrow Wilson—as the paragon of an efficient bureaucratic state, a model of constitutional monarchy, and an emblem of the rule of law (Oren 2003). It was only with the approaching war that the US image of Germany changed. Similarly, Anglo-American relations during much of the 1800s are nowadays typically depicted as amicable, even though they were quite contentious. On at least two occasions these countries almost came to exchanging blows (Layne 1994). Unfortunately, international relations discourse, including the designation of revisionist and status-quo states, often reflects retrospective political construction rather than objective analysis (Pan 2012).

There have been several prior attempts to assess China's revisionism (e.g., Chan 2004b, 2016; Chan et al. 2019; Feng 2009; Johnston 2003; Kastner and Saunders 2012; Khong 2013/2014; Womack 2015). But in contrast to most of these studies, we have pursued in this book a comparative approach, one that juxtaposes Beijing's words and deeds with those of its international counterparts, especially Washington. We emphasize this feature because obviously we cannot declare a country to be revisionist or status-quo oriented without some benchmark based on other countries' conduct or, for that matter, without considering the context provided by its own past behavior (that is, by inquiring how much its behavior has changed over time). We have introduced a variety of indicators, such as Beijing and Washington's public rhetoric about the legitimate use of force and promotion of regime change, their professed adherence to traditional norms with respect to sovereignty and sphere of influence, their participation in and engagement with international institutions, their accession to international accords and conventions, and the alignment of their respective voting positions in the United Nations with this organization's other member states. These indicators can be generally grouped to reflect two dimensions of international order—those referred to by He and Feng (2020) as norm-based and rule- or institution-based aspects of this order.

We have also tried to assess Beijing and Washington's external political and economic orientations by examining their leaders' travels to other countries and their commercial relations with other countries. For instance, do these data show that China has tended to align itself with countries that have been described, at least in the Western media, as rogue states, such as Iran, North Korea, Syria, Sudan, Zimbabwe, Burma, and Venezuela, such that one may argue that Beijing is in the process of forming an anti-Western or anti-US coalition? Alternatively, do China's profiles with respect to its leaders' foreign trips and its overseas trade and foreign investment point to a strong and, in some cases, an increasing emphasis on relations with established powers such as Britain, France, Germany, and, of course, the United States? Similarly, what conclusions can we draw from indicators such as UN roll call votes? Has China or the United States become more out of step with the international community, finding itself increasingly outside of emerging international consensus on a variety of issues? We can make similar assessments based on these countries' respective decisions to join or remain in international organizations and accords, or to leave and abandon them.

Three features of our analysis are noteworthy. First, we compare China—currently, the most obvious rising power that can potentially challenge the existing international order—with other countries from the ranks of both established and (re)emergent powers. In contrast, most existing studies tend to examine China in isolation, that is, without any concern to determine how Beijing's words and deeds compare with those of its international counterparts. We therefore try to improve on existing studies by making explicit comparisons between China and other countries to assess the extent of their *relative* revisionism or status-quo commitment. After all, as professors we do not give a test to only one student while exempting the rest of class before we assign grades to our students.

Second, we try to track changes in each of the pertinent country's revisionist or status-quo orientation. Do our indicators suggest that China has become more revisionist as it gains more power, or, conversely, has it shown a greater status-quo orientation over time? Similarly, what trends, if any, can we discern for the United States? These questions address important theoretical questions. For example, as a rising power gains increasing stature and capability, should we expect its foreign policy orientation to be influenced by the logic of more intense competition brought on by the prospect of power transition, or, alternatively, should we expect this orientation to increasingly manifest the effects of socialization due to this country's greater incorporation into the existing international community and its integration into the existing international institutions? As for the established powers, including the incumbent hegemon, do their foreign policy orientations suggest an increasing disenchantment with and a decreasing commitment to existing international norms and institutions as they experience a relative decline in their stature and capability? Or do they remain committed to the existing international order despite the erosion of their international position? Our assessments are based on benchmarks established by a country's own conduct at a prior time and, of course, the contemporaneous conduct of its counterparts. Naturally, the time to tell whether a country is really as committed to the rules of international order as it professes is when these rules seem not to serve its interests as well as previously. It is easy to proclaim one's commitment to the international order when one is reaping large and disproportionate benefits from it. Whether this proclamation is made by a fair weather supporter becomes clearer if it continues this commitment when its benefits begin to fall.

Third, we rely on multiple indicators to gauge China's and its international peers' revisionist or status-quo orientations. We recognize that each individual indicator may be imperfect, but we seek to overcome this limitation by emphasizing the collective import of our evidence. We try to be transparent and systematic in interpreting this evidence, so that other analysts may be able to suggest how our data and analysis may be improved. To the extent that data of different kinds and from different sources point to the same general conclusion, we gain more confidence in the validity of our conclusion.

Our analysis in Chapter 3 shows that while China has become more embedded in multilateral diplomacy and has altered its policy positions to become more aligned with the prevailing global consensus, the United States has moved in the opposite direction in recent decades. Indications from a variety of evidence point rather consistently to Beijing's increasing integration into the international community and Washington's increasing alienation from it. China has changed from its revolutionary stance and from its political and economic isolation during the first two and half decades of the People's Republic and has now become an active participant in various international organizations. Conversely, and especially since the advent of the Trump administration (but certainly also predating this administration), the United States has withdrawn from many multilateral institutions and has increasingly voiced its discontent with the views endorsed and shared by most other states. For example, it is the lone holdout against the Paris climate accord (until Biden reversed Trump's decision to withdraw from it), one of only two countries that have not joined the Basel Convention regulating the cross-border shipment of plastic waste, and among a small minority that have stayed out of the United Nations Convention on the Law of the Sea and, along with China, the International Criminal Court. As shown in the book's Appendix, the United States has declined to ratify some international conventions and treaties after many *decades* of delay. Even on issues that Washington has declared to be especially important to its foreign policy, it has found itself frequently in the minority in roll call votes in the United Nations. In contrast, Beijing is much more likely to be in the voting majority.

Evidence such as those just mentioned should be common knowledge among scholars who study international relations and especially specialists on Chinese and US foreign policy. It has led a number of these analysts to consider the United States to be more a "revisionist" state and/or China more of a "status-quo" one, or at least not a "revisionist" one (e.g., Breslin 2010; Ding 2010; Hurd 2007; Ikenberry 2017a; Jervis 2003; Johnston 2003; Lind 2017; Qin 2010; Schweller 2015; Walt 2005; Wilson 2019; Xiang 2001). Because this body of evidence seems rather conclusive to us, we are puzzled by the still widely held view suggesting the opposite, including the Trump administration's official designation of China and Russia as "revisionist powers" in the US National Security Strategy document published in December 2017 (White House 2017). The meme that China violates "rule-based order" has surged on the internet since then (Breuer and Johnston 2019), crowding out alternative views of this country. This prevailing view among Western commentators and the lay public reflects Gramsci's (1971) observation about the influence of hegemonic ideas whose power can persist in the absence of strong evidence and even in the presence of contrary evidence. It also reminds us of the debate about "China's new assertiveness." This narrative of a supposed turn in Chinese foreign policy toward a more confrontational and aggressive stance during 2009–2010 went unchallenged among experts of Chinese foreign policy, and its popularity suggests the grip of orthodoxy and the highly politicized nature of scholarship on China (Jerden 2014; Johnson 2013). Significantly, much of the existing literature treats international conflicts as a matter of material contest while overlooking the social basis and nature of such interactions. Murray (2019) warns that by neglecting the latter considerations, current discussions reflecting a bifurcated US policy approach toward China (engagement versus containment) can be seriously flawed.

Revisionists' Strategies

Challenging the dichotomous view of "status quo" versus revisionism, we develop behavioral measures of revisionism which, we emphasize, are a matter of degree both relative to a country's own past and to its counterparts' conduct. This evidence suggests to us that all states, including the United States and China, can be revisionist with respect to certain issue areas and in certain contexts (Foot and Walter 2011; Johnston 2019). Our ensemble of indicators also suggests that while a rising China has become less revisionist, a declining United States has become more so. Both countries challenge some domains of the international order while supporting others. As we have said earlier, states can be expected to play both offense and defense in their foreign policy. In our view, international order is a multifaceted concept, and its components are in constant flux and can even be in contradiction with one another. Thus, this order is evolutionary and is being constantly negotiated and renegotiated. It should not be taken as a settled matter whereby states can be assessed to be either in support of or in opposition to it. Moreover, in our view, the mere rise and fall of material capabilities due to the different rates of growth among states cannot be taken as the standard to measure revisionism so long as states do not challenge the key tenets of international order—the existing institutional arrangements that shape and guide their interactions as well as their views on mutual adjustment and accommodation in operating in the international system.

There are two types of international institutions: primary institutions and secondary institutions (Buzan 2004b, 2018). While primary institutions refer to the widely accepted norms and principles that constitute the international system's foundation governing interstate relations, secondary institutions—consisting of intergovernmental organizations, treaties, and agreements—are the major domains of interactions among states, including revisionist ones. We have studied data on Chinese and US treaties. This information presents a glimpse of these countries' evolving attitudes toward and relations to the secondary institutions of international order. States can rely on both hard and soft revisionist strategies to alter the existing institutional order. Hard revisionism based on the exercise of military power is more likely to cause conflict. In contrast, soft revisionism relies on institutional strategies, and it promises to be more peaceful in introducing transitions of international order.

Two factors—perceived benefits from the existing institutions and comparative advantage in the institution-related issue area—shape a state's different preferences for its soft revisionist strategies in dealing with institutions. If a state enjoys a comparative advantage and perceives a high level of benefits from an existing international institution, it is more likely to pursue a strategy of institutional reform to revise the rules and procedures inside the existing institution. However, when a state perceives low benefits or a significant decline in these benefits from the current institution, a strong comparative advantage will encourage it to choose a strategy of competition by creating an alternative institution, which can not only challenge the relevance and legitimacy of the existing institution, but also enable this revisionist state to better pursue its interests. Naturally, the two variables just mentioned are not simply traits that inhere in individual states. They reflect instead a state's position in its relations with others and are therefore situational. A state's strategic choice is naturally also contingent on its expectation of other states' likely reactions, and this choice is therefore again not likely to be made without regard to its anticipation of how others will respond to its actions.

When a state does not enjoy a comparative advantage in a specific issue area, its perceived benefits from an existing institution will prevent it from leaving the institution. This state is more likely to use the institution's rules and procedures to block or obstruct any initiative that in its judgment can potentially harm its interests. However, if the perceived benefits from the existing institution are perceived to be low or declining significantly, this state is more likely to adopt an exit strategy to withdraw from it. This option will enable it to escape the potential constraints of the existing institution and, concomitantly, its departure will undermine the legitimacy and relevance of this institution.

All states are likely to harbor some revisionist intentions in the sense that they can all be expected to act in a way that would bring the ordering rules and principles of international relations and shared expectations and standards of behavior into closer alignment with their own values and interests. However, not all states have the capability or willingness to mount a revisionist challenge. Both the United States and China are large beneficiaries of the existing international order. As great powers, they also possess the greatest capability to alter this order. How their revisionism tends to be manifested is likely to be determined by the interplay of these variables.

As mentioned before, the current literature tends to focus on a rising power's increased capability to challenge the existing order without, however, giving enough recognition to the fact that it is now drawing a larger share of benefits from this order and it should therefore be less motivated to undermine this order. Conversely, a declining hegemon may become more dissatisfied with this order and may demand that this order be altered because its share of benefits has declined. It should accordingly have a smaller incentive to defend the existing order and a stronger motivation to seek this order's revision. As the incumbent hegemon, this state can also be expected to continue to command large comparative advantages in many important issue areas and in many forums, although its influence in other issue areas and forums can be greatly attenuated. The Trump administration's decision to reduce US financial contribution to the expenses of maintaining NATO as an organization and its efforts to pressure its allies (including non-NATO allies such as Japan and South Korea) to pay more for US military protection are illustrative of a strategy of institutional reform when a state perceives itself to be still receiving important benefits and commanding a significant comparative advantage. This situation also seems to fit with the Trump administration's demand to renegotiate the North American Free Trade Agreement. When an incumbent hegemon finds itself facing an institution, forum, or situation with diminished benefits and mounting constraints and, at the same time, perceives itself to be in an isolated position with reduced influence and attenuated comparative advantage, an exit strategy is likely to be adopted. This rationale seems to explain the Trump administration's decisions to leave the Iran nuclear deal, the Paris climate accord, the Trans-Pacific Partnership (TPP), and the United Nations Human Rights Council, as well as some other institutions affiliated with the United Nations, such as the World

Health Organization. Parenthetically, after the United States withdrew from the TPP, member states of ASEAN joined Australia, China, Japan, New Zealand, and South Korea in November 2020 to sign the Regional Comprehensive Economic Partnership (RCEP), the largest trade pact in the world.

As we have argued before, international outcomes can rarely be determined unilaterally by a single state, even a dominant one (although dominance obviously means the ability to have more influence). Other states also have a vote in influencing these outcomes. When both the ruling and rising states adopt soft revisionist strategies, their interactions promise to be more peaceful, although not without discord and rivalry. Conversely, the danger of war rises when both sides adopt hard revisionist strategies that abet and involve competing in armament races, building rival alliances, challenging the other great power's traditional sphere of influence, and initiating recurrent crises and militarized disputes. These actions contribute to creating a dangerous combination in the presence of a real or perceived power transition, making an armed collision more likely (Thompson 2003). But what about situations in which one state in a dyad pursues a soft strategy and the other adopts a hard one?

In one possible scenario, a rising state chooses hard revisionism, but a ruling state decides to adopt soft revisionism. In an alternative scenario, a rising state pursues soft revisionism, but a ruling (or stronger) state undertakes hard revisionism. The former situation comes close to describing the hard-line policies adopted by Washington in demanding London's recognition of its primacy in the Western Hemisphere in the late 1800s, and London's eventual decision to appease Washington and to accommodate US hegemony in this region (Bourne 1967; Layne 1994; Kennedy 2010; Rock 1989, 2000). The latter situation resembles the preventive war launched by Germany against Russia/the Soviet Union in 1914 and again in 1941. Both Wilhelmine/Nazi Germany and Czarist Russia/the Soviet Union were, of course, rising powers at that time (we have, however, distinguished Wilhelmine Germany from Nazi Germany and Czarist Russia from the Soviet Union in our earlier discussion on whether they should all be considered revisionist). Russia/the Soviet Union, however, sought appeasement to avoid a premature confrontation so that it could buy time to further develop its strength. German leaders, however, felt pressure from a closing window of opportunity and decided on both occasions to start a preventive war against a rival that was expected to become stronger and thus able to more effectively challenge its dominant position in the future.

Prospect Theory and Its Implications

What steps would help to alleviate anxieties that typically accompany large changes in interstate power relations? Which reassurance gestures would be credible, and which signals would be dismissed as insincere and may even be interpreted as a sign of weakness? What are the likely red lines for both sides? And how can domestic politics confuse interstate communication, compound distrust, and create echo chambers that further entrench and deepen mutual attributions of malevolence (Chan 2017)? Conversely, how can each side undertake policies that can help to relax a counterpart's domestic political pressures, facilitate its coalition politics to reduce the danger of confrontation, and provide feasible exit options for its leaders to defuse crises without losing face or credibility domestically and internationally (Quek and Johnston 2017/2018)? We confess that we do not have all the answers to these questions, but we do have some general ideas about feasible, appropriate, and prudent policy.

We start from the position that whether China—or for that matter, the United States—will be a revisionist or status-quo power is not in the stars, but rather in the hands of their government officials and opinion leaders. Whether these individuals have the requisite acumen to play skillfully "two-level games" (Putnam 1988) with concurrent attention to domestic and international conditions and consequences will hold the key to their successful management of mutual expectations. For instance, can one country's policies inadvertently cause its counterpart's leaders to be put in a domain of loss in domestic politics, thereby increasing the danger of conflict escalation (He 2016a; He and Feng 2013)? To put matters starkly in the context of rising Chinese capabilities, Beijing's leaders will have to navigate adroitly between the inevitable Scylla of escalating popular aspirations for an elevated international status and the concomitant Charybdis of mounting foreign apprehensions and even alarm about the emergence of an excessively ambitious and hence dangerous challenger to the international order.

Our views are especially informed by prospect theory (Boettcher 2005; He 2016a; Kahneman and Tversky 1979; McDermott 1998). A key insight of this theory suggests that when people—and by implication, states—see themselves in a domain of loss, they are likely to be more willing to take risks to avoid prospective losses or to gamble to recover losses already suffered. Conversely, when they see themselves in a domain of gain, they are likely to act cautiously or conservatively. Put differently, states will run greater risks to maintain their position than to improve their position. This view is significant because it expects a country experiencing relative decline (or one that expects to experience such decline) to be more inclined to undertake risky policies to reverse its recent (or impending) setback, whereas a country making relative gains will be more risk-averse. This proposition of course points in an opposite direction from those narratives based on offensive realism and power-transition theory. As a rising state, China has more to fear from the United States as the incumbent hegemon, a country that still holds an overwhelming advantage in relative power but one that is also undergoing an erosion in its dominant position.

The logic of prospect theory suggests that at this point, compared to China, the United States is more likely to be aggressive and assertive in pushing its demands and more inclined to practice brinksmanship in its diplomacy. It is also important to note that prospect theory offers a proposition contrary to power-transition theory. As long as China continues to grow, it is likely to postpone its demand for immediate and full status satisfaction and other concessions for tangible and intangible resources. It is likely to act cautiously and even modestly in the belief that time is on its side and its bargaining position will improve over time. However, if China's growth starts to stall and it faces an imminent decline (absolutely or relative to its peers), Beijing's policies can be expected to become more aggressive and assertive. In short, contrary to power-transition theory, we can expect a declining China to become more bellicose, whereas a growing China can be predicted to be a more satisfied country (all else being equal) and one that is more reluctant to destabilize international relations or challenge international order.

As just alluded to, the determination of a state's motivation is a basic concern of prospect theory. Is it motivated by a sense of insecurity (to prevent or recover from losses) or greed (to acquire additional gains)? Is it responding to vulnerability or opportunity? These questions require the analyst to understand the pertinent leaders' reference point, which determines whether they perceive themselves to be in the domain of gain or loss. Different policy implications follow from this distinction (e.g., Davis 2000; Levy 1996). For instance, actions that subject one's counterpart to potential domestic political vulnerability or a loss of international reputation are likely to encounter more vigorous pushback. Similarly, a state would be willing to accept a larger amount of uncertainty and risks when confronting the possibility of losses than when contemplating the prospect of making gains. This observation in turn implies that threats are much less likely to be effective than promises when dealing with a counterpart which sees itself in the domain of loss. Even a highly credible threat suggesting serious repercussions may not work against a counterpart which is willing to accept great uncertainty and run large risks to prevent or reverse a significant loss—whereas a modicum of reassurances and rewards may be more effective in influencing its behavior (Davis 2000). This proposition in turn leads us to expect that a rising China will be more forthcoming with concessions in its disputes with the United States, such as in their recent rounds of trade negotiations.

As mentioned previously, differences in where countries have established their reference points can produce discrepant expectations and hence a source for their disagreements. Rising states readily shift their reference point to reflect their recent gains, whereas declining states are more reluctant to alter their reference point, which would require them to acknowledge their loss or setback. This resulting difference in timing can cause rising states to become aggrieved because they do not feel that their accomplishments have been quickly and fully recognized and respected by other countries. Conversely, delays on the part of declining states to adjust their self-appointed roles and self-identities in international relations can incline them to be less willing to accommodate newcomers and to commit the error of imperial overstretching (when their overseas commitments outstrip their available resources)

The logic of prospect theory suggests that it would require a greater amount of deterrence to prevent the United States from taking reckless action because as a declining hegemon, it is in a domain of (actual or prospective) loss and should be therefore more disposed to adopt risky policies that can precipitate a crisis or confrontation than China, which, as a rising latecomer, is in a domain of gain and should therefore be more risk averse. One can try to infer the likely policy disposition of countries by another line of reasoning. As the strongest country in the world, it would take a massive countervailing coalition to restrain the United States. This countervailing coalition is less likely to form in a unipolar era, because its prospective members would face the threat of formidable retribution from a powerful hegemon and they can be "picked off" by it before this coalition has had a chance to develop (Brooks and Wohlforth 2005; Ikenberry et al. 2009; Jervis 2009). Given its immense power, the United States as the incumbent dominant power does not have to place its trust in other countries' reassurances. It can instead resort to unilateral action to, say, nullify the possibility of any nuclear threat coming from Iraq or North Korea, instead of having to rely on their leaders' promises. As Kydd (2005) has remarked, the more powerful a country is, the more demanding it will be in insisting on proof that a counterpart's promises are credible. This proposition suggests that, everything else being equal, it will require a greater amount of reassurance to convince the United States simply because it commands overwhelming power to take matters into its own hands. Thus, ironically, even though reassurances should be more effective than deterrence or threats when dealing with a state in decline, the threshold for a very powerful country like the United States to accept reassurances from other states will be higher than for China and other less powerful countries. These latter states will necessarily have to accept greater uncertainties in their foreign relations, because they lack comparable capabilities to act unilaterally to assuage their doubts about the sincerity or reliability of other countries' leaders.

As another example of a policy implication from prospect theory, the so-called endowment effect suggests that it would be more difficult to reverse gains already made by a counterpart than to negotiate concessions by it to forgo some future gains. In addition, efforts intended to compel a counterpart to cease an ongoing policy or action are more difficult to undertake and less likely to succeed than efforts seeking to prevent this policy or action in the first place. Furthermore, coercive policies are more likely to fail in the wake of prior successes because its repetition will place a counterpart in a situation of even larger losses and will thus provoke even more strenuous resistance and greater risk-taking from it. This last observation runs counter to the advice that one should continue an approach, such as coercive diplomacy, that has worked in the past. For example, on the eve of World War I, Russian leaders decided to stand firm even though, and indeed precisely because, they had yielded to German pressure on prior occasions involving crises in the Balkans; they feared that further concessions would irreparably harm their reputation (Levy and Mulligan 2017). Similar reasoning would lead one to expect that despite prior successes of US policy of extended deterrence, if there should be another episode of Beijing resorting to armed coercion against Taiwan, this US policy will be *less* effective because, having suffered prior setbacks, Chinese leaders would not have initiated another encounter unless they were more optimistic about its outcome *and* more resolved to avoid another setback which would further compound their reputation cost (Chan 2014).

Finally, conflict can stem from the tendency for people (and states) to update their reference point quickly when they are in the domain of gain, while their counterpart in the domain of loss resists making this cognitive shift. Because people have difficulty coming to terms with their losses, this temporal discrepancy (that the adjustment to a new reference point by the side suffering loss tends to occur only belatedly and reluctantly, in contrast to the side making gain) suggests another important source of conflict. That declining states fail to adjust their reference point quickly for psychological reasons reinforces the tendency for bureaucratic inertia and ideological rigidity to perpetuate a state's inflated view of its own role and importance in international relations, causing it to fail to downsize its international mission and reduce its commitments abroad when suffering a decline in its power. A state's imperial overstretching (Kennedy 1987) can thus continue for a long time, even though the accumulating evidence pointing to the deleterious effects of this policy and to a process of precipitous and persistent decline should be evident to its leaders for some considerable amount of time, such as in the case of Soviet leaders before Mikhail Gorbachev.

Promises are likely to be more effective than threats against a counterpart caught in the domain of loss. Given this counterpart's strong motivation to avoid loss, even a modest amount of enticement will have a significant impact on it. In contrast, it would require a much greater amount of coercion to achieve the same impact—indeed, such coercion could cause even greater prospective loss for this counterpart and thus incline it to adopt even more desperate and dangerous actions in response in its effort to avert this occurrence. Naturally, as already mentioned, this coercion will be more difficult to succeed if it seeks to compel this counterpart to stop a current policy or to surrender gains already made than if it seeks to only prevent this counterpart from taking some possible undesirable action in the future. Moreover, everything else being equal, deterring a counterpart in the domain of loss will be more difficult than one that is in the domain of gain. Thus, rather than curtailing imperial Japan's aggression, the US strategic embargo denying vital raw material to that country made its leaders more fearful, desperate, and acceptant of great risks to extricate themselves from their acute resource predicament, disposing them to gamble their nation's fate on attacking the United States at Pearl Harbor—even when they realized that their country was eight or nine times weaker than the United States (Russett 1969).

If both parties to a relationship, such as China and the United States, are status-quo powers, they should reassure each other that they will "play nice." As it should have become abundantly clear by now, by "status quo" and "playing nice" we have in mind conforming to the prevailing "rules of the game." We do *not* mean by these terms a commitment to not alter the current interstate distribution of power. As Gilpin (1981) has observed, different rates of growth are constantly causing power shifts among states, causing some of them to make relative gain and others to suffer relative decline. It is difficult, even impossible, to imagine that we can freeze the interstate distribution of power to preserve it as "*the* status quo." As power-transition theorists make clear, the determinants of national growth tend to be located inside each country, and international conditions play only a relatively small role in determining this growth compared to the influence of domestic factors. It should be obvious that when we ask a state to be a "responsible stakeholder," we do not mean that it should foreswear prospective future growth and submit to the perpetuation of its current (subordinate) position in the international hierarchy.

"Status-quo" states, even soft revisionist states, should then reassure each other that they would abide by the prevailing international order and not seek to alter its rules and norms by violent, unilateral action. They should demonstrate to others that they are serious about keeping this commitment. Naturally, as we have learned from Fearon (1995, 1997), such reassurance is less likely to be dismissed as empty talk if it is backed up by costly actions. This remark in turn returns us to our analysis of actions undertaken by a country to bind itself and its future leaders to multilateral treaties and to become enmeshed in extensive international economic networks so that any policy reversal will be very costly in both tangible and intangible (e.g., reputation) terms. A state's declared commitment to the international order is especially credible when the political positions and economic interests of its powerful domestic stakeholders are closely identified with and tied to this commitment and when they will be seriously jeopardized by a decision to abandon this commitment.

Germany's deep and extensive enmeshment in the European Union and NATO provides such credible commitment to its neighbors, such that a defection by Berlin to return to its pre-1945 policies has become simply and literally unthinkable—economically, militarily, socially, and politically. Alarm bells would go off in Germany's neighboring countries if Berlin were to make any move communicating that it is abandoning those multilateral ties and international institutions that have heretofore bound it to peaceful external relations. Powerful domestic stakeholders inside Germany can also be expected to play an important part in providing this reassurance and early warning, as they would be the first ones to mobilize against such defection. Analogously, Japan's "peace constitution" that foreswears militarism also serves an example of "self-binding" that has contributed to reassuring its neighbors. Domestic debates about revising this constitution to give Japan's military a larger role abroad also serves as a bellwether of this country's future intentions. Although hardly comparable to the German example, Taiwan's increasing economic integration with China is somewhat suggestive of such reassurance, even though the leaders of its Democratic Progressive Party have routinely and publicly declared a determination to seek the island's political independence. Yet, Taiwan's economic integration with China and the vast amount of its investments located in the mainland convey a nonverbal reassurance to Beijing that Taipei will not declare de jure political independence (Chan 2009). These economic ties are tantamount to hostages given to Beijing, indicating that the island's economy would suffer enormously if cross-Strait economic ties were to be cut or disrupted. China's purchase of large sums of US debt provides another example of costly commitment, indicating that Beijing wants to reassure Washington that it does not intend to upset their relationship because such a development would impose large costs to its own existing holdings (Chan 2012). Naturally, the intense trade relationship between China and the United States is also suggestive of costly commitment, as important stakeholders in both countries have strong vested interests in preserving this relationship and they can be seriously hurt, politically and economically, if it were to deteriorate.

These remarks do not imply that such serious deterioration is impossible, as China and the United States have been involved in an increasingly tense and acrimonious trade dispute. We are also aware that states that have traded and invested heavily with and in each other, such as Britain and Germany, have gone to war in the past. Our general point, however, is that the deeper and more extensive a country's relations with another, the more difficult and costly for it to disrupt and reverse these relations. Germany's postwar deep and extensive enmeshment in NATO and the European Union's multilateral institutions provides a costly and convincing commitment, signaling to its neighbors that Berlin will not repeat its past aggressive policies. We are, of course, not implying that China's engagement with its neighbors is comparable to Germany's. We maintain, however, that although scholars and pundits may debate about Beijing's revisionism, it has become more difficult over time to image that it can or will return to the days when it was politically isolated and economically closed to the rest of the world—unless China is forced by other countries, espe-cially the United States, to return to this situation by their collective attempt at imposing economic blockade and political isolation against it (recall that the Western powers had sought strenuously to deny China's representation in the United Nations and refused to extend diplomatic recognition to Beijing in the 1950s and 1960s). A voluntary reversal on Beijing's part has become increas-ingly unthinkable because it would require fundamental changes in China's domestic political and economic arrangements, changes that would require ex-tensive, heated debates and would engender mobilized opposition from benefi-ciaries of the current system.

Before closing this section, we should add that sometimes signals do not have to be costly to be credible to foreign audiences. For instance, our previous ref-erence to Japan's domestic debate to revise its constitution provides useful in-formation to foreigners about this country's future intentions, even though this discourse may not be costly in the sense used by Fearon (1995, 1997). Similarly, it is sometimes difficult for a government to coordinate or reconcile messages intended for different audiences (Yoder et al. 2019). For instance, Beijing may want to play the nationalist card to enhance its domestic legitimacy, while trying at the same time to reassure foreigners about its peaceful intentions. As Goddard (2018b: 198) states succinctly, "talk matters"—even supposedly "cheap talk." She shows that a state's legitimating strategy—that is, its statements seeking to ex-plain and justify its policies to domestic and foreign audiences—plays an impor-tant role in shaping people's beliefs and expectations and their interpretations of its actions and intentions. These statements can reassure and even resonate with foreigners, or can upset and even alarm them. Although President Trump's "America First" rhetoric may have been useful in mobilizing and consolidating his base in domestic political competition, it can unsettle and even alienate his foreign audiences. In contrast, Xi Jinping and his immediate predecessors have sought to reassure foreigners that China's rise will be peaceful and that it is com-mitted to its course of economic reform and globalization.

Beijing's public rhetoric has characterized China both as a rising power and as a developing country (Pu 2019). It has therefore tried to identify itself as a global actor, as well as a part of the developing world. Such duality is of course not unusual. For example, Japan depicts itself routinely both as an Asian country and as a member of "the developed West." In the context of Goddard's (2018a) network analysis, these examples show that China and Japan's "speech acts" can be deployed to suggest that these countries are concurrently integrated deeply in global institutional networks and also well positioned to play a "broker" or "intermediary" role with respect to important subsets of states. Statements from the Trump administration sent the opposite message, suggesting that the United States was pulling out from various international institutions and multilateral diplomacy and that it was turning to a more unilateral approach in its foreign policy.

How to Manage US-China Relations

What policies can dampen revisionist impulses on the part of a rising latecomer and convert it into a "responsible stakeholder"? Conversely, what policies can exacerbate this latecomer's sense of relative deprivation and increase its grievance against the established powers and the international order that they supposedly represent? These questions of course presume that we have some ideas about what a rising latecomer wants. Does it want to have a larger share of the benefits (including status) conferred by the existing international order? Or does it want to fundamentally alter and thus overturn and replace this order? What factors are important and relevant in shaping its preferences? How do its preferences—or self-perceived interests—interact with this state's evolving self-identities (Rousseau 2006)? How will these preferences (or interests and identities) likely be influenced by its counterpart's adoption of a policy of engagement or containment?

For example, will attempts to involve a rising China in webs of international economic interdependence be more effective in dampening the danger of its involvement in militarized disputes than, say, a policy to promote democracy in its neighborhood and even in China itself (Thies and Nieman 2017)? Could the latter policy have the counterproductive effect of increasing this danger by empowering China's mass public that tends to be more nationalistic than its leaders? The interstate system's structure only enables a material-based inference of a rising state's motivations or incentives; we will need to also develop, more importantly, an ideational interpretation of the genesis and transformation of these motivations and incentives. That is, we need to consider how the Chinese people and their leaders see their country's roles, identities, and status in international relations. In general, it seems to us that the current literature places too much emphasis on the competitive logic of international relations, and it does not give enough attention to the possibility that a newcomer can be socialized into the existing order and can change its views on its roles, interests, and even identities to become a more "responsible stakeholder" (Johnson 2008; Legro 2007). Naturally, the possibility of such "conversion" does not necessarily imply a smooth and unproblematic process (e.g., Allan et al. 2018; Buzan 2010; Kupchan 2014). This process is rather likely to involve constant mutual adjustments or, to use Goh's (2019) terminology, repeated rounds of renegotiation about the nature of international order among various stakeholders, including China. We should also be reminded that whereas a newcomer can be socialized to accept and internalize prevailing global norms, an "old timer" may become disenchanted and "un-socialized" to abandon and reject these same norms.

When addressing the question of how to manage Sino-American relations, it would be important to acknowledge the obvious: that these relations are multifaceted and variegated. They include both cooperation and competition. A natural starting point for leaders of both countries is to recognize and work to enlarge those areas where they have convergent interests and can therefore cooperate to achieve joint gains. Efforts to combat terrorism, cope with global warming, stabilize the international financial system, and prevent nuclear proliferation come naturally to mind. Both Beijing and Washington also have a common interest in ensuring regional peace and stability in the Asia Pacific and a multilateral regime that sustains open, free, and fair trade. These are "low hanging fruits" for which it is easier for these countries to reach agreement and to build a basis for trust before proceeding to the more difficult and contentious issues.

Both China and the United States have shown revisionist tendencies (Medeiros 2019 calls both "selective revisionists"), and their relationship has become more competitive and contentious in recent years. How should these countries' leaders address and manage their competition? Obviously, we do not share the perspective endorsed by the prevailing discourse, framing this competition or rivalry as a matter of an ambitious upstart trying to displace a dominant power and to upend the existing international order. For one thing, as should have become abundantly clear by now, we do not see the dominant power and the international order to be synonymous. We also do not share the view that China's authoritarian political system is the cause that fosters Sino-American competition—that somehow, a power transition (real or perceived) between these countries would not be concerning if only China were a democracy. Countries with different political systems have in the past managed to get along, and there are many historical instances when they have been successful in turning enmity to amity (Kupchan 2010). As another consideration, relations between Beijing and Washington were friendlier and even rising to the level of forming a tacit alliance when China's political system was significantly more authoritarian and its civil society less open and vibrant, during much of the 1970s and 1980s. China's mass public tends to be more nationalist and less moderate than its elite (including government officials), so that in our view a larger voice and easier access for popular opinion in China's political processes can constrain Beijing's policy space and actually incline its leader to become more bellicose (Weiss 2014). We therefore find ourselves in general agreement with the view that countries undergoing the democratizing process are more prone to become engulfed in foreign conflicts, including wars (Mansfield and Snyder 2007). The idea that if only China were to become a democracy, the problems troubling Sino-American relations would go away, strikes us as one of those facile assumptions that have beset research in this area. For these reasons, our recommendations do not address China's domestic politics because the real challenge to the United States is a *rising* China, no matter whether it is a democracy or not. As we have emphasized, it is important not to place China's leaders (or for that matter, leaders of any country involved in a crisis) in a domain of loss whereby they may be motivated to adopt riskier or more reckless policy. We propose three policy recommendations that focus on addressing Beijing and Washington's bilateral relationship.

First, we see nuclear balance or mutual deterrence between the United States and China to hold the key to avoiding a large-scale conflict between these countries. A report from the Stockholm International Peace Research Institute (2019) suggests that among the five great powers with nuclear weapons, Russia has 6,500 warheads, the United States 6,185, France 300, China 290, and Britain 200. These figures suggest that the United States enjoys a large numerical advantage over China. More relevant, however, is Washington's qualitative edge and its pursuit of "Star War" initiatives and space-based armament that can threaten China (and Russia) with the prospect of a successful first strike. Thus, continued qualitative improvements in the US nuclear arsenal can overwhelm China's limited number of warheads—undermining seriously the logic of mutual assured destruction that had provided the decisive stabilizing factor in Soviet-American relations during the Cold War (Lieber and Press 2006; Posen 2003).

If the United States and China can maintain credible mutual strategic deterrence, it will greatly enhance the prospect of avoiding a military conflict between them. A nuclear war between them would be highly destructive, not only for these countries but also for the rest of the world. As just remarked, however, mutual nuclear deterrence can be destabilized by the development of advanced technology, including missile defense systems. This deterrence only works if both countries have a second-strike capability, which can now be cast in doubt by the development and deployment of missile defense systems. The United States has withdrawn from the Anti-Ballistic Missile Treaty originally signed with the Soviet Union, and China has not been a party to such an agreement.

The development and deployment of tactical nuclear weapons presents another factor that can destabilize nuclear deterrence and thus make a resort to military force more "thinkable." Tactical nuclear weapons may loosen the restraint on getting into a military confrontation or war because, unlike strategic nuclear weapons, they can be used with more precision and less collateral damage. China's tactical nuclear capabilities have lagged far behind those of the United States, even though it has tried hard to keep up (Schneider 2019). To make things worse for Beijing, there are asymmetric beliefs about nuclear escalation. Chinese strategists seem to believe that nuclear conflict can easily spiral out of control. US officials, however, appear to think otherwise, because they are more confident about maintaining control in the event of a limited nuclear war with other states.

This perceptual gap regarding mutual deterrence and nuclear balance may cause misperceptions and miscalculations, producing unintended nuclear escalation in a future crisis (Cunningham and Fravel 2019).

As already remarked, we have witnessed a gradual demise of various arms control regimes. In 2001, President George W. Bush pulled the United States out from the 1972 Anti-Ballistic Missile Treaty with Russia. In August 2019, President Donald Trump withdrew the United States from the Intermediate-Range Nuclear Forces Treaty with Russia. The demise of the latter treaty has intensified concerns about the future of nuclear arms control—the new START (Strategic Arms Reduction Treaty)—between the United States and Russia, although the Biden administration extended the new START for five more years in February 2021. Given its limited nuclear capabilities, China has not been a party to arms control agreements between Russia/the Soviet Union and the United States. However, as China continues to boost its military capabilities, driven by its economic growth, it will become another major player in designing such regimes in the future. It is imperative that Washington and Beijing negotiate and establish effective arms control regimes to maintain nuclear balance and mutual deterrence between them. With the Trump administration's creation of a new branch of military force, the space force, there is also an urgent need for the United States and China to reach an understanding about the development and deployment of space weapons. And, of course, cyberwarfare would be another area for these countries to establish some basic "rules of the game."

Second, the United States needs to avoid risky behavior by resorting to military means to respond to China's soft revisionist challenges, such as Washington's declared intention to "pivot" or "rebalance" to Asia. This remark does not deny that Beijing has undertaken some hard revisionist policies, such as improving its military capabilities and consolidating its position on those land features in the South China Sea under its control. This said, China's military capabilities are still far from matching those of the United States. Due to states' different rates of growth, great powers will naturally rise and fall in the international system. However, as Kennedy (2010: 15) points out, "hegemons always prefer History to freeze, right there, and forever. History, unfortunately, has a habit of wandering off all on its own." It is reasonable for a hegemon to try to prolong its primacy in the international system. How it seeks to contain or defuse the challenge coming from a rising power, however, will affect whether the transitions of power and order will be peaceful or violent.

When facing diminished power and prestige, a declining hegemon is placed in a domain of loss, a situation that, according to prospect theory (Kahneman and Tversky 1979; for an application in Asian security, see He 2016) discussed in the previous section, is likely to incline it to engage in risky behavior in the hope of recovering its influence and status. Therefore, some scholars warn that this country may be disposed to initiate a preventive war or other confrontational policy against a rising power in the hope that such action can secure its continued dominance (Copeland 2000; Taliaferro 2004). Recent US actions, such as precipitating a trade confrontation with China, banning its high-tech companies, and lobbying other countries to exclude Huawei from their 5-G markets, seem to point in this direction. People in China believe that these actions represent US efforts to block their country's ascent.

Since China became the world's second largest economy in 2010, the United States has started to adopt a more confrontational posture against it. President Barack Obama launched a policy of pivoting or rebalancing US power to the Asia Pacific during his second term. In the eyes of Chinese leaders, it is a containment strategy against China's rise, although Obama publicly denied that Washington had this intent (Lieberthal and Wang 2012; Yan 2013). After Trump came to power, the United States no longer tried to hide its intention to contain China. As mentioned before, Trump's 2017 national security document officially designated China as a revisionist power and strategic competitor. The director of the Federal Bureau of Investigation, Christopher Wray, stated publicly that the United States should launch a "whole-of-society" approach to address the threat coming from China, a threat "which is not just a whole-of-government threat, but a whole-of-society threat on their end" (Kranz 2018: n.p.). It seems that conflict between the two countries has been expanded to include their respective societies in addition to their governments. Indeed, Washington's actions to escalate its trade dispute with Beijing and to block China's high-tech firms such as Huawei from accessing foreign markets and suppliers have been interpreted by many Chinese as additional evidence that tension between the two countries has further escalated to include economic and technological rivalry.

In the most recent exchange of tit for tat, the United States asked China to close its consulate in Houston, and China retaliated by demanding that the US consulate in Chengdu be shut down. Moreover, the United States had escalated its investigation and detention of Chinese nationals on suspicions of espionage, and Trump announced his intention to ban Chinese-owned video app TikTok from the United States by executive order. Bilateral tension between the two countries has clearly been escalating, especially after the start of the Covid-19 pandemic. Trump publicly called this pandemic "kung flu" and the "Chinese flu" because it came from Wuhan, and had claimed that it had originated in a Chinese lab in that city, although he declined to offer any evidence. He has also used the term "rape" to describe China's alleged predatory commercial policy toward the United States.

The Trump administration's announcement of forced sale of at least part of TikTok's US-based assets is essentially similar to Beijing's requirement for Apple to operate in China. As such, Beijing is being given a dose of its own medicine.

This demand is tantamount to requiring the company to divest its corporate control by forming a joint venture with a local firm and to make large investments and employ large numbers of local employees in the host country. The United States has complained about this Chinese policy for many years. Having now made the same demand, ostensibly on national security grounds, it is also subject to the table being turned on it by the European Union, Japan, India, and others that can follow this example and subject large US technology companies operating in their country to the same treatment.

It is normal for an existing hegemon to contain and undermine a rising power. However, it will be dangerous and risky if it relies primarily on military means, engages exaggerated rhetoric, and adopts a "whole-of-society" approach. China's military, economic, and technological capabilities are still far from reaching the level that would permit it to compete with the United States (Beckley 2011/ 2012; Brooks and Wohlforth 2016a, 2016b; Nye 2019; Posen 2003). China is also hardly a peer competitor of the United States for regional influence in Europe, the Western Hemisphere, and the Middle East. Washington commands a formidable coalition arrayed against Beijing which has few allies that can tip the balance of power in its favor in a possible showdown between the two countries. Moreover, as mentioned previously, the mere increase in a country's economic and military power should not be interpreted as evidence of its intention to displace the incumbent hegemon or to overthrow the existing international order by force. Most of China's revisionism lies in its policies seeking to alter international institutions. Military means are unlikely to be effective in addressing China's institutional revisionism. Resorting to these means may instead produce unnecessary tension and may even trigger conflicts between the two countries. We concur with Doran's (1991) power-cycle theory, suggesting that adaptation and adjustment, rather than opposition and balance, are more appropriate strategies for dealing with a rising power. We also share Kennedy's (2010) view that appeasement as a policy has been mischaracterized and misused in much of the prevailing academic and popular discourse, and it should not be overlooked in the pursuit of statecraft (see also Ripsman and Levy 2008; Rock 2000; Treisman 2004).

US officials will need to think carefully about how to deal with China's challenges wisely and effectively. If China does not use hard revisionist strategies to challenge the existing international order, a US response based on a "strategic" vision of power and approach to statecraft (in the sense of "strategic state" discussed by Rosecrance 1986) will be not only unnecessary, but also counterproductive in sustaining its hegemony (Kennedy 2010). Rather, US policymakers should consider how to use institutional strategies, especially institutional balancing, to shape China's policy preferences and influence its behavior within the existing institutional order—rather than taking a leading role itself in dismantling the institutional structure supporting this order (Ikenberry 2017a; Schweller 2015). The United States will not be a hegemon forever. It can, however, affect China's policy choice and its behavior to transform the international order in a peaceful, orderly, and consensual way (Ikenberry 2001, 2008, 2011, 2012).

Last but not least, China needs to consider how to reassure the United States during the process when international order is undergoing change. It must work to overcome ultra-nationalism fueled by grievances about the past and overconfidence about the future on the part of both its mass public and portions of its policy elite. As a rising power, time will be on China's side if it can continue its pace of economic growth. According to prospect theory, Chinese leaders are currently in a domain of gain, which should encourage them to avoid reckless confrontation and to pursue instead a conservative course of action. China should not provoke the United States, especially in the security arena. Even when facing pressure from the United States, such as over Taiwan and in the South China Sea disputes, China should avoid direct military confrontation. Chinese leaders should especially avoid actions that would inflame US public and elite opinion, or that would place US officials in a perceived domain of loss that would dispose them to adopt more confrontational policies. Although, as we have stressed, it is difficult for a rising state to reassure its declining counterpart that it will continue to "play nice" in the future when it gains more power, Beijing should demonstrate to and reassure Washington that its policies of "peaceful rise" and engagement with the rest of the world will be very costly and difficult to reverse. It should show by its actions that it is committed to these policies, and that it will continue and even expand its role as a responsible stakeholder by making larger contributions to the provision of collective goods, such as supporting UN peacekeeping missions, preventing nuclear proliferation, combating international terrorism and global warming, and stabilizing the world's financial and trade regimes.

Actions, especially costly actions that would make a future reversal of Chinese policy very difficult, costly, and unpopular, will be necessary to give credibility to Beijing's verbal assurances to Washington claiming that China is not just biding its time for an opportunistic moment to commit aggression. Its ability and willingness to resist playing its strong hand in its immediate neighborhood and when facing serious provocations—such as during the recent unrest in Hong Kong—are especially informative and useful for providing such reassuring signals. At the same time, Washington should avoid actions that are likely to complicate Beijing's domestic politics, such that it will alter the nature of political discourse in China to the advantage of hard-liners and placing incumbent leaders there in a perceived or likely domain of loss (such as with respect to their domestic control or legitimacy) and thereby forcing their hands to take a harder line. Recent US moves to impose sanctions against Hong Kong's officials and to revoke Hong Kong's special trading status are symbolic gestures that may be politically expedient and popular at home but are unlikely to improve matters and may even have the effect of hurting and constraining further those whom they are supposed to help.

This view echoes Putnam's (1988) analysis of "two-level games," suggesting that Washington has an important role to play in influencing the nature and course of domestic political discourse in China—it can ease the problems faced by the more moderate Chinese officials in coping with pressure coming from their more hard-line colleagues and ultranationalist elements in the mass public. As mentioned before, the actions and rhetoric of hard-liners in each country can feed on each other, thereby escalating acrimonies and recriminations. By the same logic, moderates in both countries can be de facto partners in a transnational effort to foster mutual trust, defuse crises, and avoid confrontation.

Institutionalized (Peaceful) Order Transition?

Thucydides's oft-quoted remark about the Spartans' fear of Athens's rise suggests an anxiety and even insecurity on the part of a dominant power about losing its hegemonic position. Naturally, fear can also motivate a rising power because it can be concerned about the danger of a preventive war initiated by the dominant power against it to avert this possibility. Thus, a systemic war can happen because of a rising power's (often premature) bid for hegemonic power or a declining albeit still dominant power's worries about a closing window of opportunity. If fear, anxiety, and a sense of vulnerability are the chief motivations behind both countries' foreign policies, then mutual reassurances should be given priority in efforts to avoid unwanted conflict. Reassurances should be tried first, because they require less resources and effort than deterrence. Moreover, should reassurances fail, the dominant power will still have the option of turning to even stronger efforts of deterrence and containment, backed up by its superior capabilities. From the perspective of the rising power, an exclusive or even primary reliance on deterrence and opposition would also be distinctively suboptimal because this policy would require much more effort and resources on its part and because this policy's effectiveness against a more powerful hegemon is quite doubtful (especially as it is highly probable that this counterpart will respond in kind, thereby setting off a spiral of mutual recrimination and retaliation). Such a posture can have the unwanted consequence of abetting a cycle of reciprocal escalation that traps both countries in an intensifying security dilemma. Path dependency means that actions undertaken today can foreclose some options while creating others tomorrow.

The power transition between the United States and China is much more complicated than the logic of Thucydides's Trap. As this book has cautiously presented, if dialogues and diplomatic channels are kept open, and the United States and China can successfully reach a grand bargain to reassure each other, then we may have another peaceful transition between two leading powers. However, given the recent Trump-Xi showdown on multiple fronts, two potentially dangerous scenarios loom large—a possible hot war and a new Cold War—if these two countries fail to manage their strategic competition wisely. Given the deterrence power of nuclear weapons, an all-out war may be still unthinkable, but an accidental conflict cannot be ruled out.

The first dangerous scenario is the escalation of territorial disputes between China and its neighbors, which in turn draws in the United States, leading to a possible hot war between the two. Although China does not have any territorial disputes with the United States, the strategic competition between these two countries has been compounded by Beijing's territorial disputes with its neighbors in the South China Sea and the East China Sea, as well as across the Taiwan Strait. The Trump administration's "free-and-open-Indo-Pacific (FOIP) strategy" in 2017 aimed to counter China's "assertiveness" in the region (He and Li 2020). In particular, Washington revived the Quadrilateral Security Dialogue—the informal strategic forum known as the "Quad 2.0"—between the United States, Australia, Japan, and India in 2017. It is widely believed that Quad 2.0 has the potential to become an Asian NATO to contain China in the future, especially given the recent border disputes between China and India, which pushed New Delhi to move closer to other Quad countries. Moreover, the United States has reversed its previous not-take-a-position policy in the South China Sea to publicly back other claimants against China. The Trump administration also publicly claimed that the US alliances with Japan and the Philippines will cover those territories in which these two countries have challenged China's sovereignty claims, namely the Diaoyu/Senkaku islands and the South China Sea. More recently, in a break with past practice since Washington and Beijing established diplomatic relations, the United States sent high-ranking officials (such as Secretary of Health and Human Services Alex Azar) to Taiwan, and this development triggered a series of Chinese military exercises across the Taiwan Strait.

It is clear that the United States has intended to mobilize an anti-China security arrangement and even a military alliance so that China's rise can be curbed and even contained. It is a reasonable strategy from a hegemon's perspective. However, it will increase the danger of military conflicts between China and the United States because Washington may become entrapped in an escalating territorial dispute between China and its neighbors. In such a situation, the United States may be exploited by a regional actor such as Taiwan, which has its own agenda to get Washington involved (being much weaker than China, many of

China's neighbors would want to internationalize their bilateral disputes with Beijing in the hope that the involvement by a third party such as the United States would offset their disadvantage if they were to be left alone to face China). Christensen and Snyder (1990) have described this process as chain-ganging, whereby alliance commitments engulf great powers in what was originally a local conflict and turned it into a large, global conflagration. Recalling the "guns of August," Kevin Rudd (2020) has warned about a similar development in the Asia Pacific because any strategic miscalculation or military accident can potentially trigger a hot and even nuclear conflict in the South China Sea, the East China Sea, or over the Taiwan Strait. It would lead to, even if accidental, an apocalypse for the whole world.

The second dangerous trend in US-China relations is an extension of the trade war to a more encompassing tech war which spirals into an ideological war, eventually becoming a new Cold War. Despite absolute gains from economic interdependence between the world's two largest economies, we have witnessed the negative impact of their trade war since early 2018. Although the two countries reached a temporary truce by signing the Phase I trade agreement in early 2020, the Covid-19 pandemic dampened the hope of further improving their bilateral relations. At the beginning of the pandemic's outbreak in January and February 2020, President Trump publicly praised China's actions and the WHO's response. But after this contagion hit the United States hard in March, his narrative changed to blaming China for covering up this disease in Wuhan in its early stages, thus significantly delaying other countries' responses. China retaliated and accused the West, especially the United States, of squandering the valuable time that China had bought for the rest of the world by locking down Wuhan. The escalating war of words between the United States and China about the origins of the virus spilled over to other areas, especially the technology sector. Washington has taken concrete actions to decouple bilateral relations by blocking global chip supplies to China's telecommunication giant Huawei, and to ban Chinese social-media companies TikTok and WeChat. It also imposes restrictions on Chinese apparel and tech goods allegedly produced by forced labor in Xinjiang.

More dangerously, Washington launched an ideological war against China in late June 2020. During the Trump administration, numerous rhetorical attacks were directed at the Chinese Communist Party (CCP) by high-ranking US officials. National Security Adviser Robert O'Brien, FBI Director Christopher Wray, Attorney General William Barr, and Secretary of State Mike Pompeo were dubbed the "four horsemen of the apocalypse," tasked by Trump to overthrow the CCP. Symbolically, Pompeo's July 23, 2020, talk at the Richard Nixon Presidential Library, calling for a new "alliance of democracies" to confront the CCP, evoked former British prime minister Winston Churchill's "Iron Curtain" speech of more than seventy years ago and seemed to highlight the beginning of a new Cold War with China (Pompeo 2020). In his Labor Day remarks, Trump raised the prospect of "decoupling" the American economy from China, and claimed, "We will make America into the manufacturing superpower of the world and end our reliance on China once and for all" (Greeley 2020: n.p.).

China has thus far not chosen to ratchet up officially its ideological rhetoric. While the United States explicitly targeted the CCP and the communist ideology, China has refrained from doing the same toward Western democracy. In an interview with Chinese state-run news agency Xinhua on August 5, 2020, China's foreign minister Wang Yi (2020: n.p.) firmly rejected the idea of a new Cold War by saying that "today's China is not the former Soviet Union. We have no intention of becoming another US. China does not export ideology." It seems that the United States has launched a new Cold War that China, at least until recently, has declined to engage. However, this is a rapidly changing situation and there are signs showing that Beijing may be pushing back (as shown in the meeting of the two countries' high-level foreign policy officials in Alaska in March 2021), and that it is preparing for a long-term contest with the United States. Thus, the danger of a new Cold War is still looming large because it is an easy way for Washington to rally other "like-minded" countries to counter China's rise. Besides weaponizing economic interdependence through a trade war, Washington is escalating its ideological campaign in order to isolate and contain China. However, a democratic crusade driven by "an end of history" mentality is a dangerous delusion. A new Cold War between the United States and China may serve some politicians' political interests in the short run, but it can lead to a political, social, and economic catastrophe for decades.

Both China and the United States should be aware of these two dangerous scenarios in managing their strategic relations. Beijing should have learned from the experiences of Berlin and Moscow that getting into an arms race with an established dominant power is not likely to be a rewarding policy. Washington should also have learned from the two world wars that systemic conflicts are likely to cause massive devastation and exhaustion to the primary belligerents and redound to the advantage of a third party that benefits from this opportunity to become preponderant at their expense. Both countries can also draw helpful lessons from the peaceful Anglo-American power transition. Mutual accommodation and timely concessions by London had enabled the United States to focus on its domestic growth without having to be distracted by external threats, and they had facilitated greatly Britain's efforts to contain Germany and to win its wars against the latter country. In contrast, Habsburg Spain's imperial overstretch and its policy of taking on all perceived challengers led eventually to its exhaustion and demise (Treisman 2004).

Naturally, our remarks are not meant to suggest that reassurance and deterrence are mutually exclusive policies. Their differences pertain to priority and sequencing, and they can and should work together to support each other in sta-bilizing Sino-American relations. As we have argued, it is important to main-tain mutual nuclear deterrence as a critical element in this endeavor. Thus, when referring to deterrence and opposition in the preceding paragraph, we are addressing a matter of relative emphasis. We also have in mind diplomatic state-craft as distinct from policies relying primarily or even exclusively on hard re-visionism or the practices of power politics, especially those based on military means. We see such policies to be largely ineffective and even counterproductive in coping with various strategies of soft revisionism seeking the transformation of international order's secondary institutions. Worse still, these policies can lead to a conflict spiral caused by self-fulfilling prophecy, one that disposes both countries to develop a mirror image of the other's overweening ambition and im-placable hostility.

It is of course also true that if both countries pursue a path of soft revisionism, they can frustrate each other's policies and may perpetuate an impasse, rather than reaching a compromise. We can also envisage soft revisionism escalating subsequently to hard revisionism. In order to secure a stable, amicable relation-ship between China and the United States, these countries will need to move be-yond soft revisionism to mutual accommodation and even smart appeasement (appeasement has been given a bad connotation in recent political discourse, just like revisionism; Kennedy 2010; Paul 2016a; Ripsman and Levy 2008; Rock 2000; Treisman 2004). History provides us with not just cases where power transitions appear to have been followed by war, but also instances where peace has endured in the wake of such transitions and, moreover, numerous examples of adver-saries managing to establish trust and cooperation to eventually become friends (Kupchan 2010; Rock 2000).

Will the transformation of international order or the transition of interna-tional leadership from an established hegemon to its successor be peaceful? As suggested by our discussion throughout this book, the answer will depend on the strategies and behavior adopted by both China and the United States. Moreover, their strategies and behavior have a reciprocal influence so that neither country can unilaterally determine the future of international relations. But these coun-tries, as the most powerful members of the international community, will have the greatest capability to shape the future of international relations. Although other countries also have an important interest in the stability and prosperity of the international system, China and the United States have the largest stake and the greatest responsibility in realizing this accomplishment.

In contrast to the past, today's world is characterized by weapons of awesome destructive power, deep and wide economic interdependence among states, and expanding social networks among people and their rising political awareness. No country or organization can address multifaceted security, economic, social, and environmental challenges alone. Nor can a single power decide the nature of international order and the process of its evolution, although some countries may have an outsized influence in shaping them. The future of the international order and its transition process are still undetermined. This process is ongoing, and a large part of it appears to involve soft revisionism. If soft revisionism continues to dominate this process, transition to a future international order promises to be more peaceful than past struggles (whether actually or ostensibly) over this order that have brought about or have threatened to bring about systemic war (Levy 2008; Organski 1958; Organski and Kugler 1980; Tammen et al. 2000). We believe that contemporary conditions have made it less likely that such episodes will be repeated, although obviously this danger has not vanished entirely. Whether our cautious optimism is warranted will depend on the joint efforts by the United States, China, and other states in the globalized world. A peaceful order transition may not be easy. But it is possible. It is also possible that, for reasons given in this book, an order will persist, regardless of power shifts among the world's leading states.

US Multilateral Treaties
Pending Ratification

US Multilateral Treaties Pending Ratification	Treaty Conclusion Time (month/day/year)	Did China Join?	United States Action	US Signing Time (month/day/year)
ILO Freedom of Association and Protection of the Right to Organize Convention, 1948	6/17/1948	No	Pending in the Senate	6/17/1948
ILO Equal Remuneration Convention, 1951	5/23/1953	Entry into force 11/2/1990	Pending in the Senate	6/17/1948
ILO Convention on Employment Policy	7/9/1964	Entry into force 12/17/1997	Pending in the Senate	7/9/1964
Vienna Convention on the Law of Treaties	5/23/1969	Acceded 9/3/1997	Pending in the Senate	4/24/1970
International Covenant on Economic, Social and Cultural Rights	12/16/1966	Signed 10/27/1997; ratified 2/28/2001	Pending in the Senate	10/5/1977
American Convention on Human Rights	11/2/1969	No	Pending in the Senate	6/1/1977
Convention on the Elimination of All Forms of Discrimination Against Women	12/18/1979	Signed 7/17/1980; ratified 11/4/1980; entry into force 9/3/1981	Pending in the Senate	7/17/1980

US Multilateral Treaties Pending Ratification	Treaty Conclusion Time (month/day/year)	Did China Join?	United States Action	US Signing Time (month/day/year)
Amendment to the 1973 Convention on International Trade in Endangered Species of Wild Fauna and Flora (CITES)	4/3/1983	No	Pending in the Senate	4/3/1983
Protocol II Additional to the Geneva Conventions of August 12, 1949, and Relating to the Protection of Victims of Non-International Armed Conflicts	6/10/1977	Ratified 9/2/1983; entry into force 3/14/1984	Pending in the Senate	12/12/1977
Convention on Biological Diversity	6/5/1992	Signed 6/11/1992; ratified 1/5/1993; entry into force 12/29/1993	Pending in the Senate	6/4/1993
United Nations Convention on the Law of the Sea	12/10/1982	Signed 12/10/1982; ratified 6/7/1996; entry into force 07/07/1996	Pending in the Senate	7/29/1994
Comprehensive Nuclear-Test-Ban Treaty	9/10/1996	Signed 9/24/1996; not ratified	Pending in the Senate	9/24/1996
ILO Discrimination (Employment and Occupation) Convention, 1958	6/25/1958	Entry into force 1/12/2006	Pending in the Senate	6/25/1958
Inter-American Convention against the Illicit Manufacturing of and Trafficking in Firearms, Ammunition, Explosives, and Other Related Materials	11/13/1997	No	Pending in the Senate	11/14/1997

US Multilateral Treaties Pending Ratification	Treaty Conclusion Time (month/day/year)	Did China Join?	United States Action	US Signing Time (month/day/year)
Rotterdam Convention on the Prior Informed Consent Procedure for Certain Hazardous Chemicals and Pesticides in International Trade	9/10/1998	Signed 8/24/1999; ratified 3/22/2005	Pending in the Senate	9/11/1998
Convention on the Safety of United Nations and Associated Personnel	12/9/1994	Acceded 9/22/2004	Pending in the Senate	12/19/1994
Stockholm Convention on Persistent Organic Pollutants	5/22/2001	Signed 5/23/2001; ratified 8/13/2004; entry into force 11/11/2004	Pending in the Senate	5/23/2001
1996 Protocol to the Convention on the Prevention of Marine Pollution by Dumping of Wastes and Other Matter, 1972	11/7/1996	Ratified 6/29/2006; entry into force 10/29/2006	Pending in the Senate	3/31/1998
Agreement on the Conservation of Albatrosses and Petrels, with Annexes	6/19/2001	No	Pending in the Senate	6/19/2001
Annex VI on Liability Arising from Environmental Emergencies to the Protocol on Environmental Protection to the Antarctic Treaty (Annex VI)	6/14/2005	No	Pending in the Senate	6/14/2005

US Multilateral Treaties Pending Ratification	Treaty Conclusion Time (month/day/year)	Did China Join?	United States Action	US Signing Time (month/day/year)
Protocol I, II, and III to the South Pacific Nuclear Free Zone Treaty (Treaty of Rarotonga)	3/25/1996	Signed Protocol II and III, 2/10/1987; ratified 10/21/1988	Pending in the Senate	3/25/1996
Protocols I and II to the African Nuclear-Weapon-Free Zone Treaty (Pelindaba Treaty)	4/11/1996	Signed 4/11/1996; ratified 9/6/1996	Submitted by the administration 5/2/2011; pending in the Senate	4/11/1996
Protocol Amending the Convention on Mutual Administrative Assistance in Tax Matters	5/27/2010	No	Pending in the Senate	5/27/2010
Convention on the Rights of the Child	11/20/1989	Signed 8/29/1990; ratified 3/2/1992	Pending in the Senate	2/16/1995
Convention on the Rights of Persons with Disabilities	12/13/2006	Signed 3/30/2007; ratified 8/1/2008	Pending in the Senate	7/30/2009
Protocol to the Treaty on a Nuclear-Weapon-Free Zone in Central Asia (CANWFZ)	5/6/2014	Signed 5/6/2014; ratified 8/17/2015	Pending in the Senate	5/6/2014
The Beijing Treaty on Audiovisual Performances	6/24/2012	Signed 6/26/2012; ratified 7/9/2014	Pending in the Senate	6/26/2012
United Nations Convention on Independent Guarantees and Stand-By Letters of Credit	12/11/1995	No	Pending in the Senate	12/11/1997

US Multilateral Treaties Pending Ratification	Treaty Conclusion Time (month/day/year)	Did China Join?	United States Action	US Signing Time (month/day/year)
The Arms Trade Treaty	4/2/2013	No	Pending in the Senate	9/25/2013
United Nations Convention on Transparency in Treaty-Based Investor-State Arbitration	12/10/2014	No	Pending in the Senate	3/17/2015

References

Alagappa, Muthiah. 2003. "The Study of International Order: An Analytical Framework." In: Muthiah Alagappa (ed.), *Asian Security Order: Instrumental and Normative Features*. Stanford, CA: Stanford University Press, 33–69.

Allan, Bentley, Srdjan Vucetic, and Ted Hopf. 2018. "The Distribution of Identity and the Future of International Order: China's Hegemonic Prospects." *International Organization* 72(4): 839–869.

Allison, Graham. 2017. *Destined for War: Can America and China Escape Thucydides's Trap?* Boston: Houghton Mifflin Harcourt.

Allison, Graham. 2018. "The Myth of the Liberal Order: From Historical Accident to Conventional Wisdom." *Foreign Affairs* 97(4): 124–133.

Allison, Roy. 2017. "Russia and the Post-2014 International Legal Order: Revisionism and Realpolitik." *International Affairs* 93(3): 519–543.

Altman, Dan. 2020. "The Evolution of Territorial Conquest after 1945 and the Limits of the Territorial Integrity Norm." *International Organization* 74(3): 490–522.

Axelrod, Robert. 1984. *The Evolution of Cooperation*. New York: Basic Books.

Bacevich, Andrew J. 2002. *American Empire: The Realities and Consequences of U.S. Diplomacy*. Cambridge, MA: Harvard University Press.

Baldwin, David A. 1993. *Neorealism and Neoliberalism: The Contemporary Debate*. New York: Columbia University Press.

Barbieri, Katherine. 2002. *The Liberal Illusion: Does Trade Promote Peace?* Ann Arbor: University of Michigan Press.

Barnett, Michael, and Raymond Duvall. 2005. "Power in International Politics." *International Organization* 59(1): 471–506.

Barnhart, Michael A. 1987. *Japan Prepares for Total War: The Search for Economic Security, 1919–1945*. Ithaca, NY: Cornell University Press.

Baschuk, Bryce. 2020. "U.S. Violated Trade Rules with Tariffs on China, WTO Says." September 15. https://www.bloomberg.com/news/articles/2020-09-15/wto-rules-that-u-s-tariffs-on-china-violate-trade-rules-kf4189y0.

Baumgartner, Frank, and Bryan D. Jones. 1993. *Agendas and Instability in American Politics*. Chicago: University of Chicago Press.

Beckley, Michael. 2011/2012. "China Century? Why America's Edge Will Endure." *International Security* 36(3): 41–78.

Behravesh, Maysam. 2018. "State Revisionism and Ontological (In)security in International Politics: The Complicated Case of Iran and Its Nuclear Behavior." *Journal of International Relations and Development* 21(4): 836–857.

Bellamy, Alex J. 2009. *Responsibility to Protect*. Cambridge: Polity Press.

Bley, Bonnie. 2019. "The New Geography of Global Diplomacy: China Advances as the United States Retreats." *Foreign Affairs* (November). https://www.foreignaffairs.com/articles/china/2019-11-27/new-geography-global-diplomacy.

Bodansky, Daniel. 2010. "The Copenhagen Climate Change Conference: A Postmortem." *American Journal of International Law* 104(2): 230–240.

Boettcher, William A., III. 2005. *Presidential Risk Behavior in Foreign Policy: Prudence or Peril?* New York: Palgrave.

Bourne, Kenneth. 1967. *Britain and the Balance of Power in North America, 1815–1908.* Berkeley: University of California Press.

Breslin, Shaun. 2010. "China's Emerging Global Role: Dissatisfied Responsible Great Power." *Politics* 30(1): 52–62.

Breuer, Adam, and Alastair I. Johnston. 2019. "Memes, Narratives and the Emergent US-China Security Dilemma." *Cambridge Review of International Affairs* 32(4): 429–477.

Brooks, Stephen G. 1997. "Dueling Realisms." *International Organization* 51(3): 445–477.

Brooks, Stephen G. 1999. "The Globalization of Production and the Changing Benefits of Conquest." *Journal of Conflict Resolution* 43(5): 646–670.

Brooks, Stephen G., and William C. Wohlforth. 2005. "Hard Times for Soft Balancing." *International Security* 30(1): 72–108.

Brooks, Stephen G., and William C. Wohlforth. 2016a. "The Rise and Fall of the Great Powers in the Twenty-First Century: China's Rise and the Fate of America's Global Position." *International Security* 40(3): 7–53.

Brooks, Stephen G., and William C. Wohlforth. 2016b. *America Abroad: The United States' Global Role in the 21st Century.* New York: Oxford University Press.

Broz, J. Lawrence, Zhiwen Zhang, and Gaoyang Wang. 2020. "Explaining Foreign Support for China's Global Economic Leadership." *International Organization* 74(3): 417–452.

Bull, Hedley. 1977. *The Anarchical Society: A Study of Order in World Politics.* New York: Columbia University Press.

Buzan, Barry. 2004a. *The United States and the Great Powers: World Politics in the Twenty-First Century.* Cambridge: Polity Press.

Buzan, Barry. 2004b. *From International to World Society? English School Theory and the Social Structure of Globalisation.* Cambridge: Cambridge University Press.

Buzan, Barry. 2010. "China in International Society: Is 'Peaceful Rise' Possible?" *Chinese Journal of International Politics* 3(1): 5–36.

Buzan, Barry. 2018. "China's Rise in English School Perspective." *International Journal of the Asia Pacific* 18(3): 449–476.

Buzan, Barry, and Michael Cox. 2013. "China and the U.S.: Comparable Cases of 'Peaceful Rise'?" *Chinese Journal of International Politics* 6(2): 109–132.

Buzas, Zoltan I. 2013. "The Color of Threat: Race, Threat Perception, and the Demise of the Anglo-Japanese Alliance, 1902–1923." *Security Studies* 22(4): 573–606.

Campbell, Kurt M. 2016. *The Pivot: The Future of American Statecraft in Asia.* New York: Hachette Book Group.

Carr, Edward H. 1946. *The Thirty Years' War, 1919–1939: An Introduction to the Study of International Relations.* New York: Harper Row.

Chan, Steve. 2004a. "Exploring Some Puzzles in Power-Transition Theory: Some Implications for Sino-American Relations." *Security Studies* 13(3): 103–141.

Chan, Steve. 2004b. "Can't Get No Satisfaction? The Recognition of Revisionist States." *International Relations of the Asia Pacific* 4(2): 207–238.

Chan, S. 2008. *China, the U.S., and the Power-Transition Theory: A Critique.* New York: Routledge.

Chan, Steve. 2009. "Commerce between Rivals: Realism, Liberalism, and Credible Communication across the Taiwan Strait." *International Relations of the Asia-Pacific* 9(3): 435–467.

Chan, Steve. 2012. "Money Talks: International Credit/Debt as Credible Commitment." *Journal of East Asian Affairs* 26(1): 77–103.

Chan, Steve. 2014. "Extended Deterrence in the Taiwan Strait: Discerning Resolve and Commitment." *American Journal of Chinese Studies* 21(2): 83–93.

Chan, Steve. 2016. "On States' Status-Quo and Revisionist Dispositions: Discerning Power, Popularity and Satisfaction from Security Council Vetoes." *Issues & Studies* 51(3): 1–28.

Chan, Steve. 2017. *Trust and Distrust in Sino-American Relations: Challenge and Opportunity.* Amherst, NY: Cambria Press.

Chan, Steve. 2020a. *Thucydides's Trap? Historical Interpretation, Logic of Inquiry, and the Future of Sino-American Relations.* Ann Arbor: University of Michigan Press.

Chan, Steve. 2020b. "Response by Steve Chan." Hi-Diplo/ISSF XII-2 on *Thucydides's Trap? Historical Interpretation, Logic of Inquiry, and the Future of Sino-American Relations.* https://networks.h-net.org/node/28443/discussions/6721850/h-diploissf-roundtable-12-2-thucydides%E2%80%99s-trap-historical.

Chan, Steve. 2020c. "The World in Which China Will Have to Operate in the Foreseeable Future: The Persistence of U.S. Structural Power." Paper presented at the Workshop on China's Influence, University of Hong Kong, Hong Kong, December 11–13.

Chan, Steve, Weixing Hu, and Kai He. 2019. "Discerning States' Revisionist and Status-Quo Orientations: Comparing China and the U.S." *European Journal of International Relations* 27(2): 613–640.

Chin, Gregory, and Ramesh Thakur. 2010. "Will China Change the Rules of Global Order?" *Washington Quarterly* 33(4): 119–138.

China Daily. 2015. "China Reaffirms the Key Principle of 'Common but Differentiated Responsibility.'" December 1. http://www.chinadaily.com.cn/world/XiattendsPariscli mateconference/2015-12/01/content_22597769.htm.

Christensen, Thomas J. 2001. "Posing Problems without Catching Up: China's Rise and Challenges for U.S. Security Policy." *International Security* 25(4): 5–40.

Christensen, Thomas J., and Jack Snyder. 1990. "Chain Gangs and Passed Bucks: Alliance Patterns in Multipolarity." *International Organization* 44(2): 137–168.

Cioffi-Revilla, Claudio. 1998. "The Political Uncertainty of Interstate Rivalries: A Punctuated Equilibrium Model." In: Paul Diehl (ed.), *The Dynamics of Enduring Rivalries.* Chicago: University of Chicago Press, 1998, 64–97.

Claar, Martin, and Norrin M. Ripsman. 2016. "Accommodation and Containment: Great Britain and Germany Prior to the Two World Wars." In: T. V. Paul (ed.), *Accommodating Rising Powers: Past, Present, and Future.* Cambridge: Cambridge University Press, 150–172.

Clark, Ian. 2005. *Legitimacy in International Society.* Oxford: Oxford University Press.

Clark, Ian. 2009. "Toward an English School Theory of Hegemon." *European Journal of International Relations* 15(2): 203–228.

Colaresi, Michael P. 2005. *Scare Tactics: The Politics of International Rivalry.* Syracuse, NY: Syracuse University Press.

Cooley, Alexander, Daniel Nexon, and Steven Ward. 2019. "Revising Order or Challenging the Balance of Power? An Alternative Typology of Revisionist and Status-Quo States." *Review of International Studies* 45(4): 689–708.

Copeland, Dale C. 2000. *The Origins of Major War.* Ithaca, NY: Cornell University Press.

Cox, Robert. 1987. *Production, Power, and World Order: Social Forces in the Making of History.* New York: Columbia University Press.

Crawford, Timothy W. 2003. *Pivotal Deterrence: Statecraft and the Pursuit of Peace*. Ithaca, NY: Cornell University Press.

Cunningham, Fiona S., and M. Taylor Fravel. 2019. "Dangerous Confidence? Chinese Views on Nuclear Escalation." *International Security* 44(2): 61–109.

Daalder, Ivo H., and James M. Lindsay. 2005. *America Unbound: The Bush Revolution in Foreign Policy*. New York: Wiley.

Danilovic, Vesna, and Joe Clare. 2007. "Global Power Transitions and Regional Interests." *International Interactions* 33(3): 289–304.

Danzman, Sarah B., Thomas Oatley, and William K. Winecoff. 2017. "All Crises Are Global: Capital Cycles in an Imbalanced International Political Economy." *International Studies Quarterly* 61(4): 907–923.

Davidson, Jason W. 2006. *The Origins of Revisionist and Status-Quo States*. London: Palgrave Macmillan.

Davis, James W., Jr. 2000. *Threats and Promises: The Pursuit of International Influence*. Baltimore, MD: Johns Hopkins University Press.

Deng, Yong. 2008. *China's Struggle for Status: The Realignment of International Relations*. Cambridge: Cambridge University Press.

Deutsch, Karl W., Sidney A. Burrell, Robert A. Kann, Maurice Lee, Jr., Martin Lichtenman, Raymond E. Lindgren, Francis L. Loewenheim, and Richard W. Van Wagenen. 1957. *Political Community and the North Atlantic Area: International Organization in the Light of Historical Experience*. New York: Greenwood.

DiCicco, Jonathan M. 2017. "Power Transition Theory and the Essence of Revisionism." In: William R. Thompson (ed.), *Oxford Encyclopedia of Empirical International Relations*. Oxford: Oxford University Press, 188–214. http://www.acsu.buffalo.edu/~fczagare/PSC%20504/DiCicco%20PT%20and%20Revisionism.pdf.

DiCicco, Jonathan M., and Jack Levy. 1999. "Power Shifts and Problem Shifts: The Evolution of the Power Transition Research Program." *Journal of Conflict Resolution* 43(6): 675–704.

DiCicco, Jonathan M., and Jack Levy. 2003. "The Power Transition Research Program: A Lakatosian Analysis." In: Colin Elman and Miriam F. Elman (eds.), *Progress in International Relations Theory: Appraising the Field*. Cambridge, MA: MIT Press, 109–157.

Ding, Sheng. 2010. "Analyzing Power from Perspective of Soft Power: A New Look at China's Rise to the Status-Quo Power." *Journal of Contemporary China* 19(64): 255–272.

Domke, William. K. 1988. *War and the Changing Global System*. New Haven, CT: Yale University Press.

Doran, Charles F. 1991. *Systems in Crisis: New Imperatives of High Politics at Century's End*. Cambridge: Cambridge University Press.

Drezner, Daniel W. 2017. "Perception, Misperception, and Sensitivity: Chinese Economic Power and Preferences after the 2008 Financial Crisis." In: Robert S. Ross and Oystein Tunsjo (eds.), *Strategic Adjustment and the Rise of China*. Ithaca, NY: Cornell University Press, 69–99.

Drezner, Daniel W. 2019. "Counter-Hegemonic Strategies in the Global Economy." *Security Studies* 28(3): 505–531.

East, Maurice A. 1972. "Status Discrepancy and Violence in the International System." In: James N. Rosenau, Vincent Davis, and Maurice A. East (eds.), *The Analysis of International Politics*. New York: Free Press, 299–319.

Edelstein, David M. 2002. "Managing Uncertainty: Beliefs about Intentions and the Rise of Great Powers." *Security Studies* 12(1): 1–40.

Etzioni, Amitai. 2015. "Spheres of Influence: A Reconceptualization." *Fletcher Forum of World Affairs* 29(2): 117–132.

Farrell, Henry, and Abraham L. Newman. 2019. "Weaponized Interdependence: How Global Economic Networks Shape State Coercion." *International Security* 44(1): 42–79.

Fearon, James D. 1995. "Rationalist Explanations for War." *International Organization* 49(3): 379–414.

Fearon, James D. 1997. "Signaling Foreign Policy Interests: Tying Hands versus Sinking Costs." *Journal of Conflict Resolution* 41(1): 68–90.

Feng, Huiyun. 2009. "Is China a Revisionist Power?" *Chinese Journal of International Politics* 2(3): 313–334.

Feng, Yongping. 2006. "The Peaceful Transition of Power from the UK to the US." *Chinese Journal of International Politics* 1(1): 83–108.

Finnemore, Martha. 2003. *The Purpose of Intervention: Changing Beliefs about the Use of Force*. Ithaca, NY: Cornell University Press.

Finnemore, Martha. 2009. "Legitimacy, Hypocrisy, and the Social Structure of Unipolarity: Why Being a Unipole Isn't All What It's Cracked Up to Be." *World Politics* 61(1): 58–85.

Foot, Rosemary, and Andrew Walter. 2011. *China, the United States, and Global Order*. Cambridge: Cambridge University Press.

Foot, Rosemary. 1998. "China in the ASEAN Regional Forum: Organizational Processes and Domestic Modes of Thought." *Asian Survey* 38(5): 425–440.

France 24. 2019. "Russia's Undiplomatic Return to the Council of Europe." https://www.france24.com/en/20190628-russia-undiplomatic-return-council-europe-ukraine.

Fravel, M. Taylor. 2012. "All Quiet in the South China Sea: Why China Is Playing Nice (For Now)." *Foreign Affairs*. March. https://www.foreignaffairs.com/articles/china/2012-03-22/all-quiet-south-china-sea.

Friedberg, Aaron L. 1988. *The Weary Titan: The Experience of Relative Decline, 1895–1905*. Princeton, NJ: Princeton University Press.

Friedman, Max P., and Tom Long. 2015. "Soft Balancing in the Americas: Latin American Opposition to U.S. Intervention, 1898–1936." *International Security* 40(1): 120–156.

Fung, Courtney. 2019. *China and Intervention at the UN Security Council: Reconciling Status*. Oxford: Oxford University Press.

Gause, F. Gregory, III. 2019. "'Hegemony' Compared: Great Britain and the United States in the Middle East." *Security Studies* 28(3): 565–587.

Gilli, Andrea, and Mauro Gilli. 2019. "Why China Has Not Caught Up Yet: Military-Technological Superiority and the Limits of Imitation, Reverse Engineering, and Cyber Espionage." *International Security* 43(3): 141–189.

Gilpin, Robert. 1981. *War and Change in World Politics*. Cambridge: Cambridge University Press.

Glaser, Charles. 2019. "A Flawed Framework: Why the Liberal International Order Concept Is Misguided." *International Security* 43(4): 51–87.

Gochman, Charles S. 1980. "Status, Capabilities, and Major Power Conflict." In: J. David Singer (ed.), *The Correlates of War II: Testing Some Realpolitik Models*. New York: Free Press, 83–123.

Goddard, Stacie E. 2018a. "Embedded Revisionism: Networks, Institutions, and Challenges to World Order." *International Organization* 72(4): 763–797.

Goddard, Stacie E. 2018b. *When Right Makes Right: Rising Powers and World Order.* Ithaca, NY: Cornell University Press.

Goddard, Stacie. 2020. "The Authors Respond." *Journal of East Asian Studies* 20(2): 172–175.

Goh, Evelyn. 2004. "The ASEAN Regional Forum in United States East Asian Strategy." *The Pacific Review* 17(1): 47–69.

Goh, Evelyn. 2013. *The Struggle for Order: Hegemony, Hierarchy, and Transition in the Cold-War East Asia.* Oxford: Oxford University Press.

Goh, Evelyn. 2019. "Contesting Hegemonic Order: China in East Asia." *Security Studies* 28(3): 614–644.

Goldstein, Avery. 2005. *Rising to the Challenge: China's Grand Strategy and International Security.* Stanford, CA: Stanford University Press.

Gramsci, Antonio. 1971. *Selections from the Prison Notebooks of Antonio Gramsci.* New York: International.

Greeley, Brendan. 2020. "Trump Raises Prospect of 'Decoupling' US Economy from China." *Financial Times,* September 8. https://www.ft.com/content/06047bc5-81dd-4475-8678-4b3181d53877.

Grieco, Joseph. 1988. "Anarchy and the Limits of Cooperation: A Realist Critique of the Newest Liberal Institutionalism." *International Organization* 42(3): 485–507.

Grieco, Joseph. 1993. "The Relative-Gains Problem for International Cooperation." *American Political Science Review* 87(3): 729–35.

Gries, Peter, and Yiming Ying. 2019. "Are the US and China Fated to Fight? How Narratives of 'Power Transition' Shape Great Power War or Peace." *Cambridge Review of International Affairs* 32(4): 456–482.

Gurr, Ted R. 1970. *Why Men Rebel.* Princeton, NJ: Princeton University Press.

Hast, Susanna. 2014. *Spheres of Influence in International Relations: History, Theory and Politics.* Burlington, VT: Ashgate.

He, Kai. 2008. "Institutional Balancing and International Relations Theory: Economic Interdependence and Balance of Power Strategies in Southeast Asia." *European Journal of International Relations* 14(3): 489–518.

He, Kai. 2009. *Institutional Balancing in the Asia Pacific: Economic Interdependence and China's Rise.* New York: Routledge.

He, Kai. 2016a. *China's Crisis Behavior: Political Survival and Foreign Policy after the Cold War.* Cambridge: Cambridge University Press.

He, Kai. 2016b. "China's Bargaining Strategies for a Peaceful Accommodation after the Cold War." In: T. V. Paul (ed.), *Accommodating Rising Powers: Past, Present, and Future.* Cambridge: Cambridge University Press, 201–221.

He, Kai, and Huiyun Feng. 2008. "If Not Soft Balancing, Then What? Reconsidering Soft Balancing and U.S. Policy toward China." *Security Studies* 17(2): 363–395.

He, Kai, and Huiyun Feng. 2012. "Debating China's Assertiveness: Taking China's Power and Interests Seriously." *International Politics* 49(5): 633–644.

He, Kai, and Huiyun Feng. 2013. *Prospect Theory and Foreign Policy Analysis in the Asia Pacific: Rational Leaders and Risky Behavior.* London: Routledge.

He, Kai, and Huiyun Feng. 2019. "Leadership Transition and Global Governance: Role Conception, Institutional Balancing, and the AIIB." *The Chinese Journal of International Politics* 12(2): 153–178.

He, Kai, and Huiyun Feng. 2020. "Introduction: Rethinking China and International Order: A Conceptual Analysis." In: Huiyun Feng and Kai He (eds.), *China's*

Challenges and International Order Transition: Beyond the "Thucydides Trap." Ann Arbor: University of Michigan Press, 1–24.

He, Kai, Huiyun Feng, Steve Chan, and Weixing Hu. Forthcoming. "Rethinking Revisionism in World Politics." *Chinese Journal of International Politics.*

He, Kai, and Mingjiang Li. 2020. "Understanding the Dynamics of the Indo-Pacific: US–China Strategic Competition, Regional Actors, and Beyond." *International Affairs* 96(1): 1–7.

Herz, John H. 1957. "The Rise and Demise of the Territorial State." *World Politics* 9(4): 473–493.

Herz, John H. 1968. "The Territorial State Revisited: Reflections on the Future of the Nation-State." *Policy* 1(1): 11–34.

Hilton, Isabel, and Oliver Kerr. 2017. "The Paris Agreement: China's 'New Normal' Role in International Climate Negotiations." *Climate Policy* 17(1): 48–58.

Hirschman, Albert O. 1970. *Voice, Exit, and Loyalty: Responses to Decline in Firms, Organizations, and States.* Cambridge, MA: Harvard University Press.

Holsti, Ole R. 1962. "The Belief System and National Images: A Case Study." *Journal of Conflict Resolution* 6(3): 244–252.

Hu, Weixing. 2012. "Explaining Change and Stability in Cross-Strait Relations: A Punctuated Equilibrium Model." *Journal of Contemporary China* 21(78): 933–953.

Hu, Weixing. 2020. "The United States, China, and the Indo-Pacific Strategy: The Rise and Return of Strategic Competition." *The China Review* 20(3): 127–142.

Huang, Cary. 2015. "China-Led Asian Bank Challenges US Dominance of Global Economy." *South China Morning Post.* April 11. https://www.scmp.com/news/china/economy/article/1763525/china-led-asian-bank-challenges-us-dominance-global-economy

Huntington, Samuel P. 1996. *The Clash of Civilizations and the Remaking of the World Order.* New York: Simon & Schuster.

Hurd, Ian. 2007. "Breaking and Making Norms: American Revisionism and Crises of Legitimacy." *International Politics* 44(2–3): 194–213.

Hurrell, Andrew. 2007. *On Global Order: Power, Values, and the Constitution of International Society.* Oxford: Oxford University Press.

Ikenberry, G. John. 2001. *After Victory: Institutions, Strategic Restraint, and the Rebuilding of Order after Major Wars.* Princeton, NJ: Princeton University Press.

Ikenberry, G. John. 2008. "The Rise of China and the Future of the West: Can the Liberal System Survive?" *Foreign Affairs* 87(1): 23–37.

Ikenberry, G. John. 2011. "The Future of the Liberal World Order: Internationalism after America." *Foreign Affairs* 90(3): 56–68.

Ikenberry, G. John. 2012. *Liberal Leviathan: The Origins, Crisis, and Transformation of the American World Order.* Princeton, NJ: Princeton University Press.

Ikenberry, G. John. 2017a. "The Plot against American Foreign Policy: Can the Liberal Order Survive?" *Foreign Affairs* 96(3): 2–9.

Ikenberry, G. John. 2017b. "The Rise, Character, and Evolution of International Order." In: Orfeo Fioretos (ed.), *International Politics and Institutions in Time.* Oxford: Oxford University Press, 59–75.

Ikenberry, G. John, and Daren Lim. 2017. "China's Emerging Institutional Statecraft: The Asian Infrastructure Bank and the Prospects for Counter-Hegemony." Project on International Order and Strategy at Brookings. https://www.brookings.edu/wp-content/uploads/2017/chinas-emerging-institutional-statecraft.pdf.

Ikenberry, G. John, Michael Mastanduno, and William C. Wohlforth. 2009. "Introduction: Unipolarity, State Behavior, and Systemic Consequences." *World Politics* 61(1): 1–27.

Ikenberry, G. John, and Daniel H. Nexon. 2019. "Hegemony Studies 3.0: The Dynamics of Hegemonic Orders." *Security Studies* 28(3): 395–421.

Jacques, Martin. 2019. "When China and the U.S. Collide: The End of Stability and the Birth of a New Cold War." Jeju Peace Institute Peace Net. http://jpi.or.kr/eng/regular/policy_view.sky?code=EnOther&id=5360.

Jerden, Bjorn. 2014. "The Assertive China Narrative: Why It Is Wrong and How So Many Still Bought into It." *Chinese Journal of International Politics* 7(1): 47–88.

Jervis, Robert. 1976. *Perception and Misperception in International Politics*. Princeton, NJ: Princeton University Press.

Jervis, Robert. 1978. "Cooperation under the Security Dilemma." *World Politics* 30(2): 167–214.

Jervis, Robert. 2003. "Explaining the Bush Doctrine." *Political Science Quarterly* 118(3): 365–388.

Jervis, Robert. 2005. *American Foreign Policy in a New Era*. New York: Routledge.

Jervis, Robert. 2009. "Unipolarity: A Structural Perspective." *World Politics* 61(1): 188–213.

Johnston, Alastair I. 2003. "Is China a Status Quo Power?" *International Security* 7(4): 5–56.

Johnston, Alastair I. 2008. *Social States: China in International Institutions, 1980–2000*. Princeton, NJ: Princeton University Press.

Johnston, Alastair I. 2013. "How New and Assertive Is China's New Assertiveness?" *International Security* 37(4): 7–48.

Johnston, Alastair I. 2019. "China in a World of Orders: Rethinking Compliance and Challenge in Beijing's International Relations." *International Security* 44(2): 9–60.

Kahneman, Daniel, and Amos Tversky. 1979. "Prospect Theory: An Analysis of Decision under Risk." *Econometrica* 47: 263–291.

Kang, Choong-Nam, and Douglas M. Gibler. 2013. "An Assessment of the Validity of Empirical Measures of State Satisfaction with the Systemic Status Quo." *European Journal of International Relations* 19(4): 695–719.

Kang, David C. 2003. "Getting Asia Wrong: The Need for New Analytical Frameworks." *International Security* 27(4): 57–85.

Kang, David C. 2007. *China Rising: Peace, Power, and Order in East Asia*. New York: Columbia University Press.

Kang, David C. 2010. *East Asian before the West: Five Centuries of Trade and Tribute*. New York: Columbia University Press.

Kang, David C. 2020. "Thought Games about China." *Journal of East Asian Studies* 20(2): 135–150.

Karabell, Zachary. 2009. *Superfusion: How China and America Became One Economy and Why the World's Prosperity Depends on It*. New York: Simon & Schuster.

Kastner, Scott L., Margaret M. Pearson, and Chad Rector. 2016. "Invest, Hold Up, or Accept? China in Multilateral Governance." *Security Studies* 25(1): 142–179.

Kastner, Scott L., Margaret M. Pearson, and Chad Rector. 2018. *China's Strategic Multilateralism: Investing in Global Governance*. Cambridge: Cambridge University Press.

Kastner, Scott L., and Phillip C. Saunders. 2012. "Is China a Status Quo or Revisionist State? Leadership Travel as an Empirical Indicator of Foreign Policy Priorities." *International Studies Quarterly* 56(1): 163–177.

Keal, Paul. 1983. *Unspoken Rules and Superpower Dominance*. New York: St. Martin's.

Kegley, Charles W., Jr., and Gregory Raymond. 1994. *A Multipolar Peace? Great-Power Politics in the Twenty-First Century*. New York: St. Martin's.

Kelley, Judith. 2007. "Who Keeps International Commitments and Why? The International Criminal Court and Bilateral Nonsurrender Agreements." *American Political Science Review* 101(3): 573–589.

Kennedy, Paul. 1987. *The Rise and Fall of Great Powers*. New York: Vintage Books.

Kennedy, Paul. 2010. "A Time to Appease." *The National Interest* 108 (July–August): 7–17. https://nationalinterest.org/article/a-time-to-appease-3539.

Keohane, Robert O. 1984. *After Hegemony: Cooperation and Discord in the World Political Economy*. Princeton, NJ: Princeton University Press.

Khong, Yuen Foong. 1992. *Analogies at War: Korea, Munich, Dien Bien Phu, and the Vietnam Decisions of 1965*. Princeton, NJ: Princeton University Press.

Khong, Yuen Foong. 2001. "Negotiating 'Order' during Power Transitions." In: Charles A. Kupchan, Emanuel Adler, Jean-Marc Coicaud, and Yuen Foong Khong (eds.), *Power in Transition: The Peaceful Change of International Order*. Tokyo: United Nations University Press, 34–67.

Khong, Yuen Foong. 2013/2014. "Primacy or World Order: The United States and China's Rise: A Review Essay." *International Security* 38(3): 153–175.

Kim, Woosang S. 1991. "Alliance Transitions and Great Power War." *American Journal of Political Science* 35(4): 833–850.

Kim, Woosang. 1992. "Power Transitions and Great Power War from Westphalia to Waterloo." *World Politics* 45(1): 153–172.

Kim, Woosang. 2002. "Power Parity, Alliance, Dissatisfaction, and Wars in East Asia, 1860–1993." *Journal of Conflict Resolution* 46(5): 654–671.

Kindleberger, Charles P. 1973. *The World in Depression: 1929–1939*. Berkeley: University of California Press.

Kirshner, Jonathan. 2012. "The Tragedy of Offensive Realism: Classical Realism and the Rise of China." *European Journal of International Relations* 18(1): 53–75.

Kissiner, Henry A. 1957. *A World Restored: Mettternich, Castlereagh and the Problems of Peace, 1812–22*. Boston: Houghton Mifflin.

Kissinger, Henry A. 2014. *World Order*. New York: Penguin.

Kranz, Michal. 2018. "The Director of the FBI Says the Whole of Chinese Society Is a Threat to the US—and That Americans Must Step Up to Defend Themselves." *Business Insider*. February 13. https://www.businessinsider.com/china-threat-to-america-fbi-director-warns-2018-2.

Krasner, Stephen D. 1999. *Sovereignty: Organized Hypocrisy*. Princeton, NJ: Princeton University Press.

Krickovic, Andrej, and Chang Zhang. 2020. "Fears of Falling Short versus Anxieties of Decline: Explaining Russia and China's Approach to Status-Seeking." *Chinese Journal of International Politics* 13(2): 219–251.

Krickovic, Andrej. 2018. "Russia's Reactionary Revisionism." Paper presented at the annual meeting of the International Studies Association, San Francisco, April 4–7.

Kupchan, Charles A. 2010. *How Enemies Become Friends: The Sources of Stable Peace*. Princeton, NJ: Princeton University Press.

Kupchan, Charles A. 2014. "The Normative Foundations of Hegemony and the Coming Challenge to Pax Americana." *Security Studies* 23(2): 219–257.

Kydd, Andrew H. 2000. "Trust, Reassurance, and Cooperation." *International Organization* 54(2): 325–357.

Kydd, Andrew H. 2005. *Trust and Mistrust in International Relations*. Princeton, NJ: Princeton University Press.

Lake, David A. 2009. *Hierarchy in International Relations*. Ithaca, NY: Cornell University Press.

Lardy, Nicholas R. 2004. *Integrating China into the Global Economy*. Washington, DC: Brookings Institution Press.

Larson, Deborah W., and Alexei Shevchenko. 2010. "Status Seekers: Chinese and Russian Responses to U.S. Primacy." *International Security* 34(4): 63–95.

Larson, Deborah W., and Alexei Shevchenko. 2019. *Quest for Status: Chinese and Russian Foreign Policy*. New Haven, CT: Yale University Press.

Layne, Christopher. 1994. "Kant or Cant: The Myth of the Democratic Peace." *International Security* 19(2): 5–49.

Lebow, R. Ned. 1984. "Windows of Opportunity: Do States Jump through Them?" *International Security* 9(1): 147–186.

Lebow, R. Ned. 2010. *Why Nations Fight: Past and Future Motivations for War*. Cambridge: Cambridge University Press.

Lebow, R. Ned. 2018. *The Rise and Fall of Political Orders*. Cambridge: Cambridge University Press.

Lebow, Richard N., and Benjamin Valentino. 2009. "Lost in Transition: A Critical Analysis of Power Transition Theory." *International Relations* 23(3): 389–410.

Lee, Jeong-ho. 2019. "US Using Trade War to Stop China Overtaking It: Ex-Singapore Diplomat Kishore Mahbubani." *South China Morning Post*. September 4. https://www.scmp.com/week-asia/politics/article/3025557/us-using-trade-war-stop-china-overtaking-it-ex-singapore

Legro, Jeffrey W. 2007. "What Will China Want: The Future Intentions of a Rising Power." *Perspectives on Politics* 5(3): 515–534.

Legro, Jeffrey. 2015. *Rethinking the World: Great Power Strategies and International Order*. Ithaca, NY: Cornell University Press.

Lemke, Douglas, and William Reed. 1996. "Regime Type and Status Quo Evaluations: Power Transition Theory and Democratic Peace." *International Interactions* 22(2): 143–164.

Lemke, Douglas, and Suzanne Werner. 1996. "Power Parity, Commitment to Change, and War." *International Studies Quarterly* 40(2): 235–260.

Levin, Dov H. 2017. "When the Great Power Gets a Vote: The Effects of Great Power Electoral Interventions on Election Returns." *International Studies Quarterly* 60(2): 189–202.

Levin, Dov H. 2018. "A Vote for Freedom? The Effects of Partisan Electoral Interventions on Regime Type." *Journal of Conflict Resolution* 63(4): 839–868.

Levin, Dov H. 2020. *Meddling in the Ballot Box: The Causes and Effects of Partisan Electoral Interventions*. Oxford: Oxford University Press.

Levy, Jack S. 1987. "Declining Power and the Preventive Motivation for War." *World Politics* 40(1): 82–17.

Levy, Jack S. 1996. "Loss Aversion, Framing and Bargaining: The Implications of Prospect Theory for International Conflict." *International Political Science Review* 17(2): 177–193.

Levy, Jack S. 2008. "Power Transition Theory and the Rise of China." In: Robert S. Ross and Zhu Feng (eds.), *China's Ascent: Power, Security, and the Future of International Politics*. Ithaca, NY: Cornell University Press, 11–33.

Levy, Jack S. 2020. "Review by Jack S. Levy: Hi-Diplo/ISSF XII-2 on Steve Chan's *Thucydides's Trap? Historical Interpretation, Logic of Inquiry, and the Future of Sino-American Relations*." https://networks.h-net.org/node/28443/discussions/6721850/h-diploissf-roundtable-12-2-thucydides%E2%80%99s-trap-historical.

Levy, Jack S., and William Mulligan. 2017. "Shifting Power, Preventive Logic, and the Response of the Target: Germany, Russia and the First World War." *Journal of Strategic Studies* 40(5): 731–769.

Levy, Jack S., and William R. Thompson. 2005. "Hegemonic Threats and Great-Power Balancing in Europe, 1495–1999." *Security Studies* 14(1): 1–33.

Levy, Jack S., and William R. Thompson. 2010. "Balancing on Land and at Sea: Do States Ally against the Leading Global Power?" *International Security* 35(1): 7–43.

Li, Mingjiang. 2012. "China's Non-Confrontational Assertiveness in the South China Sea." *East Asia Forum*. June 14. https://www.eastasiaforum.org/2012/06/14/china-s-non-confrontational-assertiveness-in-the-south-china-sea/

Liberman, Peter. 1993. "The Spoils of Conquest." *International Security* 18(2): 125–153.

Liberman, Peter. 1996. *"Does Conquest Pay? The Exploitation of Occupied Industrial Societies*. Princeton, NJ: Princeton University Press.

Lieber, Keir A., and Gerard Alexander. 2005. "Waiting for Balancing: Why the World Is Not Pushing Back." *International Security* 30(1): 109–139.

Lieber, Keir A., and Daryl G. Press. 2006. "The End of MAD: The Nuclear Dimension of U.S. Primacy." *International Security* 30(4): 7–44.

Lieberthal, Kenneth, and Jisi Wang. 2012. *Addressing U.S.-China Strategic Distrust*. Washington, DC: John L. Thornton Center, Brookings Institution.

Lim, Yves-Heng. 2015. "How (Dis)satisfied Is China? A Power Transition Theory Perspective." *Journal of Contemporary China* 24(92): 280–297.

Lind, Jennifer. 2017. "Asia's Other Revisionist Power: Why U.S. Grand Strategy Unnerves China." *Foreign Affairs* 96(2): 74–82.

Lind, Jennifer, and William C. Wohlforth. 2019. "The Future of the Liberal Order Is Conservative: A Strategy to Save the System." *Foreign Affairs* 98(2): 70–80.

Lipscy, Phillip Y. 2017. *Renegotiating the World Order: Institutional Change in International Relations*. Cambridge: Cambridge University Press.

Lynas, Mark. 2009. "How Do I Know China Wrecked the Copenhagen Deal? I Was in the Room." *The Guardian*. December 23. https://www.theguardian.com/environment/2009/dec/22/copenhagen-climate-change-mark-lynas.

MacDonald, Paul, and Joseph Parent. 2018. *Great Power Decline and Retrenchment*. Ithaca, NY: Cornell University Press.

MacDonald, Paul, and Joseph Parent. 2020. "The Authors Respond." *Journal of East Asian Studies* 20(2): 176–179.

Macias, Amanda. 2020. "WTO Says U.S. Tariffs on Chinese Goods Violated International Trade Rules." CNBC. September 15. https://www.cnbc.com/2020/09/15/wto-says-us-tariffs-on-chinese-goods-violated-international-trade-rules.html.

Macias, Amanda, and Jacob Pramuk. 2019. "Trump Tells UN He Will Not Accept 'Bad' TradeDeal with China." CNBC. September 24. https://www.cnbc.com/2019/

09/24/trump-says-he-will-not-accept-a-bad-trade-deal-with-china.html?__
source=twitter%7Cmain.

Mansfield, Edward D., and Brian Pollins (eds.). 2003. *Economic Interdependence and International Conflict: New Perspectives on an Enduring Debate*. Ann Arbor: University of Michigan Press.

Mansfield, Edward D., and Jack Snyder. 2007. *Electing to Fight: Why Emerging Democracies Go to War*. Cambridge, MA: MIT Press.

Maoz, Zeev. 2010. *Networks of Nations: The Evolution, Structure, and Impact of International Networks, 1816–2001*. Cambridge: Cambridge University Press.

March, James G., and Johan P. Olsen. 1998. "The Institutional Dynamics of International Political Orders." *International Organization* 52(4): 943–969.

March, James G., and Johan P. Olsen. 2004. "The Logic of Appropriateness." Arena-Centre for European Studies, University of Oslo. https://www.sv.uio.no/arena/english/research/publications/arena-publications/workingpapers/working-papers2004/wp04_9.pdf.

Massie, Suzanne. 2014. "Opinion: US Intervention in Ukraine Arrogant, Heavy-Handed." Mideastrussia. May 16. https://mideastrussia.wordpress.com/2014/05/16/opinion-us-intervention-in-ukraine-arrogant-heavy-handed/

Mastanduno, Michael. 2019. "Partner Politics: Russia, China, and the Challenge of Extending U.S. Hegemony after the Cold War." *Security Studies* 28(3): 479–504.

Mattes, Michaela, and Greg Vonnahme. 2010. "Contracting for Peace: Do Nonaggression Pacts Reduce Conflict?" *Journal of Politics* 73(4): 925–938.

May, Ernest R. 1973. *Lessons of the Past: The Use and Misuse of History in American Foreign Policy*. Oxford: Oxford University Press.

Mayall, James. 2000. *World Politics: Progress and Its Limits*. Cambridge: Polity Press.

McDermott, Rose. 1998. *Risk-Taking in International Relations: Prospect Theory in American Foreign Policy*. Ann Arbor: University of Michigan Press.

McDowell, Daniel. 2015. "New Order: China's Challenge to the Global Financial System." *World Politics Review*. April 14. https://www.worldpoliticsreview.com/articles/15531/new-order-china-s-challenge-to-the-global-financial-system

McFaul, Michael, Stephen Sestanovich, and John J. Mearsheimer. 2014. "Faulty Powers: Who Started the Ukraine Crisis?" *Foreign Affairs* 93(6): 167–178.

McLauchlin. Theodore. 2016. "Great Power Accommodation and the Processes of International Politics." In: T. V. Paul (ed.), *Accommodating Rising Powers: Past, Present, and Future*. Cambridge: Cambridge University Press, 293–313.

Mearsheimer, John J. 2001. *The Tragedy of Great Power Politics*. New York: Norton.

Mearsheimer, John J. 2018. *Great Delusion: Liberal Dreams and International Realities*. New Haven, CT: Yale University Press.

Mearsheimer, John J. 2019. "Bound to Fail: The Rise and Fall of the Liberal International Order." *International Security* 43(4): 7–50.

Medeiros, Evan S. 2009. *China's International Behavior: Activism, Opportunism, and Diversification*. Santa Monica, CA: RAND.

Medeiros, Evan S. 2019. "The Changing Fundamentals of US-China Relations." *Washington Quarterly* 42(3): 93–119.

Mercatante, Steve D. 2012. *Why Germany Nearly Won: A New History of the Second World War in Europe*. Santa Barbara, CA: Praeger.

Midlarsky, Manus I. 1975. *On War: International Violence in the International System*. New York: Free Press.

Modelski, George. 1987. *Long Cycles in World Politics*. Seattle: University of Washington Press.

Morgan, Patrick M. 2003. *Deterrence Now*. Cambridge: Cambridge University Press.

Morgenthau, Hans J. 1948. *Politics among Nations: The Struggle for Power and Peace*. New York: Knopf.

Most, Benjamin A., and Harvey Starr. 1989. *Inquiry, Logic and International Politics*. Columbia: University of South Carolina Press.

Murray, Michelle. 2010. "Identity, Insecurity, and Great Power Politics: The Tragedy of German Naval Ambition before the First World War." *Security Studies* 19(4): 656–688.

Murray, Michelle. 2019. *The Struggle for Recognition in International Relations: Status, Revisionism, and Rising Powers*. New York: Oxford University Press.

Musgrave, Paul. 2019. "International Hegemony Meets Domestic Politics: Why Liberals Can be Pessimists." *Security Studies* 28(3): 451–478.

Nexon, Daniel H. 2009. "The Balance of Power in the Balance." *World Politics* 61(2): 330–359.

Nikkei Asian Review. 2019. "Trump Ups Security Demands on Japan and South Korea." https://asia.nikkei.com/Politics/International-relations/Trump-ups-security-demands-on-Japan-and-South-Korea.

Niksch, Larry A. 2006. *North Korea's Nuclear Weapons Program*. Washington, DC: Congressional Research Service, Library of Congress. https://fas.org/sgp/crs/nuke/IB91141.pdf.

Norrlof, Carla, and William C. Wohlforth. 2019. "*Raison de l'Hégémonie* (The Hegemon's Interest): Theory of the Costs and Benefits of Hegemony." *Security Studies* 28(3): 422–450.

Nye, Joseph S., Jr. 2004. *Soft Power: The Means to Success in World Politics*. New York: Public Affairs.

Nye, Joseph S., Jr. 2017. "The Kindleberger Trap." Belfer Center for Science and International Affairs, Harvard Kennedy School. https://www.belfercenter.org/publication/kindleberger-trap.

Nye, Joseph S., Jr. 2019. "The Rise and Fall of American Hegemony from Wilson to Trump." *International Affairs* 95(1): 63–80.

Oren, Ido. 2003. *Our Enemies and US: America's Rivalries and the Making of Political Science*. Ithaca, NY: Cornell University Press.

Organski, A. F. K. 1958. *World Politics*. New York: Knopf.

Organski, A. F. K., and Jacek Kugler. 1980. *The War Ledger*. Chicago: University of Chicago Press.

Pan, Chengxin. 2012. *Knowledge, Desire and Power in Global Politics: Western Representations of China's Rise*. Cheltenham, UK: Elgar.

Pang, Xun. 2014. "Dissimilarity of Trade Network Positions and Foreign Policy Divergence: Structure or Strategy?" Paper presented at the conference on "China's Threat," Tsinghua University, Beijing, July 6–7.

Pape, Robert A. 2005. "Soft Balancing against the United States." *International Security* 30(1): 7–45.

Paris, Roland. 2020. "The Right to Dominate: How Old Ideas about Sovereignty Pose New Challenges for World Order." *International Organization* 74(3): 453–489.

Paul, T. V. 2005. "Soft Balancing in the Age of U.S. Primacy." *International Security* 30(1): 46–71.

Paul, T. V. (ed.). 2016a. *Accommodating Rising Powers: Past, Present, and Future.* Cambridge: Cambridge University Press.

Paul, T.V. 2016b. "The Accommodation of Rising Powers in World Politics." In: T. V. Paul (ed.), *Accommodating Rising Powers: Past, Present, and Future.* Cambridge: Cambridge University Press, 3–32.

Paul, T. V. 2018. *Restraining Great Powers: Soft Balancing from Empires to the Global Era.* New Haven, CT: Yale University Press.

Pempel, T. J. 2016. "Soft Balancing, Hedging, and Institutional Darwinism: The Economic-Security Nexus and East Asian Regionalism." *Journal of East Asian Studies* 10(2): 209–238.

Perlez, Jane. 2015. "China Creates a World Bank of Its Own, and the US Balks." *New York Times.* December 4. https://www.nytimes.com/2015/12/05/business/international/china-creates-an-asian-bank-as-the-us-stands-aloof.html.

Pollack, Jonathan D. 2005. "The Transformation of the Asian Security Order: Assessing China's Impact." In: David Shambaugh (ed.), *Power Shift: China and Asia's New Dynamics.* Berkeley: University of California Press, 329–346.

Pompeo, Michael. 2020. "Communist China and the Free World's Future." Speech at the Richard Nixon Presidential Library and Museum, Yorba Linda, California, July 23. https://www.state.gov/communist-china-and-the-free-worlds-future/.

Posen, Barry R. 2003. "Command of the Commons: The Military Foundation of U.S. Hegemony." *International Security* 28(1): 5–46.

Powell, Robert. 1991. "The Problem of Absolute and Relative Gains in International Relations Theory." *American Political Science Review* 85(4): 1303–1320.

Powell, Robert. 1999. *In the Shadow of Power: States and Strategies in International Politics.* Princeton, NJ: Princeton University Press.

Pu, Xiaoyu. 2019. *Rebranding China: Contested Status Signaling in the Changing Global Order.* Stanford, CA: Stanford University Press.

Putnam, Robert D. 1988. "Diplomacy and Domestic Politics: The Logic of Two-Level Games." *International Organization* 42(3): 427–460.

Qin, Yaqing, 2010. "International Society as a Process: Institutions, Identities, and China's Peaceful Rise." *Chinese Journal of International Politics* 3(2): 129–153.

Quek, Kai, and Alastair I. Johnston. 2017/18. "Can China Back Down? Crisis De-Escalation in the Shadow of Popular Opposition." *International Security* 42(3): 7–36.

Rathbun, Brian C. 2012. *Trust in International Cooperation: International Security Institutions, Domestic Politics and American Multilateralism.* Cambridge: Cambridge University Press.

Ray, James L. 1974. "Status Inconsistency and War Involvement among European States, 1816–1970." *Peace Science Society Papers* 23: 69–80.

Ren, Xiao. 2015. "A Reform-Minded Status Quo Power? China, the G20, and Reform of the International Financial System." *Third World Quarterly* 36(11): 2023–2043.

Renshon, Jonathan. 2016. "Status Deficits and War." *International Organization* 70(3): 513–550.

Renshon, Jonathan. 2017. *Fighting for Status: Hierarchy and Conflict in World Politics.* Princeton, NJ: Princeton University Press.

Reus-Smit, Christian. 1997. "The Constitutional Structure of International Society and the Nature of Fundamental Institutions." *International Organization* 51(4): 555–589.

Reus-Smit, Christian. 2004. *American Power and World Order.* Cambridge: Polity Press.

Reus-Smit, Christian. 2007. "International Crises of Legitimacy." *International Politics* 44(2–3): 157–174.

Revkin, Andrew, and John Broder. 2009. "A Grudging Accord in Climate Talks." *New York Times*. December 19. https://www.nytimes.com/2009/12/20/science/earth/20accord. html.

Ripman, Norrin, and Jack Levy. 2008. "Wishful Thinking or Buying Time: The Logic of British Appeasement in the 1930s." *International Security* 33(2): 148–181.

Risse, Thomas. 2002. "Constructivism and International Institutions: Toward Conversations across Paradigms." In: Ira Katznelson and Helen Milner (eds.), *Political Science: The State of the Discipline*. New York: American Political Science Association, 597–623.

Roach, Stephen. 2015. "China's Global Governance Challenge." *YaleGlobal Online*. June 9. https://yaleglobal.yale.edu/content/chinas-global-governance-challenge

Roach, Stephen, Zha Daojiong, Scott Kennedy, and Patrick Chovanec. 2015. "Washington's Big China Screw-up." *Foreign Policy*. March 26. https://foreignpolicy.com/2015/03/26/washingtons-big-china-screw-up-aiib-asia-infrastructure-investment-bank-china-containment-chinafile/.

Rock, Stephen R. 1989. *Why Peace Breaks Out: Great Power Rapprochement in Historical Perspective*. Chapel Hill: University of North Carolina Press.

Rock, Stephen R. 2000. *Appeasement in International Politics*, Lexington: University of Kentucky Press.

Rosato, Sebastian. 2014/2015. "The Inscrutable Intentions of Great Powers." *International Security* 39(3): 48–88.

Rosecrance, Richard. 1986. *The Rise of the Trading State: Commerce and Conquest in the Modern World*. New York: Basic Books.

Rousseau, David L. 2006. *Identifying Threats and Threatening Identities: The Social Construction of Realism and Liberalism*. Stanford, CA: Stanford University Press.

Rudd, Kevin. 2020. "Beware the Guns of August—in Asia: How to Keep U.S.-Chinese Tensions from Sparking a War." *Foreign Affairs*. August 3. https://www.foreignaffairs.com/articles/united-states/2020-08-03/beware-guns-august-asia.

Ruggie, John G. 1982. "International Regimes, Transactions, and Change: Embedded Liberalism in the Postwar Economic Order." *International Organization* 36(2): 379–415.

Ruggie, John G. 1998. *Constructing the World Polity: Essays on International Institutionalization*. London: Routledge.

Russett, Bruce M. 1969. "Refining Deterrence Theory: The Japanese Attack on Pearl Harbor." In: Dean G. Pruitt and Richard C. Snyder (eds.), *Theory and Research on the Causes of War*. Englewood Cliffs, NJ: Prentice-Hall, 127–135.

Russett, Bruce M. 1985. "The Mysterious Case of Vanishing Hegemony: Or, Is Mark Twain Really Dead?" *International Organization* 39(2): 207–232.

Russett, Bruce M., and John R. Oneal. 2001. *Triangulating Peace: Democracy, Interdependence and International Organizations*. New York: Norton.

Russett, Bruce M., John R. Oneal, and David R. Davis. 1998. "The Third Leg of the Kantian Tripod for Peace: International Organizations and Militarized Disputes, 1950–1985." *International Organization* 52(3): 441–467.

Saltzman, Ilai Z. 2012. "Soft Balancing as Foreign Policy: Assessing American Strategy toward Japan in the Interwar Period." *Foreign Policy Analysis* 8(2): 131–150.

Sample, Susan G. 2018. "Power, Wealth, and Satisfaction: When Do Power Transitions Lead to Conflicts?" *Journal of Conflict Resolution* 62(9): 1905–1931.

Sartori, Giovanni. 1970. "Concept Misinformation in Comparative Politics." *American Political Science Review* 64(4): 1033–1053.

Schake, Kori. 2017. *Safe Passage: The Transition from British to American Hegemony.* Cambridge, MA: Harvard University Press.

Schneider, Mark B. 2019. "Why You Should Fear China's Nuclear Weapons."*The National Interest.* May 6. https://nationalinterest.org/blog/buzz/why-you-should-fear-chinas-nuclear-weapons-56212?page=0%2C1.

Schuman, Frederick. 1948. *International Politics: The Destiny of the Western State System.* New York: McGraw-Hill.

Schwarz, Benjamin. 2005. "Comment: Managing China's Rise." *The Atlantic Monthly.* June. http://www.theatlantic.com/magazine/archive/2005/06/managing-chinas-rise/303972/.

Schweller, Randall L. 1992. "Domestic Structure and Preventive War: Are Democracies More Pacific?" *World Politics* 44(2): 235–269.

Schweller, Randall L. 1994. "Bandwagoning for Profit: Bringing the Revisionist State Back In." *International Security* 19(1): 72–107.

Schweller, Randall L. 1998. *Deadly Imbalances: Tripolarity and Hitler's Strategy of World Conquest.* New York: Columbia University Press.

Schweller, Randall L. 2001. "The Problem of International Order Revisited: A Review Essay." *International Security* 26(1):161–186.

Schweller, Randall L. 2006. *Unanswered Threats: Political Constraints on the Balance of Power.* Princeton, NJ: Princeton University Press.

Schweller, Randall L. 2015. "Rising Powers and Revisionism in Emerging World Orders." *Russia in Global Affairs.* http://eng.globalaffairs.ru/valday/Rising-Powers-and-Revisionism-in-Emerging-International-Orders-17730.

Schweller, Randall L., and Xiaoyu Pu. 2011. "After Unipolarity: China's Visions of International Order in an Era of U.S. Decline." *International Security* 36(1): 41–72.

Shifrinson, Joshua. 2018. *Falling Giants: How Great Powers Exploit Power Shifts.* Ithaca, NY: Cornell University Press.

Shih, Chih-yu, and Jiwu Yin. 2013. "Between Core National Interest and a Harmonious World: Reconciling Self-Role Conceptions in Chinese Foreign Policy." *Chinese Journal of International Politics* 6(1): 59–84.

Shirk, L. Susan. 2007. *China: Fragile Superpower.* Oxford: Oxford University Press.

Silver, Laura, Kat Devlin, and Christine Huang. 2020. "Unfavorable Views of China Reach Historical Highs in Many Countries." *Pew Research Center: Global Attitudes & Trends.* October 6. https://www.pewresearch.org/global/2020/10/06/unfavorable-views-of-china-reach-historic-highs-in-many-countries/

Simmons, Beth A. 2000. "International Law and State Behavior: Commitment and Compliance in International Monetary Affairs." *American Political Science Review* 94(4): 819–835.

Simmons, Beth A., and Daniel J. Hopkins. 2005. "The Constraining Power of International Treaties: Theory and Method." *American Political Science Review* 99(4): 623–631.

Smith, Jeff M. (ed.). 2018. *Asia's Quest for Balance: China's Rise and Balancing in the Indo-Pacific.* Lanham, MD: Rowman & Littlefield.

Snidal, Duncan. 1985. "The Limits of Hegemonic Stability Theory." *International Organization* 39(4): 579–614.

Snidal, Duncan. 1991. "Relative Gains and the Pattern of International Cooperation." *American Political Science Review* 85(3): 701–726.

Snyder, Glenn H. 1997. *Alliance Politics*. Ithaca, NY: Cornell University Press.

Snyder, Jack. 1993. *Myths of Empire: Domestic Politics and International Ambition* Ithaca, NY: Cornell University Press.

Starrs, Sean. 2013. "American Economic Power Hasn't Declined—It Globalized! Summoning the Data and Taking Globalization Seriously." *International Studies Quarterly* 57(4): 817–830.

Stockholm International Peace Research Institute. 2019. "World Nuclear Forces." https://www.sipri.org/yearbook/2019/06.

Stockholm International Peace Research Institute. 2020. "2020 Fact Sheet (for 2019)" SIPRI Military Expenditure Database. https://en.wikipedia.org/wiki/List_of_countries_by_military_expenditures#As_a_share_of_GDP

Strange, Susan. 1987. "The Persistent Myth of Lost Hegemony." *International Organization* 41(4): 551–574.

Swaine, Michael D., 2010. "Perceptions of an Assertive China." *China Leadership Monitor* 32(2): 1–19.

Taliaferro, Jeffrey W. 2004. *Balancing Risks: Great Power Intervention in the Periphery*. Ithaca, NY: Cornell University Press.

Tammen, Ronald L., Jacek Kugler, and Douglas Lemke. 2017. "Foundations of Power Transition Theory." In: William R. Thompson (ed.), *Oxford Encyclopedia of Empirical International Relations*. Oxford: Oxford University Press. https://oxfordre.com/politics/view/10.1093/acrefore/9780190228637.001.0001/acrefore-9780190228637-e-296.

Tammen, Ronald L., Jacek Kugler, Douglas Lemke, Allan Stam III, Mark Abdollahian, Carole Alsharabati, Brian Efird, and A. F. K. Organski. 2000. *Power Transitions: Strategies for the 21st Century*. New York: Chatham House.

Tannenwald, Nina. 1999. "The Nuclear Taboo: The United States and the Normative Basis of Nuclear Non-Use." *International Organization* 53(3): 433–468.

Tannenwald, Nina. 2005. "Stigmatizing the Bomb: Origins of the Nuclear Taboo." *International Security* 29(4): 5–49.

Tessman, Brock, and Wojtek Wolfe. 2011. "Great Powers and Strategic Hedging." *International Studies Review* 13: 214–240.

Thies, Cameron. 2015. "China's Rise and the Socialization of Rising Powers." *Chinese Journal of International Politics* 8(3): 281–300.

Thies, Cameron, and Mark D. Nieman. 2017. *Rising Powers and Foreign Policy Revisionism*. Ann Arbor: University of Michigan Press.

Thompson, Alexander. 2006. "Coercion through IOs: The Security Council and the Logic of Information Transmission." *International Organization* 61(1): 1–34.

Thompson, William R. 2003. "A Streetcar Named Sarajevo: Catalysts, Multiple Causation Chains, and Rivalry Structures." *International Studies Quarterly* 47(3): 453–474.

Toft, Monica D. 2017. "Why Is America Addicted to Foreign Interventions?" *The National Interest*. https://nationalinterest.org/feature/why-america-addicted-foreign-interventions-23582?nopaging=1.

Tow, William T. 2019. "Minilateral Security's Relevance to US Strategy in the Indo-Pacific: Challenges and Prospects." *The Pacific Review* 32(2): 232–244.

Treisman, David. 2004. "Rational Appeasement." *International Organization* 58(2): 344–373.

Turner, Oliver, and Nicola Nymalm. 2019. "Morality and Progress: IR Narratives on International Revisionism and the Status Quo." *Cambridge Review of International Affairs* 32(4): 407–428. https://doi.org/10.1080/09557571.2019.1623173.

Van Evera, Stephen. 1999. *Causes of War: Power and the Roots of Conflict*. Ithaca, NY: Cornell University Press.

Vasquez, John A. 1993. *The War Puzzle*. New York: Cambridge University Press.

Vasquez, John A. 1996. "When Are Power Transitions Dangerous? An Appraisal and Reformulation of Power Transition Theory." In: Jacek Kugler and Douglas Lemke (eds.), *Parity and War: Evaluations and Extensions of the War Ledger*. Ann Arbor: University of Michigan Press, 35–56.

Vasquez, John A. 2009. *The War Puzzle Revisited*. Cambridge: Cambridge University Press.

Vasquez, John A., and Marie T. Henehan. 2011. *Territory, War, and Peace*. New York: Routledge.

Voeten, Erik. 2004. "Resisting the Lonely Superpower: Responses of States in the United Nations to U.S. Dominance." *Journal of Politics* 66(3): 729–754.

Voeten, Erik. 2013. "Data and Analyses of Voting in the UN General Assembly." In: Bob Reinalda (ed.), *Routledge Handbook of International Organization*. London: Routledge, 54–66.

Voeten, Erik, Anton Strezhnev, and Michel Bailey. 2009, updated in 2017. United Nations General Assembly Voting Data, hdl:1902.1/12379, Harvard Dataverse, V17, UNF:6:o5 OiqHLeXMiv9Q8w8+3sVw==.

Volgy, Thomas J., Renato Corbetta, Keith A. Grant, and Ryan G. Baird (eds.). 2011. *Major Powers and the Quest for Status in International Politics: Global and Regional Perspectives*. New York: Palgrave Macmillan.

Volgy, Thomas J., and Stacey Mayhall. 1995. "Status Inconsistency and International War: Exploring the Effects of Systemic Change." *International Studies Quarterly* 39(1): 67–84.

Von Stein, Jana. 2005. "Do Treaties Constrain or Screen? Selection Bias and Treaty Compliance." *American Political Science Review* 99(4): 611–622.

Walker, Stephen G. 2013. *Role Theory and the Cognitive Architecture of British Appeasement Decisions: Symbolic and Strategic Interaction in World Politics*. New York: Routledge.

Wallace, Michael D. 1973. *War and Rank among States*. Lexington, KY: Heath.

Walt, Stephen M. 1987. *The Origins of Alliances*. Ithaca, NY: Cornell University Press.

Walt, Stephen M. 2002. "Keeping the World 'Off Balance:' Self-Restraint in American Foreign Policy." In: G. John Ikenberry (ed.), *America Unrivaled: The Future of the Balance of Power*. Ithaca, NY: Cornell University Press, 121–154.

Walt, Stephen M. 2005. *Taming American Power: The Global Response to U.S. Primacy*. New York: Norton.

Waltz, Kenneth N. 1979. *Theory of International Politics*. Reading, MA: Addison-Wesley.

Walzer, Michael. 1977. *Just and Unjust Wars: A Moral Argument with Historical Illustrations*. New York: Basic Books.

Wan, Ming. 2015. *The Asian Infrastructure Investment Bank: The Construction of Power and the Struggle for the East Asian International Order*. New York: Palgrave Macmillan.

Wang, Jisi. 2020. "The COVID New (Ab)Normal: Identity Politics—A Third Approach to Analyzing China-U.S. Relations." *Asia Society*. September 14. https://asiasociety.org/policy-institute/covid-new-abnormal-identity-politics-third-approach-analyzing-china-us-relations.

Wang, Yi. 2020. "Interview on Current China-US Relations Given by State Councilor and Foreign Minister Wang Yi to Xinhua News Agency." Ministry of Foreign Affairs of the People's Republic of China. August 6. https://www.fmprc.gov.cn/mfa_eng/zxxx_662805/t1804328.shtml.

Ward, Steven. 2017. *Status and the Challenge of Rising Powers*. Cambridge: Cambridge University Press.

Ward, Steven. 2019. "Logics of Stratified Identity Management in World Politics." *International Theory* 11(2): 218–238.

Weeks, Jessica L. 2008. "Autocratic Audience Costs: Regime Type and Signaling Resolve." *International Organization* 62(1): 35–64.

Weeks, Jessica. 2012. "Strongmen and Straw Men: Authoritarian Regimes and the Initiation of Interstate Conflict." *American Political Science Review* 106(2): 326–347.

Weiss, Jessica Chen. 2012. "Authoritarian Signaling, Mass Audiences, and Nationalist Protest in China." *International Organization* 67(1): 1–35.

Weiss, Jessica Chen. 2014. *Powerful Patriots: Nationalist Protest in China's Foreign Relations*. Oxford: Oxford University Press.

Weiss, Jessica Chen. 2019. "A World Safe for Autocracy? China's Rise and the Future of Global Politics." *Foreign Affairs* 98(4): 92–102.

Werner, Suzanne, and Jacek Kugler. 1996. "Power Transitions and Military Buildups: Resolving the Relationship between Arms Buildups and War." In: Jacek Kugler and Douglas Lemke (eds.), *Parity and War: Evaluations and Extensions of the War Ledger*. Ann Arbor: University of Michigan Press, 187–207.

White House. 2017. "National Security Strategy of the United States of America." Washington, DC. https://www.whitehouse.gov/wp-content/uploads/2017/12/NSS-Final-12-18-2017-0905.pdf.

White House. 2020. "United States Strategic Approach to the People's Republic of China." https://www.whitehouse.gov/wp-content/uploads/2020/05/U.S.-Strategic-Approach-to-The-Peoples-Republic-of-China-Report-5.20.20.pdf.

Wike, Richard, Janell Fetterolf, and Mara Mordecai. 2020. "U.S. Image Plummets Internationally as Most Say Country Has Handled Coronavirus Badly." *Pew Research Center: Global Attitudes & Trends*. September 20. https://www.pewresearch.org/global/2020/09/15/us-image-plummets-internationally-as-most-say-country-has-handled-coronavirus-badly/.

Wilson, Jeffrey D. 2019. "The Evolution of China's Asian Infrastructure Investment Bank: From Revisionist to Status-Seeking Agenda." *International Relations of the Asia-Pacific* 19(1): 147–176.

Wohlforth, William C. (ed.). 2003. *Cold War Endgame: Oral History, Analysis, Debates*. University Park: Pennsylvania State University Press.

Wohlforth, William C. 2009. "Unipolarity, Status Competition, and Great Power War." *World Politics* 61(1): 28–57.

Wolf, Reinhard. 2014. "Rising Powers, Status Ambitions, and the Need to Reassure: What China Could Learn from Imperial Germany's Failures." *Chinese Journal of International Politics* 7(2): 185–219.

Wolfers, Arnold. 1962. *Discord and Collaboration: Essays in International Politics*. Baltimore, MD: Johns Hopkins University Press.

Wolfowitz, Paul. 1997. "Bridging Centuries–Fin de Siècle All over Again." *The National Interest*. https://nationalinterest.org/article/bridging-centuries-fin-de-siecle-all-over-again-518.

Womack, Brantly. 2015. "China and the Future Status Quo." *Chinese Journal of International Politics* 8(2): 115–137.

World Economic Forum. 2016. "The World's Top Economy: The U.S. vs. China in Five Charts." https://www.weforum.org/agenda/2016/12/the-world-s-top-economy-the-us-vs-china-in-five-charts/.

Wuthnow, Joel, Xin Li, and Lingling Qi. 2012. "Diverse Multilateralism: Four Strategies in China's Multilateral Diplomacy." *Journal of Chinese Political Science* 17(3): 269–290.

Xiang, Lanxin. 2001. "Washington's Misguided China Policy." *Survival* 43(3): 7–24.

Yan, Xuetong. 2013. "Strategic Cooperation without Mutual Trust: A Path forward for China and the United States." *Asia Policy* 15(1): 4–6.

Yan, Xuetong. 2014. "From Keeping a Low Profile to Striving for Achievement." *Chinese Journal of International Politics* 7(2): 153–184.

Yoder, Brandon K. 2019. "Hedging for Better Bets: Power Shifts, Credible Signals, and Preventive Conflict." *Journal of Conflict Resolution* 63(4): 923–949.

Yoder, Brandon K., Kurt T. Gaubatz, and Rachel A. Shutte. 2019. "Political Groups, Coordinating Costs, and Credible Communication in the Shadow of Power." *Political Science Quarterly* 134(3): 507–536.

Yoder, Brandon K., and Kyle Haynes. 2015. "Always Inscrutable or Context-Dependent? A Critique of Sebastian Rosato's 'The Inscrutable Intentions of Great Powers.'" ISSF Article Review 45. November 27. https://issforum.org/articlereviews/45-greata-powers.

Zacher, Mark W. 2001. "The Territorial Integrity Norm." *International Organization* 55(2): 215–250.

Zakaria, Fareed. 1998. *From Wealth to Power: The Unusual Origins of America's World Role*. Princeton, NJ: Princeton University Press.

Zakaria, Fareed. 2008a. *The Post-American World*. New York: Norton.

Zakaria, Fareed. 2008b. "The Future of American Power: How America Can Survive the Rise of the Rest." *Foreign Affairs* 87(3): 18–43.

Zeren, Ali, and John A. Hall. 2016. "Seizing the Day or Passing the Baton? Power, Illusion, and the British Empire." In: T. V. Paul (ed.), *Accommodating Rising Powers: Past, Present, and Future*. Cambridge: Cambridge University Press, 111–130.

Zhang, Ketian. 2019. "Cautious Bully: Reputation, Resolve, and Beijing's Use of Coercion in the South China Sea." *International Security* 44(1): 117–159.

Zhang, Ketian. 2020. "Strategies, Signals, and Conflict Propensity: Rising States, Declining States, and Contemporary US-China Relations." *Journal of East Asian Studies* 20(2): 161–172.

Index